DATE			

SWEARING AND PERJURY IN
SHAKESPEARE'S PLAYS

By the same author:

Shakespeare's Use of Off-stage Sounds
John Webster, 'The Devil's Law-Case'

Swearing and Perjury in Shakespeare's Plays

FRANCES A. SHIRLEY
Professor of English
Wheaton College, Norton, Massachusetts

London
GEORGE ALLEN & UNWIN
Boston   Sydney

First published in 1979

GEORGE ALLEN & UNWIN LTD
40 Museum Street, London WC1A 1LU

© George Allen & Unwin (Publishers) Ltd, 1979

British Library Cataloguing in Publication Data

Shirley, Frances A
    Swearing and perjury in Shakespeare's plays.
    1. Shakespeare, William – Knowledge – Swearing
    2. Swearing in literature
    I. Title
    822.3'3   PR3069.S/   78–40626

ISBN 0–04–822040–X

Typeset in 10 on 11 point Times by
Northampton Phototypesetters Ltd
and printed in England
by Biddles Ltd, Guildford, Surrey.

Acknowledgements

I wish to express my gratitude to Wheaton College for several research grants that enabled me to work in England, and to the staffs of the British Museum and the University of Birmingham Shakespeare Institute for their assistance while I was there. My thanks go also to the reference librarians of Wheaton College and to the faculty secretaries for their invaluable help. Professor Arthur Colby Sprague has supplied several references as well as numerous suggestions about the opening chapter. His interest in the topic led me to include some of the material, in a different format, in a *festschrift* in his honour. I wish to thank the Pennsylvania State University Press for their permission to re-use some parts of that article from *The Triple Bond* (edited by Joseph Price, University Park, Pa., 1975).

To My Parents

Contents

Introduction

Today we are not surprised to hear occasional oaths in stage plays or television dramas, and we may even think fleetingly how effective a particular example is in emphasising a point or helping to delineate character. But it is not until we look at Shakespeare's works that we see how much can be achieved by the careful use of swearing. Strangely, no one seems to have examined this aspect of the plays. Various footnotes touch on particular utterances, editors comment on oaths that are omitted from the Folio text, and very recently E. R. C. Brinkworth has shown that church courts in Stratford, by punishing this and other sins, might have made young Shakespeare more aware of its enormity.[1] A thoroughgoing study of this special-ised aspect of language as it functions in the plays can increase our appreciation in a way analogous to the heightened understanding fostered by the many books and articles that focus on Shakespeare's imagery.

The word 'swearing' requires some definition, for it is now often considered synonymous with 'cursing', and was occasionally so used about 1600. I have, however, limited myself to what Elizabethans generally considered oaths and swearing: the calling to witness of something, divine or otherwise, to seal vows of allegiance and promises of love or to attest the truth of a statement; and the inclusion of a similar phrase in a more exclamatory fashion to add emphasis to one's speech. There may be an attendant self-curse, as when Buckingham asks God to punish him if he breaks his oath of friendship in *Richard III*, and this I have sometimes noted. But I have not branched into the whole realm of the formal curse, the request that some supernatural power punish another person, although my mention of *Richard III* probably calls to mind Queen Margaret's cursing rather than Richard of Gloucester's swearing.[2] The phrases with which we are concerned range from 'I protest' to the more readily recognizable 'by my faith' or 'by God's wounds', and their common contractions, 'faith' or 'zounds'.

That word 'range' implies some gradation in strength as well as a relatively large selection, and makes our task a bit more difficult. Quite often a formal pledge of allegiance or other oath-taking utilises the simple 'I swear', but includes an action which points up the seriousness of the moment – a hand placed on the cross of a sword, or knees bent before an altar – or a comment that draws our attention. The more spontaneous utterances, however, are widely varied and may even be so elided that the original meanings are not immediately apparent and the force of the phrases is lost to us. Should we, for instance, hear a contemporary use 'zounds', we might smile indulgently. After all, the *Oxford Dictionary* calls the word 'archaic', although noting its meaning, while the American *Random House Dictionary* labels it 'mild'. But four centuries ago it was the strongest phrase available, and indicated either extreme stress or lack of conscience coupled with a rough tongue. The unskilled author of *The Famous Victories of Henry V* might give it to Hal as well as to others; Shakespeare, in *Henry IV, Part One*, carefully keeps the Prince from saying it, thereby expressing gradations between him and both Falstaff and Hotspur.

A second kind of scale must also be established, in so far as is possible: the social class of those most likely to swear, and even differences because of sex. Renatus Hartogs, in a recent study of obscene language, has pointed out that, if one accepts a person's profanity, one accepts the person, for this aspect of language is a quick establisher of bonds or barriers.[3] While certain people might be very casual or liberal with oaths, others, simply because of their positions or their attitudes toward themselves, would avoid perjury and would shock us by exclamatory swearing.

It is apparent that, even were I able to leap back into Shakespeare's own time, I would have some difficulty in setting up absolute standards. One butcher might use far stronger language than his neighbour, although both came from the same class. Two men might very well agree about which were the strongest oaths, but be at variance about the offensiveness of somewhat milder phrases. Yet even from the distance of almost four centuries we can assemble a great deal of material that enables us to understand better the effect Shakespeare might have intended to produce in his initial audience.

In the late 1700s, Samuel Johnson, closely followed by Edmund Malone, indicated the method we must use, declaring that obscure phrases in Shakespeare could only be comprehended if one read as widely as possible in the extant literature of the period. Johnson still had some doubts: 'Whether Shakespeare represented the real conversation of his time is not easy to determine.'[4] The method, however, serves to make us aware of the great amount of writing about swearing that has survived even to our time. And if plays by others, legal records, sermons, and the over-written indictments of frothing moralists present a common stock of examples to their divergent audiences, and this stock is also present in Shakespeare, we are probably much closer to contemporary speech than to isolated literary convention.

In the opening chapter, I shall be looking not only at the words, but also at the recurrent comments on the sin of swearing and the pressures to control it. Quite frequently, some isolated scene or speech from Shakespeare will serve as a point of departure for this investigation of the wider background against which the later critical study of many of the plays will be made. The plays themselves need to be approached in varying ways to show to best advantage Shakespeare's increasing skill in his use of oaths as well as his response to a new external factor – the statute of 1606 that sought to eliminate blasphemy from the theatre and printed texts. Generally we can profit little from tracing an individual word through the canon, although occasional comparisons are enriching, and the Spevack *Concordance* has proved invaluable.[5] Context is far more important. In plays as different as *King John* and *Love's Labour's Lost,* the relationship of swearing to plot structure provides a key. In most instances, we will find oaths illuminating some facet of character – the inclination to be fashionable in many of the comedies, the need to express tension in some of the tragedies. Within a single play, the same kind of swearing may emphasise or be a prelude to the revelation of striking contrasts between two figures. Talbot and Burgundy in *Henry VI, Part One*, and Troilus and Cressida provide military and amatory examples of constancy and infidelity, while villains, cowards and heroes may use the same words in different ways to reveal their standards of behaviour.

We are fortunate in having so large a canon to work with, although where the First Folio provides the sole text we may face disappointment. After the blasphemy law of 1606, Shakespeare found ways of writing within legal bounds, and Folio texts of these later plays presumably print the original oath. Earlier works – including, unfortunately, half of the comedies from the 1590s – were first printed in 1623. Comparisons of those plays that do exist in early Quartos with their Folio versions suggest frequent censorship. This is helpful in determining the strength of a particular word, but it also leads to a feeling of frustration. We may not miss a specific oath any more than we would a particularly vivid image that was inadvertently lost in the printing. But there will always be the nagging suspicion that Rosalind originally spiced her vocabulary with something beyond 'faith' and 'honour' when she assumed her 'swashing' and 'martial' outside, or that Sir Toby Belch once shared Falstaff's vocabulary as well as his thirst.[6]

Even with such difficulties, we are amply reminded that the blunderbuss technique of early plays like *Gammer Gurton's Needle* or *Hickscorner*, or of the later *Misogonus*, was not for Shakespeare. John Farmer, with his turn-of-the-century research into swearing and cant terms, might declare 'For variety and force it would be hard to beat the samples found in *Misogonus* and other plays in this volume',[7] but Shakespeare was controlling that sort of creative urge even as he wrote *Richard III*. He carefully kept the horror of the formal curses and the force of oaths or talk of perjury from cancelling each other out. And, as his art matured, he used increasingly subtle patterns. It is this patterning, in its many permutations, that shows us something not unlike his broader achievement with imagery, although swearing is not only more specialised but also more closely tied to popular usage and moral attitudes.

Chapter 1
The Mouth-Filling Oath

Early in the third act of *Henry IV*, *Part One*, Hotspur launches into one of the tirades so typical of him. Moments before, he has taken exception to the rebel partitioning of England and gone farther than necessary in ridiculing the testy Glendower's belief in prodigies. In answer, Glendower has produced unearthly music to accompany Lady Mortimer's Welsh air. Now Hotspur insists on a matching song from his wife, who demurs: 'not mine, in good sooth'. Apparently more annoyed by her choice of words than her refusal, he bursts out, gradually subsiding into the control of verse and finally returning to the real issue. His words not only tell us about him, but also lead into the two areas we must explore: class and strength.

> Not yours, in good sooth? Heart! you swear like a comfit-maker's
> wife. 'Not you, in good sooth!' and 'as true as I live!' and 'as God
> shall mend me!' and 'as sure as day!'
> And givest such sarcenet surety for thy oaths
> As if thou never walk'st further than Finsbury.
> Swear me, Kate, like a lady as thou art,
> A good mouth-filling oath, and leave 'in sooth'
> And such protest of pepper gingerbread
> To velvet guards and Sunday citizens.
> Come, sing.[1]

Hotspur, at this point in the play as frequent a swearer as Falstaff, should know what he is talking about. But why choose a comfit-maker's wife for contrast to a lady? It is not merely that her husband's trade has sweetened her words. The reference to Finsbury and 'Sunday citizens' in their velvet trimmings would have called to the Elizabethan minds a merchant middle class with stricter rules of behaviour than the gentry. They would have understood the use of oaths to define social distinctions, especially with Hotspur's own 'Heart!' ('By God's heart') thrown in for contrast. We may be amused that Hotspur's rigidity extends to Kate's vocabulary, but Shakespeare is telling us more. Hotspur wants in all ways to be at the top of the ladder, and cannot brook a wife who falls short of conventional standards of profanity although, ironically, his own language will become milder later in the play.

I am not, I think, reading too much into the lines. Similar understanding is expected of the audience when Falstaff characterises Master Dombledon, a tailor who has refused him credit, as 'A rascally yea-forsooth knave', adding with a rather mild oath of his own, 'I looked 'a should have sent me two-and-twenty yards of satin, as I am a true knight, and he sends me security' (*Henry IV, Part Two*, I, ii, 34–5, 41–3). Malvolio, dubbed a Puritan by Sir Toby's faction in *Twelfth Night*, may call his hand to witness, but he also uses 'I protest', a phrase synonymous with 'I swear' but as mild as 'yea-forsooth' (I, v, 82; II, iii, 113–14). Finally, characters in *The Comedy of Errors* could have been given pagan oaths – no concern of the censor when it was printed and not subject to cutting. But Shakespeare makes these merchants and a merchant's sons shy away from the 'by Jove' we might expect. Frantic with puzzlement, characters may beat their servants, draw their swords or call officers, but only in the last-act recapitulation, when Antipholus of Ephesus says Angelo had sworn, does the Second Merchant go so far as to declare, unprofanely, 'I will be sworn these ears of mine/ Heard you confess you had the chain of him/After you first forswore it on the mart' (V, i, 260–2).

Although presumably not so delicate as 'fine Mistris Simula', a hypocritical Puritan who would 'faint if she an oath but hear',[2] they tend to be careful of their language, and certainly do not underline minor statements in the manner of Falstaff or Hotspur. Even at the end, where the Duke might call upon them to swear to their statements as he conducts his inquiry, there are not the oaths that gentry employ in the denouements of some of the later works, including *Cymbeline*. Of course, Shakespeare is not totally consistent in this sort of characterisation by omission; and, if we look beyond his works, we will find numerous exceptions. But there is copious support for a generalisation that more swearing was done at the ends of the social scale than in the middle. Randle Cotgrave, while mixing his languages, sticks mainly to the upper ranks of society in making a comparison: 'Il iure comme un Gentilhomme. He swears after a thousand pound a yeare. Il jure comme un Abbé, chartier; gentilhomme; prelate. Like a Tinker, say we.'[3] There seems to be a surprising concentration on religious figures, although there is not the bias that one finds in a Martin Mar-Prelate tract of the late 1580s. Mar-Prelate is, however, attacking what is perceived to be a habit of some churchmen in the 'Epistle to the Terrible Priests of the Convocation House'. One should not trouble the Bishop of London, lest that august person be interrupted at bowls and 'sweare too bad'. And Bishop John is asked 'will you not sweare as commonly you do, like a lewd swag, and say, by my faith my masters, this geare goeth hard with us'.[4] The more writing of the time that we sample, though, the more we will find swearing coming from Cotgrave's gentlemen and tinkers, as well as from soldiers, rather than from priests and bishops.

Almost a century ago, Julian Sharman stated that 'Swearing mostly owed its favour and its audacity to the presence of really cultivated men.'[5] If we recall Ben Jonson's gull Stephen, who wants badly to be thought a gentleman and strains to sound at ease as he mouths great oaths, or the Clown in *The Winter's Tale* adopting his mark of class along with his new clothes, we see how even the social climbers would have agreed with Sharman. But there is an overgeneralisation here, for neither Bobadil, who is coaching Stephen, nor Cob the Water-Carrier is 'really cultivated', and yet there is apparent inventiveness being shown as well as satirised.[6] They have picked up and embroidered phrases, as did the 'Smithfield Ruffian' attacked by Roger Ascham when he deplored the many bad influences young people were subject to.[7] And they are at one with the people of Samuel Rid's City of Vanity, who are all engaged in inventing fashions, words and oaths.[8]

Much of the inventiveness or 'audacity' is part of oral tradition and has been lost, while evanescent secondary meanings or connotations in use by a particular social group are also often preserved only by chance. Renaissance Englishmen were more apt to spend their time compiling dictionaries of hard words or recording the sayings of their queen than setting down the language of the streets with definitions to aid succeeding generations. Thomas Harman, fortunately, kept a list of cant terms, including a few oaths, when he made his observations of the underworld in the 1560s. Rid enlarged Harman's work, and included one particularly interesting example: 'Salomon', which meant 'mass'. He advises the bystander:

Now when many doe presse the poore rogues so earnestly to sweare by the *Salomon*, doe not blame them though they refuse it; for although you know not what it means, yet they very well know: Many men I have heard take this word *Soloman* to be the chiefe commander among the beggars; but to put them out of doubt, this is not he.[9]

Given the scarcity of such information, we are lucky that Shakespeare is not so prone as some of his contemporary dramatists to invent strange oaths or to indulge in those with obscure second meanings. He uses, instead, the phrases that appear time and again in the lists of others, and his swearers range through the social groups most commonly accused of offending. There are even many comments that could have come from the tract- or character-writers of the day, including Henry IV's reference to the 'ruffian that would swear, drink, dance', or Jaques' characterisation of the soldier as 'full of strange oaths' when he catalogues the seven ages of man.[10]

Ironically, it is the Puritans, with their moral grounds for disapproving of all but the oath taken before an official, who tell us most about casual swearing and explain the meanings of some of the abbreviated phrases that Shakespeare does use. It is further irony that, just as censorship of the Rock musical *Hair* in Boston and delay of its opening in London made many people more aware of sex and nudity on stage, so the puritanical fulminations must have made the audience of Shakespeare, Jonson or Greene much more conscious of the theatre's use of oaths. The plays rarely give such illuminating glances into the thinking about profanity as do the tracts and sermons, and it is with them that we will begin. Although attitudes toward a specific phrase might change over the years, certain principles remain, and provide guidelines for determining what might be considered profane, what innocent, even what offended seemingly capricious censors and courts.

The moralists probably felt a bit on the defensive. Hosking notes, as he surveys the theatrical background of the time, that those who did not join in riotous amusement in 1600 were decried as 'puritans';[11] Bernard is speaking from experience in his allegorical guide to behaviour, *The Isle of Man*, when he comments that sin is too often glossed over and '*Filthy Ribaldry*' called '*Merriment*'.[12] Despite tendencies of people to minimise their own sins and laugh at their critics, the complaints continued. There are frequent attacks on the mental attitudes that lead to casual swearing, warnings of the damnation that awaits offenders, and calls for the enactment of civil penalties for a spiritual crime in an effort to save the souls that are being lost daily. Although occasionally pagan precedent is recalled, such as Hesiod's statement that swearing would lead to long-lasting punishment by the gods,[13] predominant references are to the Bible. Alexander Nowell cites Exodus, 20, and Leviticus, 19, reminds his readers of the Lord's Prayer's specific 'Hallowed be Thy name', and points finally to a verse in Jacob, 5: 'Swear not neither by heaven, neither by the earth, nor any other kind of oath.'[14] Nowell's target is 'this great and horrible vice of vaine swearing', and he asks strength to fight 'so great a sinne. . . . So common an evil'.[15] Like many of his fellows he uses a wide range of illustrative rumours and facts, including tales of grim punishments in the far reaches of Scotland and a sweeping reminder that heathens do not swear lightly.

This last point is important to him, for he is particularly upset by the light and frequent utterances of those whose habitual oaths have lost all believability.[16] His specific references are not to kings but to common men, counterparts of the sinners he hopes to reform, and his tales have sorry ends: 'Arthur Miller a filthy talker of ribaldries, a common swearer and blasphemer of GODS name . . . in his sicknesse in the yeare of our Lord, 1573, refused all comfortable doctrine of faith in Christ.'[17] One need not ask what happened to his soul! Despite the volume of Nowell's work and an attitude that suggests opposition to everything from 'by God' to 'by the mousefoot', like many of his contemporaries he fails to list specific examples. These men could assume, of course, that their readers knew the offensive words and needed only to be told of underlying principles.

Some critics, like Thomas Adams, felt there were regional differences, and that innocent 'rural wretches' were happier than corrupt London dwellers because 'they skill not what the studying of oaths means'.[18] Far more are like Gervaise Babington, who in the midsixteenth century was bewailing the apparently general carelessness of English parents heard to 'sweare fearfully without regarde, speake prophanely, not respecting the frailtie of the youth that heareth them'.[19] Weaned on such language, succeeding generations developed a taste for it, and even the translator of the anonymous Spanish–French rodomontade, *Al-man-sir*, seems to have felt a need to cater for this appetite. Original phrases such as 'I swore by *Pluto's* Horns, by the beard of *Mars*, by *Samsons* Whiskers, and by *Mahomets* Alcoran' are not enough, and he inserts bits like 'By the stately gravity of my fore-fathers'.[20] Although the translation comes much later than Shakespeare, it is suited to an English reputation that had been well established two centuries before.[21] Adams lamented in 'The Sinner's Passing Bell' that the streets were full of blasphemers. His sermons on 'England's Sicknesse' reminded his parishioners that 'Oathes are lowder than prayers; men scarce spend two houres of seven dayes at their supplications, whiles they sweare away the whole weeke'.[22]

It is important to note that the 'common swearers' were often, like Falstaff or Doll Tearsheet, people of more than one sin. Court records, tracts, and literary examples all tell of compound offences. Hamlet's declaration that his mother's actions make 'marriage-vows/ As false as dicers' oaths' draws on the stock association of gambling and vow-breaking. Gosson and Stubbes, two of the best-known moralistic writers, are among many who link swearing and forswearing with drinking and betting. The coarse company in gaming-places, the reckless manners that young men thought were expected of them, the tension as dice were rolled, or the influence of drink – all loosened the tongue and led to a forgetfulness of the soul's danger. The air would ring with soon-to-be-forgotten oaths or gratuitous swearing to underline statements of no import, and the playwright creating a tavern scene could give an air of verisimilitude by including at least a reference to such language.

Selecting at random from tracts of the seventeenth century, one finds that Bernard, in *The Isle of Man*, though he dwells less on swearing than one might expect, carefully lists it among other sins. Robert Boyle, who follows his scientific bent by cataloguing excuses given and details of behaviour, asks the man who swears in anger and means no harm: 'Why must your Tongue fly in your Maker's face, and vilify his Sacred name, because your Dice turn up *Size-ace* rather than *Quatre-trey*?' He adds that drunkenness is no more excuse than choler.[23] Babington, a century earlier than Boyle, created a picture of the typical sinner that makes our minds turn again to passages in the *Henry IV* plays. He complains,

> But if he blaspheme the name of the Lord by horrible swearing, if he offende most grievously in pride, in wrath, in gluttonie, and covetousnesse, if he be a drunken alestake, a *ticktack* taverner, keepe a whore or two in his owne house, and moe abroade at bord with other men, with a number such like greevous offences, what doe they? Either he is not punished at all, and most commonly so; or if he be, it is a little penance of their owne inventing, by belly or purse, or to say a certaine of prayers, to visit such an image in pilgrimage, &c.[24]

Compare Falstaff's description of his youth, made more humorous by his initial tone of abstinence followed by quick qualifications: 'I was as virtuously given as a gentleman need to be, virtuous enough; swore little, diced not above seven times a week, went to a bawdy house not above once in a quarter of an hour, paid money that I borrowed three or four times' (*Henry IV, Part One*, III, iii, 12–16). The ailing Henry IV is not amused by such an attitude, although he seems to have done little to punish those he complains about. He lacks the sensitivity to realize that Hal's swearing is neither so strong nor so casual as Falstaff's, and his vision of England after his death is as discouraging as the picture painted by many of Shakespeare's contemporaries.

> Now, neighbour confines, purge you of your scum.
> Have you a ruffian that will swear, drink, dance,
> Revel the night, rob, murder, and commit
> The oldest sins the newest kind of ways?
> Be happy, he will trouble you no more.
> England shall double gild his treble guilt,
> England shall give him office, honour, might.
> (*Henry IV, Part Two*, IV, v, 123–9)

Swearing, according to Boyle, was a relatively easy sin for a man to control, if only he would take the time and trouble to break the habit.[25] Lack of motivation was a continual concern of all the moralists, however, and they seem generally to have felt that some present punishment was the only way to make a man think of his eternal salvation. Andrew Boorde, antedating Boyle by well over a century, declared that the head of the house should take special care 'to punysshe swearers, for in all the worlde there is not such odyble swearing as is used in Englande, specyally amonge youth & chyldren, which is a detestable thyng to here it, and no man doth go aboute to punysshe it'.[26]

The kind of clever rationalisation that appeared in the 'Epistle' of one of the Martin Mar-Prelate pamphlets – 'Amen, is as much as *by my faith*, and so that our Saviour Christe ever sweare by his fayth' – may have dismayed the reformers, but they were more concerned with thoughtless utterances.[27] Although the same sort of bias Gurr warns against in puritanical descriptions of theatre audiences probably colours accounts of various sorts of blasphemy, we must remember that enough people were concerned as to make legal action feasible on an ever-increasing scale.[28] Pressures built up for making what had been a canonical sin, punished by ecclesiastical courts, a statutory crime, and we must assume that it was either active opposition or the dead weight of apathy that kept Parliament from passing a nationwide law two decades before it did. Actually the theatres, so often called a breeding-ground for sin, were regulated just as Shakespeare was completing his great tragedies. There were some local ordinances in effect in the early years of the seventeenth century, too. But a general anti-profanity statute was not enacted until 1623 – a coincidence that may have made the publishers of the First Folio careful to expurgate at least the latter half of their text.

While Captain John Smith coped in a singularly straightforward way with the strong language of the Virginia settlers, punishing an offender with a bucket of water poured down the sleeve for each oath,[29] the English at home were thinking in terms of fines – an approach retained in Maryland until 1953.[30] Boyle pointed out that a fine would not remove the guilt, but it certainly should discourage future lapses. He suggested that a person thus faced with financial as well as spiritual ruin would be well advised to avoid profane company and have a friend call attention to his unconscious and habitual swearing.[31]

Relatively recently Gerald Nokes stated that English lawyers of Shakespeare's time did not comment on religious offences.[32] This may be generally true, but the discussion of swearing seems to have been so pervasive that they and the lawmakers added their voices. How many knew that Justinian had decreed death to those who swore by the limbs of God, or that more recently the Scots had sometimes cut out the tongues of offenders, is a moot point.[33] They probably did not foresee that under the Commonwealth there would be records of similarly gruesome punishments in England.[34] Around 1600 they and others were chiefly concerned with citing precedents for financial levies. Henry VI was mentioned more than once as an example of the non-swearer who took offence at profanity and exacted fines. Nowell, in 1611, lists the English rulers who decreed generally against swearing or specifically against perjury, pointing out that Henry I 'ordained that if any within his owne Pallace did sweare, he should forfeit to the use of the poore for every oth'. There was a sliding scale, from the stiff forty shillings for a duke down through a squire or gentleman's ten shillings to the scourging for a presumably impecunious page or lackey.[35]

While these arguments were being aired, local opinion fostered some legislation that either forbade swearing specifically or included it under the vague rubric of 'disturbing the peace'. Court records include a 1592 indictment, perhaps in common law, against a man who 'reviled a sermon, swearing by God's wounds that there was never a true word in the same'.[36] The case sounds very similar to those dealt with in Stratford-upon-Avon's ecclesiastical court. There Joan Tawnte left church service 'Swearing by the name of God', and Elizabeth Wheeler uttered a string of shocking comments including 'Goodes woondes', in the 1590s.[37] Over a decade later, in 1607, an alehouse at Green Oare, Somerset, was disturbed when John Lyming indulged in 'swearing, swaggering, and blasphemy of the name of God'. Elizabeth Busher, a witch, was punished for railing and, although the actual words are not set down, there is the implication of profane swearing.[38] In the same year, in Richmond, Yorkshire, there was a standard combination of offences in the charges levelled against Alex Scarr of Cubeck, a common drunkard, swearer and blasphemer.[39] I could cite many similar records for the two decades when Shakespeare was most active, but they would add only to our sense of public concern, and not to our knowledge of oaths. The most useful are the very few that list the actual words, for they make clear that it was not God's name alone that could get one into trouble.

Gilbert Northcott had to pay 3s. 4d. for saying 'upon my life'. Thomas Courtis was fined for swearing in Court 'God is my witness', and 'I speak in the presence of God'. Christopher Gill, being reproved by Mr Nathaniel Durant, clerk, 'for having used an oath, God's life, in discourse', went and informed against the minister himself for swearing![40]

Because there had to be at least one witness under oath, convictions were sometimes hard to come by and people were understandably touchy about their accusers. This must have been especially true when punishments were decreed for something apparently far short of 'blaspheming the name of God'. When we examine more closely some of the cuts made in plays, we should remember that William Harding of Chittlehampton was punished for 'Upon my life' and Thomas Buttand for 'On my troth'![41] The theatrical censors were not being excessively idiosyncratically puritanical, for they reflected the thinking of many of their countrymen.

For the most part we do not know the social class of the men and women who were punished, or of their accusers. Brinkworth finds in the Stratford records that Edward Samon was a hayward.[42] Humphrey Trevitt must have been a man of some substance, for he paid thirty-three shillings, four pence (the price of about a hundred gallons of beer) for ten oaths.[43] We are not surprised at a social trend that appears when bills begin to be introduced into Parliament, however. In 1595, a Monsieur Rodenburg, recognising the potential volume of cases, suggested to Lord Burghley that a great part of a proposed general revenue bill might be raised from fines on swearing.[44] The proposal was dropped, and it was not until six years later that a measure 'against usual and common swearing' passed the Commons, was sent to the Lords, and actually got a first reading. It, too, was dropped.[45]

If we think back to Hotspur's reaction to Kate's 'in good sooth', or remember that the Lords would be closer to the most noted swearer of all, Queen Elizabeth, we are not surprised at their lack of enthusiasm. It would have been a ticklish matter to legislate fines for all Englishmen when Elizabeth might have greeted the statute with an oath! Perhaps, though, she would not have been completely against the law. If one examines Chamberlin's accounts of her sayings, one does find 'forsooth' far less frequently than passages like 'God's death. Villain, I will have thy head!' (shouted in response to Sir Nicholas Throckmorton's advice that she dismiss some Catholics from her council).[46] But her writing does not seem to include the kind of casual swearing Wellbred wrote to Young Knowell in the first version of Jonson's *Every Man in His Humour*.[47] She emphasised to her sister the importance of a sovereign's oath and, like Shakespeare's heroic swearers, respected a serious vow. Time and again I feel she swore to startle, knowing that she could back up what might have been mere bombast in a less powerful person. We can imagine the response when she turned from cards and suddenly demanded of Robert Carey when his father intended to take up a new post, exclaiming: 'God's wounds! I will set him by the feet and send another in his place if he dallies thus.'[48] Her language was not original, nor did it spring organically from the topic of conversation as do some literary examples. But it was quotable, and many courtiers emulated her. As Nathan Drake concludes: 'A shocking practice seems to have been rendered fashionable by the very reprehensible habit of the Queen . . . for it is said that she never spared an oath in public speech or private conversation when she thought it added energy to either.'[49]

Drake implies, and many of the quotations in Chamberlin demonstrate, a degree of calculation missing from the utterance of the casual swearers. It is worth noting, however, that in plays 'God's wounds' is spoken by men. Doll Tearsheet, the doxy of *Henry IV, Part Two*, and Zantippa, the cursed woman of *The Old Wives Tale* may use 'God's light' or 'By gogs bones', but they and their kind never go all the way.[50] Indeed, Elizabeth is said to have sworn 'like a man', and certainly would have posed a problem to anyone trying to enforce a new law regulating oaths.

Her successor, King James, seems to have taken a dimmer view of profanity, for there is little record of his swearing casually, and he was a theatrical patron when that statute of 1606 was passed, forcing authors and actors away from many of the oaths that had served so well before.[51] He was still on the throne when both houses of Parliament agreed 'to prevent and reform profane swearing and cursing', thus reinforcing the regional courts that had haphazardly 'bound over and penalized the profane'.[52] After 1623 presumably any person convicted on the oath of two witnesses would find himself in the stocks for three hours if he neglected to pay the shilling fine or, if he were under twelve, be subject to a public whipping. The law was accompanied, incidentally, by an ordinance restricting 'the haunting of inns'.[53] Joannes Ferrarius, whose work was published the year after Elizabeth's accession, would have been pleased. He complained that blasphemy was so common that even the Church winked at it; that nobles were never punished, although occasionally 'some of the baser people' were; and that the ruler was patently neglecting the duty of a prince to keep the people aware of the commandments of God.[54]

Those 'commandments of God' were both the authority behind moralistic writings and the justification for civil laws. Although to us, and presumably to many in the seventeenth century, stealing and killing are worse than a sin which often damages only one's own soul, there are some tracts that emphasise the order of the Ten Commandments. Taking 'the name of the Lord in vain' does precede murder, theft and adultery, and is the only instance where God Himself speaks of punishment.[55] (The injunction against 'false witness' is conveniently omitted from this line of thinking!) The third and ninth commandments were really together in the minds of many, however, and the old worry recurs that the habitual swearer would be less apt to think seriously about a formal oath. Although some of the strictest Puritans insisted that a man's word should be enough, most of them felt that solemn swearing was essential to the State.[56] Governmental operations would be endangered if men risked their souls as casually as a modern chain smoker lights a cigarette despite a health warning on the packet. The words are almost identical whether one reads Nowell, Boyle or someone from the intervening years:

at all times he sweareth, and by swearing dishaloweth, as much as in him lyeth, the most holy and reverent name of GOD; in so much that a common swearer, if he be in the feare of God reprehended for his vain swearing, he answereth with an other othe, that he sware not afore. I have heard ere now, a vaine fellow to be gently reprehended for ye damnable custome of swearing, and his answer hath been with an execrable oth, that such reprehension needed not, for he never sware lightly, whose wordes truely understood, he spake more truly than he was aware, not lightly, but heavily.[57]

As we shall soon see, there was one school of thought that considered something as innocent-sounding as 'by the mousefoot' dangerous. More often, however, attention centred on this dishallowing use of God's name. Boyle, more thoroughly than any of Shakespeare's contemporaries, traces the habit in an individual who might first utter 'God forgive me' or 'God help you', and then a 'Customary Exclamation' like 'O God! O Jesus!' to 'supply the want of a Complement'. When one reaches the point of saying God's name easily and without thinking, it is a short step to habitual swearing.[58]

Much of the material we have been examining so far would have had the effect, in modern parlance, of raising the consciousness of the Elizabethans and Jacobeans. It has also, for us, painted a rather broad picture of attitudes toward profanity, and we can say with more assurance that gentry seeking to follow fashion or keeping bad company, and many from the lower classes who haunted taverns, drank and gambled, would have indulged in this vice, either in anger or out of habit. Habit or thoughtlessness seems to loom large, for one cannot be thinking if 'one riskes one's soul for mere air'.[59] Although we shall return again to the matter of perjury, we already have a good sense of the serious and widespread arguments against both swearing and forswearing.

Some of the writers were most concerned with the effect on government and law when people became casual about oaths, but more were concerned about individual souls in a nation swept by a dangerous sin.

The 'Zounds' that Shakespeare found liberally sprinkled through *The Famous Victories of Henry V* or the many phrases that spice *Misogonus* were literary echoes of this evil. They contrast sharply to oaths that Babington describes as 'for glorie of God and truth and love of neighbor, not in cholor, in malice, for spite and envie'.[60] God and His attributes might safely be called to witness officially, but under these circumstances His name alone often sufficed. It was on a more popular level that the 'attributes' were mentioned, probably perfectly naturally by people who were expected to attend church regularly and learn about God's incarnation and physical suffering. Wounds, blood, body, eyelid, life, death, nails and cross or rood, the whole of the Passion, found their way into common usage, as did the bread of the Last Supper, the mass itself, and 'God's Mother' by many names.

In this list one immediately sees two examples that might have lost strength after the Reformation – the mass and any mention of the Virgin. The former seems to have been regarded in different ways during Shakespeare's lifetime, and we would need far wider evidence than we possess to decide whether, for example, it was considered milder in the 1590s, when post-Armada anti-Catholicism was rife, than in the first decades of the 1600s. Elyot in *The Governour* (1531) and Earle in his *Micro-Cosmographie* (1628) specifically call it 'out-of-date' and 'innocent'. But Thomas Lupton, a very minor writer, used it carefully in his interlude *All for Money* (1578), and it was occasionally censored after 1606,[61] as when Polonius' speech is either cut or weakened to 'Misse' in the Folio. Although the formal mass was not important to the Protestants, one might have expected 'God's bread' to retain its significance. There was a heated argument over the doctrine of transubstantiation, however, and for many this symbol would not have seemed quite so strong as the actual body or blood. Sharman noted that it had lost its pre-Reformation strength,[62] though neither it nor the mass ever became as mild as one minced oath which was originally 'by the Virgin Mary'. Legions of people used 'marry' quite safely to add a bit of emphasis to a statement, and even a censor who would pounce on 'faith' ignored it. 'By our Lady', with its elided forms such as 'By'r Lady', is on the other hand more like 'Mass'. The Virgin might no longer be an intercessor for the majority of Englishmen, but she was holy, and a reference to her might be censored.

Reforming Protestants were responsible for burning many crucifixes, but the rood remained a central symbol for all Christians. When people swore by it, however, it was not called 'God's rood', and therefore was technically milder than 'God's nails', although probably more important in the minds of many. It can be safely left in the Folio *Romeo and Juliet* to add one more bit of emphasis to the Nurse's speech, which is full of mild oaths and asseverations (I, iii, 36). The Hostess was evidently swearing more forcefully when she emphasised her anger at Falstaff with 'God's light', which was excised from the Folio (*Henry IV, Part One*, III, iii, 59).

Here I seem to be implying that the censors are reliable guides to the strength of words, while earlier I implied that some of their dicta were idiosyncratic. Actually they follow certain principles, but one has to go beyond a record of their displeasure to draw firm conclusions. Certainly they cut many things that Dr Bowdler and his family would later let stand, while ignoring words that seemed offensive to Victorians.[63] Edmund Tilney was Master of the Revels when the 1606 statute was passed, but was succeeded in 1608 by Buck (or Buc), who after fifteen years was in turn followed by Sir Henry Herbert. Enough manuscripts survive for us to learn that both Buck and Herbert worked very unevenly, sometimes going beyond their charge to prevent 'the Great abuse of the Holy Name of God in Stage plays'. In one relatively well-known instance, Sir William Davenant appealed against Herbert's 1634 black-penning of *The Wits*, and King Charles supported the author. Sir Henry could only sputter: 'The King is pleased to take faith, death, 'slight for asseverations and no oaths, to which I do humbly submit as my master's judgement; but under favour conceive them to be oaths, and enter them here to declare my opinion and submission.'[64] Perhaps because of the growing strength of Puritan opinion, Herbert was somewhat stricter than Buck; but we also have proof here of laxity in high places, when an abbreviated form of 'God's death' was considered merely an asseveration.

E. K. Chambers and others who examine the cuts all comment on their erratic nature.[65] Virginia Gildersleeve, summing up Buck's work, incidentally notices a problem peculiar to verse drama. His excisions, she says, are 'generally disastrous to the meter. "Sheart" or "Heart," and "'Slife" or "Life," he often crosses out, nor will he permit "By th' mass." But he frequently nods, and passes over "Life." "Faith" he seems never to object to.'[66] Chambers is actually mixing two considerations when he notes that 'In half a dozen places such expletives as "Life" and "heart" are excised; in many more these and others, such as "mass" and "faith," which one would have supposed to be as much or as little objectionable, remain unquestioned.'[67] First, the censor is sometimes marking, sometimes ignoring the same word. Second, the censor seems to be distinguishing between phrases where 'God's' is understood and those where it was never part of the oath. If we turn to the anonymous *Second Maiden's Tragedy*, submitted for licensing in 1611, we find that folio after folio bear no marks. Then suddenly the heavy black pen comes down frequently, noting words that were passed over a few leaves before. In one instance, even a soldier's 'By this hand' and the four following lines are cut, although the whole speech seems innocent to the twentieth-century reader.[68]

We need to examine more of the moralistic pronouncements to understand the latter marking, but I feel a conclusion can be drawn about the handling of the manuscript as a whole. Buck and his assistants, who had more to do than hunt oaths, would not have had time to examine every line of every play. Extant manuscripts seems to show a sampling, with a few pages thoroughly marked as exempla. If a theatre company did not follow these guidelines, the law still had a hold. 'All the courts of record at Westminster [were] empowered to entertain proceedings instituted by common informers for the recovery of penalties of £10' for each time a person, in a performance, 'jestingly or prophanely' used the name of God, Christ, the Holy Ghost or the Trinity.[69] This was no idle threat. We know that Ben Jonson was called from a sickbed to answer for oaths in *The Magnetic Lady* and pleaded his innocence, whereupon the actors confessed that they had made the additions.[70] One wonders how many times such embellishments escaped notice, how many times actors spoke lines from earlier plays in their unexpurgated original state or, for that matter, how many of the profane lines in Jonson's *The Alchemist*, written in 1610, were actually spoken unchanged by Doll, Face or Subtle.

It is easy for us to recognise the exceptionable phrases that include God's name, clearly said. But laziness, the twinge of conscience, or the speed born of excitement and stress led many swearers to elide or omit the possessive. 'Od's life' or 'Od's bodkins' ('God's little body') marks a middle stage, with the diminutive signalling another attempt to make the word less offensive. Occasionally the intended happens, and the meaning is forgotten. 'Gadzooks' may refer to God's hocks. Ironically, in this instance God's name remains more recognisable than the attribute. Often the elision went farther, to ''Sblood' or ''Swounds', or the more compressed ''Slud' or ''ouns', which seem like nonsense until we think what they stand for. New words were formed, like today's 'golly', not in the heat of a single moment, but as evolved parts of the vocabulary of those who needed habitual 'safe' ways to emphasise their statements. These minced oaths, however, were attacked just as vigorously by the moralists as the original expressions. Boyle was among those who complained of such crafty changes, reminding users of 'by Dod, and c.' who think they can 'justify their Oaths' by such 'disguising of them' that they are not fooling God.[71]

Shakespeare makes less use of the barely understandable mincings than some of his contemporaries. Old Gobbo has his 'Be God's sonties' (little saints? sanctities?). Ophelia sings 'By Gis' and 'by Cock' in the Saint Valentine's Day song. The former, relatively rare in print, is usually used by women when it occurs, and may be spelled 'Jis'.[72] Presumably it is a form of 'Jesus'. The latter, which I have recently heard glossed as a sexual vulgarity in keeping with some of the other startling phrases Ophelia utters, apparently meant 'by God' to the Elizabethans.[73] Farmer specifically refers to a rather common 'softened' phrase, 'by cock and pie', where 'pie' is the sacred book of offices. The combination appears in *Misogonus*, at least a decade before Shakespeare began writing, and in *Wily Beguiled*, a comedy from 1606.[74] Justice Shallow and George Page, both good members of the upper middle class, use it for conveniently unshocking emphasis as they press their hospitality on someone (*Henry IV, Part Two*, V, i, 1; *The Merry Wives of Windsor*, I, i, 272). Farmer also includes the more self-explanatory 'Cock's precious soul' in his list of oaths, but ignores the muddled 'Cockes stones bones' that rings out in Breton's *Merry Wonders*.[75]

The list of mincings could be extended almost indefinitely to include every invention set down in play or pamphlet. 'By our ladykins' becomes 'Be lakins'; and even 'By my faith', despite its mildness, is altered to 'Bum vay', perhaps only because of laziness. Hamlet, in a good mood with the boy actor, will use 'By'r lakins', although generally his elisions do not include the diminutives. In fact, tragic heroes as a rule do not use the familiar-seeming diminutions, which generally come from women, or from characters in comedy.

On the other hand, the simple elision to the *s* form is as strong as the original. Buck and Herbert cut ''Sheart' and the Folio omits ''Swounds' and ''Sblood' from pre-1606 plays. In moments of extreme stress, in fact, the elision would have been very natural. It is the form also favoured by the casual swearers when they want to mention God's attributes. Even when the *s* is missing, the meaning is understood, and it is no wonder that Buck and Herbert would find 'Life' objectionable.

There is the problem of where to draw a line. Presumably Rosalind's listeners are expected to have a list in mind when she speaks of 'all pretty oaths that are not dangerous' (*As You Like It*,

IV, i, 174). To most, evidently, one could safely call on anything not connected with God. But to others a saint was forbidden, and to some it was really worse to say 'by this hand' or 'by the mousefoot'. Babington is most particular when he enlarges his commentary on the Ten Commandments to include a warning. If we swear by those that are not gods, including Mary, Peter, Paul, faith and truth, we must remember 'what GOD saieth by the Prophet, namlie, that they that sweare by any thing that is not GOD doo flatlie forsake the true GOD himself'. Furthermore we must never 'sweare by the name of God in our common talke, although the matter be never so true, but onelie where the glorie of God is sought, or the salvation of our brethren, or before a Magistrate in witnessing the trueth, when we are thereunto lawfully called'. In such a situation, 'we must onlie sweare by the name of God. But as for Saints, Angels, Roode, Booke, Crosse, Masse, or any other thing, we ought in no case by them to sweare.'[76] One need not mention the symbols of Christian belief, he adds, because all are implied in God's own name. When one uses it, one calls also on attributes, providence, 'mercie', law and doctrine.[77]

Although, in 1613, Sir John Harrington called 'the pix' and 'the mousefoot' 'innocent', perhaps giving a clue to some of the phrases Rosalind had in mind, others found these a mark of idolatry. Stubbes, writing when Shakespeare was growing up, his less famous contemporary, Robert Crowley, and Boyle, born about a decade after Shakespeare's death, all agree remarkably in their attitude toward even the most innocent-seeming words. Boyle, with characteristic clarity, postulates the arguments that the habitual oath-monger is apt to advance: 'But I do not take God's Name in vain; for I swear not by God, or by Christ, or other Oaths of the like nature, but only by the Creatures, as by this Light, by this Bread, by Heaven, and the like; and the Creatures name I hope it no sin to take in vain.'[78] He counters, 'If God forbids swearing by heaven and earth (Matthew 5.34) surely this includes all things,' and adds that, if one swears by a thing, one must be elevating it to godhead. Otherwise, what is the point of swearing by it? The man who tries to be safe is, in fact, an idolater, and God will punish this sin as surely as He will perceive and punish a minced or mongrel oath.[79]

Stubbes attacks this sort of verbal craftiness with similar vigour. In a dialogue the simpler-minded Spudeus asks the more knowing Philoponus, 'Is it so greate a matter to sweare? Doeth not the worde of God saie, thou shalt honour me, and sweare by my name, and those that sweare by me shall bee commended?' His position is like that of one of Plato's questioners, who is immediately proven wrong by the greater wisdom of Socrates. Philoponus, of course, waxes far more emotional than the Socratic reasoner, giving an absolute answer and adding a general admonition. The lengthy speech culminates in a list, an explanation of what some of the oaths really mean, and a warning of God's wrath.

And to sweare by God at every worde, by the World, by S. Jhon [*sic*], by S. Marie, S. Anne, by Bread and Salte, by the Fire, or by any other Creature, thei thinke it nothyng blame worthie . . . to sweare by God at every woorde, is the greatest othe that can bee. For in swearyng by God, thou swearest by God the Father, by God the Sonne, and by God the holie Ghost, and by all the whole divine Nature, Power, dietie, and essence. When thou swearest by Gods harte, thou swearest by his misticall wisedome. When thou swearest by his bloud, thou swearest by his life. When thou swearest by his feete, thou swearest by his humanitie. When thou swearest by his armes, thou swearest by his power. When thou swearest by his finger, or tung, thou swearest by the holie Spirite. When thou swearest by his nosethrells, thou swearest by his inspirations. When thou swearest by his eyes, thou swearest by his providence. Therefore, learne this, and beware of swearing, you bloudie Butcher, least God destroye you in his wrathe. And if you sweare by the Worlde, by S. Jhon, Marie, Anne, Bread, Salt, Fire, or any other creature that ever God made, whatsoever it be, little or muche, it is horrible Idolatrie, and damnable in it self.[80]

This whole argument about idolatry may surprise us today, and was evidently not in the minds of those who happily substituted 'by my life' or 'by Jupiter' for 'by God'. But it must have been behind Buck's displeasure at 'by this hand' and have motivated some of those court judgments cited earlier. Stubbes felt so strongly about the evil that he wished all 'bloody swearers' could be killed or at least deprived of a limb or their tongues. God would of course eventually exact vengeance, but at least a swearer should be branded for all to see. One senses a note of despair when he finally pleads that, if there is not to be a prison sentence, there should certainly be a fine.[81] Crowley's epigrammatic piece, *Of Blasphemous Swerers*, repeats much of this and in doing so helps show just how pervasive the arguments were. Its irregular poetic lines include warnings many Puritans took to heart, the usual promises, and a catalogue of examples from the 'innocent' through the 'minced' to the very strong.

The sonne of Syrach wryteth playnelye
Of suche menne as do sweare blasphemouselye.

'The manne that sweareth muche shall by fylled,' sayeth he,
'Whyth all wicked manners, and iniquitie.
In the house of that manne the plage shall not cease;
He shalbe styll plaged either more or less.'
Christe byddeth all his affirme and denie,
Wyth yea, yea; nay, nay; affirmyng no lye.
'Whatsoever ye ad more' (saith he) 'cometh of ivell,
And is of the wycked suggestion of the devyll.'
But we can not talke wythouten othes plentye.
Some sweare by Gods mayles, hys herte, and his bodye;
And some sweare by his fleshe, his bloude, and hys fote;
And some by his guttes, hys lyfe, and herte rote.
Some other woulde seme all sweryng to refrayne,
And they invent idle othes, such is theyr idle brayne: –
By cocke and by pye, and by the goose wyng;
By the crosse of the mouse fote, and by saynte Chyckyn.
And some sweare by the Divell, such is theyr blyndness;
Not knowyng that they call these thynges to wytnes,
Of their conscience, in that they affirme or denye.
So boeth sortes commit Moste abhominable blasphemie.[82]

One aspect, closely related, that we have hinted at but not examined closely is perjury. If courts and other institutions were dependent on statements under oath, they were also dependent on man's aversion to perjuring himself. Philoponus carefully explained to Spudeus, 'you must understand that there be two maner of swearings: the one Godly, the other ungodly: the one lawfull, the other damnable. The Godly swearyng, or lawfull othe, is when we be called by the Magistrates . . . to depose a truth.'[83] Babington seems to be contradicting his earlier absolute stand when he suggests that the New Testament really takes exception not because swearing itself is intrinsically bad, 'but because forswearing is horrible'. He is arguing here that proper swearing really honours God, however, because it has a purpose and ritual and dignity absent from casual utterances.[84]

Nicholas Breton, in his character of 'The Unworthy Merchant', is dismayed that such a person would 'adventure a false oath for fradulent gaine'.[85] From what we have seen of the *Henry IV* plays, or could see in Jonson's *The Alchemist*, where the tobacconist Abel Drugger's vocabulary is very mild, it would seem that a swearing merchant would be subject to comment, and a perjuring one would be especially reprehensible.[86] After all, perjury was criticised in dicers where it was expected, and caused serious strife if it was practised in high government posts. It is the 'Knave' whose 'Words are lies, his Oathes perjuries', and the 'Atheist' who swears a grace because an oath has no import to him.[87] Shakespeare echoes this general concern with special attention to those who would break a formal oath. The troubled Duke of York resists pressure to shift his allegiance from Richard II and is horrified that others are disloyal, even though he is aware that the King is abusing his office. Hotspur, as things grow more serious for the rebels, will give up his casual profanity and talk frequently of formally sworn oaths that he thinks have been broken. Like many of the serious young men who swear a good deal, he is still very much aware of honour and of keeping one's word.

It is, of course, in the world of the tragedies and histories that the consequences of perjury are most destructive, for there even clever rationalisation cannot counteract the effects of shifting allegiances or of convenient lies underlined with vows. There are many instances like Octavius Caesar's accusation that Antony broke an oath to send 'arms and aid' which help to lay the foundations for future animosity (*Antony and Cleopatra*, II, ii). And conscience can haunt a vow-breaker. We have only to think of the Duke of Clarence, who forsook his father-in-law, Warwick, during the Wars of the Roses, and who, on the eve of his death, dreams of accusing wraiths shrieking 'false, fleeting, perjur'd Clarence'. While Richard is reminding others of his sin '(which Jesu pardon!)', the murderers are accusing George himself:

2 Murderer: For false forswearing and for murder too:
        Thou didst receive the sacrament to fight
        In quarrel of the house of Lancaster.
1 Murderer: And like a traitor to the name of God
        Didst break that vow, and with thy treacherous blade
        Uprip'st the bowels of thy sov'reign's son.
2 Murderer: Whom thou wast sworn to cherish and defend.
                              (*Richard III*, I, iv, 197–203)

The comedies provide a different level of punishment, as we shall see when we examine the structure and actions of *Love's Labour's Lost* or the unmasking of Parolles when he is supposed to retrieve a captured drum in *All's Well that Ends Well*. In the comic world, in fact, certain vows are made to be broken when a character behaves wrongly and needs to be educated to another point of view. One thinks of Bertram, who has negated his marriage vows by his subsequent oath never to sleep with his wife. Still, there is a bad taste in the mouth when he must be tricked into breaking this later vow and then prevaricates about his actions in Florence. And frequently, when the oath-breaking is a source of laughter for the audience, the characters remain serious about it. If the comic is mixed with the historic, there is, of course, even more pressure to preserve the world of the play from such sin.

Falstaff has chosen the 'baudie talke, & damnéd profanation Of Godes most holy name' with men who 'will rage, sweare, curse . . . Break glasses, & throw pottes against the wall'.[88] Prince Hal may enjoy it for a while, but gradually draws farther from it as he moves closer to his coronation, and must banish a man who stands so openly for the reprehensible. At least here there is the openness. In the tragedies, too often honest men with an aversion to perjury do not realise until too late that the villain is swearing to lies.

I have noted that continued attention to oaths would heighten people's awareness of them. I should also mention that shortly after Elizabeth's accession oaths of allegiance and supremacy were instituted for all Englishmen. Some may have taken them as casually as many Americans took state loyalty oaths during the McCarthy era. But others would have been thoughtful about these formal and carefully recorded statements of allegiance and religious like-mindedness. Surely these people would have been quick to grasp the import of swearings and forswearings that they saw on stage. Although King James I supposedly said, 'I will never believe that man whose honesty relies only upon oaths,'[89] and reliance on them gradually decreased around 1600, formal oaths were still an essential part of court and other government procedures.

Attention paid to perjury in tracts and other commentaries was small in comparison with that paid to casual swearing, however. There was little argument about what constituted it, and generally its roots were seen in the casualness with which oaths entered everyday conversation.[90] Nowell, sounding very like Crowley, admonishes, 'thinke an othe to be no grace nor no garnishing unto your speach. . . . Sweare not at all, not at all, lette your communication bee yea, yea, no, no, that which is more than this is sin.'[91] Ferrarius did not hesitate to attribute the troubles of the commonwealth to its vices, insisting that oaths, perjury and 'wrong swearing' helped to detract from overall prosperity. His finger-wagging injunction against 'by heaven . . . by the earth . . . by Jerusalem . . . or by thine own head' was capped with an admonition to use the phrase that Falstaff so scorned: 'Your communication must be yea, yea, naie, naie.'[92]

Although in a sense everyone who swore casually was defending the habit by his actions, there was very little written justification for it. The chapter on 'Fashionable Swearing' will bring us closer to people like the bragging gallant of *The Times' Whistle* who shot out oaths 'in vollies, like artillerie', while 'Swearing his manhood all mens else exceeds.'[93] Such men could scarcely attack the moralists directly, for they would be attacking Biblical precepts, too. But they could suggest that many of the non-swearers were like Mistress Simula in their hypocrisy. Dekker, in *The Seven Deadly*

Sinnes of London, spoke of the 'Puritane' who 'sweares by nothing but Indeede . . . wrapping his crafty Serpents body in the cloke of religion [while] he does those acts that would become none but a Devill'.[94] In *How a Man May Choose a Good Wife from a Bad*, Fuller's tale of dressing conservatively and speaking mildly to appeal to a 'puritan' reaches a climax when he swears 'in sooth' to put out the light and 'in troth' to go to bed with her. According to him, her apparent reluctance to yield was rationalised away: 'though I be loth,/I'll come, quoth she, be't but to keep your oath'.[95] Many other Puritans are shown with a similar scale of values and ability to find excuses for their questionable behaviour.

Ben Jonson, who had a marvellous ear for cant, touches on those who 'play the foole . . . to challenge the Author of scurrilite, because the language some where savours of Smithfield, the Booth, and the Pigbroth, or profaneness', and then launches into *Bartholomew Fair* with its satire on Puritans.[96] He is suggesting the playwright's best defence, for many dramatists felt they were presenting a theatre of the world, not working for a 'School of Abuse' or 'Bawdry'. Rather than teaching people 'to play the vice,̈ sweare, teare, and blaspheme both Heaven and Earth',[97] they were mirroring those who already practised such sins. If they were to present the sorts of people so often censured by the moralists, they would have to make the speech ring at least partially true to the audience.

They might have argued further that plays often satirised braggarts and loose-swearing soldiers and gentry, and usually exposed or punished perjurers. Had the Puritans read the plays, they would have been forced to admit that not all swearers were flattered. The problem, of course, is that many rather attractive characters swear under stress, at moments when the audience would be expected to sympathise with them. And on the stage even Stephen the Gull was more exciting than Stephen Gosson in the pulpit. There is also dramatic exaggeration: in a play like *Misogonus* one might hear more oaths in two hours than one could elsewhere. Especially after 1606, when playwrights had to invent phrases that the censor could not object to, there was a great deal of cleverness in concocting occasional oaths to spice the language of gentry and braggarts. Shakespeare and many of his contemporaries did not revise their earlier works, but Jonson's rewriting produced speeches that are more imaginative than the originals, and might well have been echoed by members of the audience.

The end product was verisimilitude in the theatre. Shakespeare occasionally wanted the kind of artificiality the formalised and poetic Gardeners of *Richard II* achieve, but more often he created servants, soldiers, rogues and young gentry whose language is what

Stubbes or Crowley might have expected. The Capulets' Nurse, Angelica, avers 'By my maidenhead at twelve year old' that she has called Juliet, simultaneously giving us a hint of her good-natured coarseness and in a way preparing us for the talk of Juliet's youth and readiness for marriage.[98] At the other end of the social scale, Mercutio uses stronger words, but shares honours with Angelica for frequency of swearing. Petruchio, as we shall see later, occasionally goes farther than a gentleman might be expected to when he uses oaths as part of his shrew-taming strategy; while Dr Caius, the explosive Frenchman in *The Merry Wives of Windsor*, would seem less volatile were his speech not continually punctuated by his accented 'by Gar'. There are many sermon-like parts of William Averell's writings that playwrights would have taken exception to, but surely they would have agreed with the tongue that speaks out in a dialogue with the body, insisting that swearing and forswearing are part of its work.[99]

Audiences might have taken some time to adjust to the relative strength of utterances in the post-1606 plays, but context would have helped them, and there was still the possibility of creating a feeling that one person swore while another abstained. Before 1606, faced with the traditional panoply of oaths, they would have had little trouble. They would have grasped instantly the exasperation and dismay of the sweating man who bursts into a cobbler's shop and explodes 'Zoones' when he discovers the pair of shoes he is after have been sold.[100] They should have realised quickly that Hal is not so profane as Hotspur or Falstaff, or that Richard III, while playing the mild man, is very careful to keep his asseverations and reactions to oaths in harmony with his assumed character.

The list of profane expressions, as we have seen, was rather limited if one included only the most exceptionable. The parts of Christ's or God's body, especially the blood and wounds of His crucifixion, were the strongest. Less forceful, especially in Protestant England, were the Virgin, saints, and some aspects of ritual. Even farther down the list there were one's own body and soul, which might be important to the swearer, but generally unexceptionable to the censors. Air, stars, ale, sword and anything else that one saw or used daily could of course be called to witness, although upon occasion it would be punished. Some of the most exotic or trivial were, in the plays at least, intended to evoke more laughter than worry. Fortunatus, in *Wily Beguiled*, lets out strings of classical references when he swears. His 'By Mars his bloody blade, and fair Bellona's bowers' is, in contrast to the earthy Cricket's 'I swear by the blood of my codpiece', suggestive, but not so strong as the 'Zounds' that marks his real anger.[101] A dandy would not surprise us in calling articles of clothing to witness, and we would be amused that he is actually deifying his outward adornments. Of course, Stubbes would have seen this as further evidence of the kind of corruption he was continually attacking.

For us today, formal oaths are easier to recognise and understand, even without the glosses that scholarly editions provide. The attitudes of the characters give a clue to their seriousness. It is the informal utterances that I have been concentrating on that may cause us trouble. We must try to understand the implications some people would have seen in the clothing oaths noted above. On the other hand, we must guard against a twentieth-century tendency to be too psychologically subtle. The Second Bandit in *The Two Gentlemen of Verona*, in a mere twenty-five lines, has one oath by his beard and one 'By the bare scalp of Robin Hood's fat friar' (IV, i, 10, 36). It would be absurd to suggest that he has any fixation on hair. On the other hand, he is presumably saying something about his appearance, and he is quite probably indicating that he thinks of himself and his band as akin to Robin and his popular heroes, rather than a mere collection of robbers. Occasionally, although we might very well illuminate some oath as particularly appropriate, Shakespeare merely took it over from his sources. Richard of Gloucester appeals to the citizens of London in his bid for power, and we can imagine him glancing at their cathedral and calling upon Saint Paul. In fact, neither Shakespeare nor Holinshed tells us why he evoked this figure, and Richard's more subtle swearing comes with other oaths.

The list of variants could be extended. Much of the material is repetitious, though, and would only serve to reinforce the impression I hope is now absolutely clear – that people were vitally concerned about swearing during Shakespeare's lifetime. The sampling is biased, of course, but the moralists would have been less vocal had they had fewer examples to work with. It remains for us to examine the wider range of Shakespeare's plays to see oaths not as parts of lists or excerpts from sermons, but as organic parts of a dialogue, helping to delineate character, stimulate action, or even provide a vehicle for satire.

Chapter 2

Oaths as Structure

An oath taken or an oath remembered often becomes the excuse for later action in the plays. Hotspur and other rebels recall Henry Bolingbroke's return from exile, when he had declared the limits of his ambition. Northumberland had then answered Old York's challenge:

> The noble duke hath sworn his coming is
> But for his own; and for the right of that
> We all have strongly sworn to give him aid;
> And let him never see joy that breaks that oath!
> (*Richard II*, II, iii, 148–51)

In *Henry IV, Part One*, when the rebel faction is challenged – this time by Henry and Prince Hal – Worcester reminds the King that he and others risked much to join Henry's cause, for 'You swore to us,/And you did swear that oath at Doncaster,/That you did nothing purpose 'gainst the state' (V, i, 41–3). Now, says Worcester speaking for the rest, Henry has aggrandised power and forgotten his oath.

At first glance this argument seems reasonable. Hotspur, to some extent honour personified, can be expected to take extreme offence at perjury. The older rebels may be less voluble in their dislike of Henry, but they are, after all, men of some repute who feel they have been betrayed. The situation, however, is far more subtle. They, in turn, have broken trust with Henry who, despite a shaky claim to the throne, is trying to keep the kingdom together. Shakespeare had reminded his audience earlier that England could face the world if it 'to itself do rest but true' (*King John*, V, vii, 118). But we have seen these rebels dividing a map of England, squabbling about a river here, a point of land there. Worcester, Hotspur and the others feel a need to justify their disloyalty publicly and to themselves. The oath taken in an earlier play becomes a rationalisation, seemingly supplanting problems of prisoners and ransoms. It is interesting that we do not see Henry deny he is forsworn, but do witness his generalisation that insurrection always hunts its pretexts (*Henry IV, Part One*, V, i, 72–82). Worcester, least truthful of the rebels, strengthens that pretext by returning from a parley and announcing to Hotspur that Henry's 'oath-breaking . . . he mended thus,/By now forswearing that he is forsworn' (V, ii, 37–8).

Without this excuse, the rebels would certainly continue on their course. There is the memory of Mortimer and the sort of ambitious disagreement that Richard II had foretold: 'Northumberland . . . Thou shalt think,/Though he divide the realm and give thee half,/It is too little, helping him to all' (*Richard II*, V, i, 55, 59–61). The vows at Doncaster, however, serve to stimulate their sense of indignation. These men with their knightly backgrounds prefer to think they are the true patriots, redressing a wrong committed by ambitious Henry, who had gathered them to him under false pretences. The last thing they would wish to believe of themselves is Falstaff's comment on Worcester: 'Rebellion lay in his way and he found it' (*Henry IV, Part One*, V, i, 28). And nothing serves so well as an oath to give action a colouring of 'principle'.

There are other plays, however, where Shakespeare uses the oath as an organising device in more artistically important ways, either to guide a character on a course of action that will influence the whole direction of the play or, generally when there is forswearing, to cast light on the way a larger number of people behave. In his first tragedy, Shakespeare had stiff old Titus Andronicus and his brother Marcus reinforce their determination to get vengeance by having them swear, and he would use the device again in *Hamlet* and *Othello*. Shylock, too, swears vengeful oaths, but after his dismissal *The Merchant of Venice* is lightened by Portia's practical joke with the rings the men have vowed to keep. On a much larger scale, young men in *Love's Labour's Lost* are continually reminded of their vow to their academe, and eventually receive punishments because they are forsworn. Even more seriously, vows broken or kept become a leitmotif running through *King John*, where the Bastard Faulconbridge's sense of honour and loyalty contrasts sharply with the self-serving behaviour of virtually every other major figure in the play.

It is ironic that the Bastard is not effusive in his pledges to King John. His sheer delight in learning that he is indeed the son of Richard the Lionhearted seems to affirm that he shares the kind of upright behaviour that popular legend attached to the first Richard. A simple 'Madame, I'll follow you unto the death' binds him to Queen Elinor as she, with the fierceness that Shakespeare's older women sometimes exhibit, encourages her son to force his rights in France (*King John*, I, i, 154).

Countless critics have commented on the Bastard's process of discovery as he finds his loyalty tested by John's actions, and his steadfastness contrasted sharply to blatant shiftings of allegiance. He is no innocent, though, and has early stated that he will not practise deceit, but will learn the ways of court society to avoid being himself taken in (I, i, 214–15). Occasionally he disengages himself from the action and comments sarcastically. Immediately after being dubbed 'Sir Richard and Plantagenet', he characterises court manners in an unflattering way. Later, he exclaims against 'commodity', that 'daily break-vow'. He has seen John give up land and France back off from a high-principled defence of Constance and Arthur. Although the Bastard does not live up to his 'Gain, be my lord, for I will worship thee!' he has ample opportunity to witness the diplomatic wrangling that could lead a man to this cynical view of life. For the play is concerned with the way 'kings [and others] break faith upon commodity' (II, i, 597).

Juxtaposed with Faulconbridge's second-act observations are Constance's anguished declarations of the wrong that has been done her. She hears of the convenient agreements and shrieks out, 'False blood to false blood joined,' refusing to believe Salisbury's report, for she has 'a king's oath to the contrary' (III, i, 2, 10). Yet she soon realises that France has indeed 'Gone to swear a peace', and her well-founded attack on Philip fits into the iterative pattern that at times drives fellow-characters and audience alike to wish for silence.[1] Faith, she says, has changed to 'hollow falsehood'. Philip attempts to calm her with another oath: 'By heaven, lady, you shall have no cause/To curse the fair proceedings of this day' (III, i, 96–7).

In the next thirty lines, Constance repeats 'forsworn' and 'perjured' half a dozen times, starting with: 'You have beguiled me with a counterfeit/Resembling majesty, which, being touched and tried,/Proves valueless. You are forsworn, forsworn' (III, i, 99–101). Austria, the Bastard's particular enemy, is included in her accusations: 'Thou art perjured too,/. . . What a fool art thou,/A ramping fool, to brag and stamp and swear/Upon my party!' (III, i, 120–3). Her words suggest a great outward display, devoid of inner worth. Austria, his captured lion's skin draped over his shoulder to attest his prowess in battle, has been reduced to a braggart, reared on his hind legs like a heraldic figure, gesticulating meaninglessly. Shakespeare's audience would have understood her pleas to higher powers – 'Arm, arm, you heavens, against these perjured kings!' – for it was commonly held that nobility, of all people, would most offend heaven with their perjury. Queen Elizabeth, back in 1554, had written to her sister Mary that 'a king's word is more than another man's oath',[2] and in later correspondence frequent 'By God's had underlined her determination to fight foreign powers.

Subject to outside forces, however, Philip swings like a pendulum.

At Angiers, he had vowed by his hand (appropriate not only to a soldier but to a sceptre-bearing king) to drive out the English. Now he is bound to John in a convenient alliance. The new treaty is inconvenient, though, for the Church, and Pandulph finds he must argue some basic priorities. In Protestant England, there would be delight in seeing a Papal legate rationalising the sort of vacillation that Faulconbridge, the true Englishman, had earlier excoriated. Within memory of the audience, the Pope had, by turn, excommunicated Elizabeth, absolved subjects of allegiance to her, and finally said that they might accept her as their ruler.[3] Philip's dilemma was not only historic but might also have a current application for those with divided loyalties. Incidentally, the matter of allegiance to God seems much in Philip's mind, for his infrequent oaths generally involve his faith even when he is not actually debating the matter.

Pandulph gives the French king a simple choice. Unless the heretic John returns to Rome, Philip will be cursed and excommunicated if he does not bear arms against England. Philip's concern about his new league, linked 'With all religious strength of sacred vows' (III, i, 299), is countered by Pandulph's assurances. When one compares Pandulph's speech with that of the Cardinal in *The Troublesome Raigne of John, King of England*, it appears terribly convoluted. In the earlier play, there had been a simple 'I doo ... aquit thee of that oath as unlawful, being made with an heretike'.[4] Here, in thirty closely reasoned lines, the absolution is given in detail:

> So mak'st thou faith an enemy to faith,
> And like a civil war set'st oath to oath,
> Thy tongue against thy tongue. O, let thy vow
> First made to heaven, first be to heaven performed,
> That is, to be the champion of our church.
> What since thou swor'st is sworn against thyself
> And may not be performèd by thyself.
> For that which thou hast sworn to do amiss
> Is not amiss when it is truly done. . . .
> It is religion that doth make vows kept,
> But thou hast sworn against religion,
> By what thou swear'st, against the thing thou swear'st,
> And mak'st an oath the surety for thy truth
> Against an oath; the truth thou are unsure
> To swear swears only not to be forsworn;
> Else what a mockery should it be to swear!
> But thou dost swear only to be forsworn;
> And most forsworn to keep what thou dost swear.
> Therefore thy later vows against thy first
> Is in thyself rebellion to thyself,
> And better conquest never canst thou make

> Than arm thy constant and thy nobler parts
> Against these giddy loose suggestions, . . .
>
> (III, i, 263–92)

The two main ideas – that two wrongs can make a right, and that religion gives an oath its validity – can be used to explain the mental processes of some other vacillators. And the Elizabethan English, although no longer allied to Rome, understood the reasoning that an oath with an infidel was not binding. But who was the infidel? In *The Troublesome Raigne*, John voices the English notion of priority. 'Obey the Pope, and breake your oath to God?' (*Part 1*, 1. 1015 [sc. V]). Philip is weak and misguided as he turns again from John.

The shifts of allegiance, often accompanied by oaths that are then forgotten in the exigencies of the moment, reach a climax in the fifth act, and are dominant thematic and structural devices. The last act opens with John's renewed vow of service to the Pope, with his crown placed again by Pandulph (V, i, 23). But the nobles, their consciences pricking after the catalytic death of Arthur, and not quite willing to believe the sworn testimony of Hubert and the Bastard, have pledged faith to the Dauphin. *The Troublesome Raigne*, making far more of pageantry at this moment, and with more obvious irony, carefully showed first the vows of Pembroke and Salisbury on the altar, then Lewis' immediate shift, on the same altar, when he promised 'by heaven's power' that he would punish the English traitors.

Shakespeare, moving at a faster pace, picks up the thread after the altar scene, but recalls it with Lewis' careful direction to have the terms written down, that they may all remember 'whereof we took the sacrament,/And keep our faiths firm and inviolable' (V, ii, 6–7). Salisbury assures him, 'Upon our sides it never shall be broken,' although he is dismayed at the thought of civil war. Lewis' counter-vow is revealed in a more tension-ridden scene than it was in *The Troublesome Raigne*. Abstract rationalisation of shifts of allegiance pales before a concrete reason to return to John's side. The dying Melun fortuitously confesses that Lewis plans

> to recompense the pains you take
> By cutting off your heads. Thus hath he sworn,
> And I with him, and many moe with me,
> Upon the altar at Saint Edmundsbury,
> Even on that altar where we swore to you
> Dear amity and everlasting love.
>
> (V, iv, 15–20)

The horror of this sort of convenient oath-breaking, in its particular setting, has impressed Melun, and his desperate situation in turn impresses the nobles who hear him. It is with a certain relief that the Englishmen have an excuse to return to 'an old right'. As the play ends, it will remain for the new blood, young Prince Henry, to talk to the 'mended faiths' of the nobles, and for Faulconbridge, the one person who has not broken faith, to make his famous statement about England resting true to itself.

In this play, it is not a single oath that helps form a structural basis. There is the cumulative effect of a number that are uttered not merely to characterise individuals, but as pledges that should bind a person to act for another. They come from people in all walks of life: from Hubert, who remembers his oath as Prince Arthur pleads for his eyesight, and who finally must send lies to cover a humane dereliction of sworn duty; and from Faulconbridge, who exclaims delightedly when the Dauphin suddenly defies Pandulph, and his faithfulness to Rome: 'By all the blood that ever fury breathed,/The youth says well' (V, ii, 127–8).

More important, there is the fact that after being ostentatiously sworn they are so continuously broken. The message is conveyed that only disaster can come from such faithlessness. Had all remained true to their original oaths, there might have been other difficulties. But opportunism would not have had its momentary victory over honour, and the Bastard Faulconbridge would not have had such opportunity to comment on the vanity of men. Nor, Shakespeare is careful to point out, would England have come so close to defeat. Painful lessons are learned by the end of the play, and could stand also as a reminder to those Elizabethans who might have been tempted to forget where their duty lay.

Several years before he wrote *King John*, Shakespeare had made different use of a single vow, religiously kept. Revenge plays tend to turn on the oath of one man to seek a private justice for some injury inflicted on a member of his family, or on one close to him. Titus Andronicus, in our eyes, may well have started the chain of disaster in this early, bloody play by refusing to heed the captive Tamora's pleas for the life of her son. Her eldest boy is deemed a religious sacrifice, and she is told, 'Patient yourself, madam, and pardon me' (*Titus Andronicus*, I, i, 124). Pardon is far from her mind, however, and Titus later pleads with equal ineffectiveness and feels he has just cause for revenge when his sons' heads are brought to him. He addresses the gory remains, as well as the sorrowing few around him: '[I] swear unto my soul to right your wrongs./The vow is made' (III, i, 278–9). The talk of revenge and woe, the stabbing of the fly, and Lavinia's grotesque identification of her attackers all produce a nervous frenzy. This is immediately supplanted by a ritualistic kneeling when Marcus reaffirms his brother's vow and this time makes it specifically cover redressing the wrongs to mutilated, ravished Lavinia:

> And swear with me, as with the woeful fere
> And father of that chaste dishonourèd dame,
> Lord Junius Brutus sware for Lucrece' rape,
> That we will prosecute by good advice
> Mortal revenge upon these traitorous Goths.
>
> (IV, i, 89–93)

These promises of revenge stand out in a play that is remarkably free of oaths, having only about a dozen if one excludes these two scenes and one long speech by Aaron in V, i, when he in turn pleads for his child. Tamora's formal vows in the first act were of faith to Saturninus when the ritual slaying was immediately followed by her marriage. Only as an aside did she promise 'to massacre them all/ And race their faction and their family' (I, i, 453–4).

The proud and determined Gothic queen almost succeeds. But Shakespeare must shift sympathy to Titus, and as the indignities to the Andronici mount we are prepared for another revenge movement. Shakespeare has shown this Roman family with an uncompromising sense of honour that may reduce their humaneness, but leaves no room for wavering. Titus, mutilated and a bit mad, waits for a chance to repay Chiron, Demetrius and Tamora in a suitably bloody way. It is ironically appropriate that she should unwittingly lead her sons into a trap when she hits upon an elaborate disguise as Revenge and self-confidently believes she can trick Titus into calling off his vengeful son Lucius. Titus' vow, shared by the others in Marcus' reaffirmation, becomes a guiding principle that moves the last half of the play and finally destroys him. When Tamora's Revenge has eaten of her sons and become a grisly self-consuming fulfilment of the old man's vow, there is nothing left for him but to remove the last reminders of this particular chain of evil. He ends his sorrow by ending Lavinia's shame, and he stabs Tamora, the breeder of those who wronged him.

As he grew more skilled in characterisation, Shakespeare would continue to be interested in vows that shaped succeeding action, but these oaths would seem more integral to the characters who swear them, functioning on several levels at once. King Lear stands firm in his banishment of Cordelia, for example, and lashes out at the wise Kent with 'thou hast sought to make us break our vows,/Which we durst never yet'. In the last chapter we will see more of this obstinate old man who regards his formal disclaimer as a symbol of regal constancy. Like Julius Caesar's, his self-image includes what he regards as honourable inflexibility, and we realise immediately that he cannot turn back. But the speech is part of a series of events, and we are as fascinated by what it shows of Lear and the cosmology of the play as we are by its structural implications.

Iago recognises that Othello will be similarly bound by an oath and, once the seemingly righteous vow of vengeance is sworn, Desdemona is doomed. The structure of the play is such, however, that this is only one of a series of episodes pointing inexorably toward disaster. One should add that *Othello* includes numerous examples of other people swearing, so that the scene is thrown into less sharp relief verbally, and functions as a climactic part of a pattern of induced oaths.

Related to Titus' and Othello's vows is Hamlet's 'Yes, by heaven' as he promises the Ghost's 'commandment all alone shall live/ Within the book and volume of my brain' (*Hamlet*, I, v, 102–3). The Ghost may impress the audience more than the actual words in this scene, but his charge and Hamlet's sense of duty are frequently recalled, and are, of course, mainsprings for the succeeding actions of a hero attempting to carry out his job. But again – and the emphasis of mountains of Hamlet criticism shows this – the interest quickly shifts from the mechanical aspects of the vow itself to the personality of the hero.

In two comedies written shortly after *King John*, however, the structural effect is more patently pivotal, and Shakespeare uses it without apology. In *The Merchant of Venice*, Shylock sounds as serious as Titus or Marcus, and even more insistent, as he vows revenge on Antonio. Comedy, however, has different rules. Titus Andronicus would not have hesitated to take a pound of flesh, careless of the consequences had he spilled a drop of blood or miscalculated the weight. But Shylock must stop short, and the fact that he does retreat from a vow because of a legal trap to some extent diminishes his character. The taste of the courtroom scene lingers, however, and Shakespeare washes it away with the ring trick, which emphasises vows of a different kind.

The play's structural contrast of serious threat and romantic love is grounded in bonds and the oaths that spring from those bonds. Portia is bound by her father's will, and its elaborate provisions lead to marriage vows not only for Portia and Bassanio but also for Gratiano and Nerissa. Antonio is bound by the terms of debt contract, but that supposedly safe and 'merry' transaction leads to the vows of vengeance that cast a momentary shadow over the romantic story.

Shylock's oaths are impressive and serve partially to reveal character. His Jewishness has been emphasised in spiteful remarks by others, especially Gratiano and Antonio, and in those often-noted humanising speeches that call attention to the similarities of Jews and

Christians. Shylock may have been a comic character in Elizabethan times, with a big nose and red wig,[5] and many of his speeches could have been regarded as grotesquely amusing perversions of the truth, deserving the coarse laughter Gratiano indulges in. But, until he submits at the trial, there is a thread of dedication running through them, emphasised by the oaths, that must surely have produced an undertone of horror and interest even in an audience bent on seeing a Jew as comic.

Although Shylock was an infidel whose oaths would no doubt have been taken even less seriously by sixteenth-century Christians than Pandulph was taking Philip's allegiance to King John, Shakespeare does create a character whose initial consistency and apparent truth to his own values lend weight to his vows. As he says, 'I will buy with you, sell with you, talk with you, walk with you . . . but I will not eat with you, drink with you, nor pray with you' (I, iii, 32–4). He emphasises religious and dietary differences, speaks of his 'Jewish gaberdine', and holds an ancient grudge against Antonio, who 'hates our sacred nation'. His parable about Jacob and the sheep, taken from Genesis, is one of many details that individualise his speech and emphasise his difference from the Christians. The gap is widened by the rather acid comments of the young Venetians and Antonio's seemingly overdone promise 'To spit on thee again, to spurn thee too'.

Later his anti-Christian warnings to Jessica help prepare us for his intransigence against Antonio, and for the fact that he will keep referring to a righteously sworn oath to back up his insistence upon the bond. He had already underlined his threat: 'Let him look to his bond. He was wont to lend money for a Christian cursy' (III, i, 42–3); and Tubal's reports of Jessica's prodigality and Antonio's impending ruin help whip him to fever pitch. By the end of the scene he has made plans for the arrest, and prepares to meet Tubal later 'at our synagogue'.

When we see him again, brushing off the jailer's talk of mercy, he continues the pattern of reiteration that has been noticed in his speech.[6] His determination to have his bond is uppermost in his mind, as his daughter and his ducats had been earlier. 'I have sworn an oath that I will have my bond.' He is careful to tell the Duke, who joins in the cry for mercy, that the oath has been religiously taken 'by our holy Sabbath' (IV, i, 36). It becomes the excuse for his intransigence when Portia mixes the request for mercy with the temptation of a triple repayment. We have not seen the initial swearing, but we are led to believe it was formally done.

Portia: Shylock, there's thrice thy money off'red thee.
Shylock: An oath, an oath! I have an oath in heaven;

Shall I lay perjury upon my soul?
No, not for Venice!
Portia: . . . Be merciful.
Shylock: . . . By my soul I swear
There is no power in the tongue of man
To alter me. I stay here on my bond.
(IV, i, 225–40, passim)

The atmosphere of Belmont lingering from the preceding scene, and our awareness that Portia has some scheme in mind, may make a person newly acquainted with the play hopeful that Antonio will escape, but at this moment Shylock certainly seems to have the advantage. The scales are ready, the knife whetted, and requests for an attendant surgeon have been rejected as not articles in the bond. But suddenly Shylock comes face to face with another strict constructionist, and Portia, on the careful technicalities of exact weight and no allotment of blood, traps him and swings the story back into the comic path. How does one get rid of Shylock, who, to our twentieth-century minds, has been disparaged by the anti-Semitic Venetians, and badly treated by his daughter? The Christians do extend to him a legalistic mercy, rather than insisting on strict application of existing law. But Shakespeare also diminishes him by making him less single-minded than a tragic revenger. The grand oath is forgotten, and he attempts to bargain, asking merely for his principal. Defeated by a series of legal twists, he finally does say, but weakly, 'Nay, take my life and all! . . . You take my life/When you do take the means whereby I live' (IV, i, 372–5). Yet his desire has been to live, as he has proven by his recoil from his absolute position as soon as there is a threat to him.

This is very different from Granville-Barker's comment that Shylock's tragedy lies in 'the betrayal of the faith on which he builds'. Granville-Barker *is* dismayed at his descent from avenger to butcher, though, and yearns for him 'to regain tragic dignity'.[7] But this can never be, for Shakespeare has made him forsworn, and serious, non-romantic characters who break oaths are seldom redeemed. Had he remained steadfast, there would at least have been a defiance, albeit tragic, that he now lacks as, unrevenged, he waits for Portia, Antonio and the Duke to decide upon the terms of his future life.

But, no matter how much we argue that Shylock deserves to lose because it was a 'monstrous bond', we are left with a bitter taste. To restore the comic mood, Shakespeare quickly introduces the matter of the rings, a parodic treatment of promise, forfeit, threat of punishment, and plea for mercy, with the solution again coming unexpectedly. Oaths had played a part in the romantic plot for, as

Arragon states, he and all the others who came for Portia's hand were 'enjoined by oath' not to reveal their choice of casket and, if they failed, to leave immediately and never woo another 'maid in way of marriage' (II, ix, 9–15). There is a presumption that both Arragon and Morocco will honourably abide by their vows. Conveniently, Bassanio is the third person we see put himself in jeopardy, and Portia resists the temptation to guide his choice, for 'then I am forsworn'. Were he to choose wrongly, however, she would, in retrospect, 'wish a sin – That I had been forsworn' (III, ii, 10–14).

Bassanio's happy choice leads him into another bond, complete with legal terms: his prize is 'confirmed, signed, and ratified' by Portia, and sealed by the gift of a ring which he must never 'part from, lose, or give away', or she will have the 'vantage to exclaim on him'. Gratiano meanwhile has been himself fashionably 'swearing till my very roof was dry/With oaths of love', and is, we later learn, similarly bound (III, ii, 204–5).

Within a minute of Shylock's exit, Portia is making her bid for that ring, and soon Nerissa, too, is seeing 'if I can get my husband's ring,/Which I did make him swear to keep for ever' (IV, ii, 13–14). They will not be disappointed in their gleeful expectation of the 'old swearing' that the rings were given to men, and they promise to 'outface them, and outswear them too'. Portia, wishing to 'give light, but . . . not be light', is willing to lie for a good cause, pretending her absence is a contemplative retreat, sealed by a secret vow breathed 'toward heaven' (III, iv, 26–9). Earlier she had wearily but wittily endured the procession of suitors under the terms laid down by her deceased father. In the fifth act, with the mixture of seriousness and clever pretence that is her trademark, she emphasises to this man she still scarcely knows the seriousness of her marriage vows.

The idyllic calm of Belmont is touched with gentle banter as Jessica speaks much as Hermia in *A Midsummer Night's Dream* might.

> In such a night
> Did young Lorenzo swear he loved her well,
> Stealing her soul with many vows of faith,
> And ne'er a true one.
>
> (V, i, 17–20)

This is soon replaced by the livelier joking of Portia and Nerissa, discomfiting those husbands who had only a scene before been dependent on the cleverness of the disguised women. We realise the accusations have started when Gratiano suddenly exclaims: 'By yonder moon I swear you do me wrong!/In faith, I gave it to the judge's clerk.' Shakespeare had presented the young men as typical romantic lovers, with Gratiano, as we have noted, making appropriate pro-

testations of his affection, while curbing his less circumspect behaviour and promising to 'swear but now and then' (II, ii, 177).

There is a difference between casual swearing – what Santayana
calls 'the fossils of piety'[8] – the sincere though often overdone
protestations of lovers that we will examine a bit more fully in
the next chapter, and the formal oaths of non-amorous allegiance.
Shakespeare obviously has most fun with the lovers' vows. He deftly
combines the women's stock accusation about men's hollow swearing
with the husbands' honest belief that they have broken one particle
of their marriage vows for a good cause. Gratiano tries briefly
to make light of the affair, calling the ring merely a 'hoop of gold'
with a trite inscription. Nerissa explodes:

> What talk you of the posy or the value?
> You swore to me when I did give it you . . .
> Though not for me, yet for your vehement oaths,
> You should have been respective and have kept it.
>
> (V, i, 151–6)

It is Portia's cue to comment that *her* husband would never do such a
thing. Bassanio can only splutter: 'No, by my honour, madam! By my
soul/No woman had it.' There is a delightful tension built between
the desperate seriousness of the men, the perfectly correct moral
stance of the women, and the fact that Portia can again solve
matters when she sees fit. The men employ a whole series of appropriate oaths that border on the trite emblematica of love, with just
a hint of mythological allusion. Bassanio admits he had been a sinner
in a good cause, then begs forgiveness, though he is cut off in a final
interchange that is one of the closest matchings of protestations and
reaction in Shakespeare, one that even Cleopatra cannot better.

Bassanio: Portia, forgive me this enforcèd wrong,
              And in the hearing of these many friends
              I swear to thee, even by thine own fair eyes,
              Wherein I see myself—
Portia: Mark you but that!
              In both my eyes he doubly sees himself,
              In each eye one. Swear by your double self,
              And there's an oath of credit.
Bassanio: Nay, but hear me.
              Pardon this fault, and by my soul I swear
              I never more will break an oath with thee.
                        (V, i, 240–8)

Antonio, who seems a bit out of place amid the bantering lovers,
finally has a function here as he joins in the pleas for mercy, assuring

Portia that Bassanio 'Will never more break faith advisedly'. The moment has come for her to relent and eventually relate her role in saving Antonio from that other bond.

The final scene has become a slightly askew replaying of the initial ring-giving, coupled with a repetition of the mercy-showing in a scene where we do not feel real mercy is needed. While Portia and Nerissa emphasise the seriousness of the earlier vows, the oaths sworn spontaneously by the pressed husbands are often more fitting to love speeches than to a serious defence. This is, of course, completely in keeping with the Belmont story, especially on a moonlight night when usury has been defeated. The nineteenth-century producers who centred all on Shylock, occasionally even cutting the last act, lost the richness this comic ending can give.

There is a similarity between some of the phrases sworn in *The Merchant of Venice* and a few of the lines that Shakespeare makes fun of in *A Midsummer Night's Dream* and *Love's Labour's Lost*, where lovers go overboard in their declarations of affection. It is in the latter play, however, that we find the most obvious use of a plot that turns on an oath and its violation, when Shakespeare again is making a serious point, this time about oaths lightly taken without real thought of the consequences. It is a play that delights in language for its own sake, at the same time weaving a fine fabric of satire about the various pretences of all the lords with their planned and discarded course of study.

Ferdinand thinks he has found the way to fame by turning his group from their natural desires to a life of contemplation in 'a little Academe'. He reminds his willing courtiers of their impending asceticism:

> You three, Berowne, Dumaine, and Longaville,
> Have sworn for three years' term to live with me,
> My fellow scholars. . . .
> Your oaths are passed; and now subscribe your names,
> That his own hand may strike his honour down
> That violates the smallest branch herein.
> If you are armed to do as sworn to do,
> Subscribe to your deep oaths, and keep it too.
>
> (I, i, 15–23)

Two of the young men leap to affirm their serious intentions. But Berowne, a forerunner of Benedick in *Much Ado about Nothing*, realises the absurdity of trying to spend three years in fasting, study and celibacy. This juxtaposition of the monastic and the courtly is doomed to failure not because study is bad but because this plan stints them on food, sleep and women for too long. Ferdinand remains firm and Berowne finally agrees that he has sworn to the entire programme, but is frank to say that necessity will make them all forsworn 'Three thousand times within this three years' space:/ For every man with his affects is born' (I, i, 147–8). In fewer than 150 lines, Shakespeare has laid the foundation for the play's demonstration of Berowne's prediction.

With the neat timing so often found in the comedies, the French princess arrives to negotiate a territorial agreement on behalf of her sick father. Immediately Shakespeare shows how excessively strict Ferdinand is. He ignores her suggestion that it is a sin to be inhospitable, and decrees that she and her three ladies-in-waiting must camp outside the walls. As he so frequently does in a range of situations, Shakespeare seems to be suggesting a more reasonable course, although the King is adamant at this moment; and later he will invite the ladies into his castle. The men and women are not total strangers – Berowne had once danced with Rosaline – but under pressure of their very new vow the men practise restrained formality. Within a day or so, recognising that they are forsworn, they begin their secret courtships, writing dreadful poetry when in a more natural situation they might have spoken their love.

Sonnet 130 anatomises Shakespeare's 'Dark Lady' in terms consciously opposite to the clichés of Elizabethan courtly versifiers; and the rhymes that Orlando hangs on trees in *As You Like It* and that the courtiers send here make more fun of the convention. These missives have a structurally more important use, too, for they are all brought out as evidence that the men have broken their vow. The word-play in the opening lines of Berowne's poem reminds us of this and, like his initial reservations, points ahead, this time to the doubts the Princess will raise.

> If love make me forsworn, how shall I swear to love?
> Ah, never faith could hold if not to beauty vowed!
> Though to myself forsworn, to thee I'll faithful prove.
>   (IV, ii, 100–2)

A tension is created by the juxtaposition of the memory of the first-act vow and these later declarations of devotion. There will be an additional twist at the end when these declarations prove false as the ladies exchange masks and the men reiterate their protestations to the wrong women.

In the third act, Berowne had seemed a bit annoyed at perjuring himself for a mere woman 'With two pitch balls stuck in her face for eyes' but, as he says, she is, 'by heaven, one that will do the deed' (III, i, 186–7). Those eyes have captured him, and even in soliloquy, partially by habit and partly because he needs to emphasise his sincerity, he utters a string of oaths: 'By this light, but for her eye,

I would not love her. . . . By heaven, I do love, and it hath taught me to rime, and to be mallicholy. . . . By the world, I would not care a pin if the other three were in [love]' (IV, iii, 8–16). One by one the others come in, reading over their attempts at poetry. 'Shot, by Heaven!' Berowne exclaims delightedly when he realises that another of Cupid's arrows has found its mark in the King. Longaville sighs that he is forsworn, and Dumaine arrives 'transformed'. Perjurers were often made to stand in the pillory with a proclamation of their offence, and the practice is called to mind by the way each man carefully carries in evidence of his love, as Berowne says, 'like a perjure, wearing papers' (IV, iii, 43).

The leitmotif of perjury springing from the first act is continued in Dumaine's jigging rhyme:

> But, alack, my hand is sworn
> Ne'er to pluck thee from thy thorn.
> Vow, alack, for youth unmeet,
> Youth so apt to pluck a sweet!
> Do not call it sin to me,
> That I am forsworn for thee.
>   (IV, iii, 106–11)

Each man in turn realises how inappropriate the King's proposed academe had been, and each hopes that the others have failed, too; for, as Dumaine says, 'Ill, to example ill,/Would from my forehead wipe a perjured note,/For none offend where all alike do dote' (IV, iii, 119–21). The King's pose of righteousness is destroyed by Berowne, who steps from his eavesdropping-place, 'to whip hypocrisy', pretending a superiority that is not his.

> O me, with what strict patience have I sat,
> To see a king transformèd to a gnat . . .
> I that am honest, I that hold it sin
> To break the vow I am engagèd in,
> I am betrayed by keeping company
> With men like you, men of inconstancy.
>   (IV, iii, 160–1; 172–5)

There is comic irony in our knowledge that Jaquenetta and Costard are on their way to the King with the misdelivered letter from Berowne to Rosaline.

The scene, with charge and countercharge, sighs and guilty sniggers, is highly amusing. But, like most scenes of perjury in Shakespeare, it has deeper connotations, carried in words like 'treason', 'sin', 'ashamed' and 'guilty'. As in the last act of *The Merchant of Venice*, so here Shakespeare is having his fun at the expense of the young men, while at the same time pointing up a more sombre theme – that one must take seriously what one swears. Initially, only Berowne had expressed reservations, and he had compromised himself by joining the idealistic but impossible academe. Now he states frankly:

> Young blood doth not obey an old decree.
> We cannot cross the cause why we were born;
> Therefore, of all hands must we be forsworn.
>
> (IV, iii, 212–14)

Later, at the King's request, he embarks on a long set speech attempting to prove 'Our loving lawful and our faith not torn'. We are reminded of Pandulph's logic with King Philip as Berowne argues that they had an earlier allegiance to more basic principles.

> Consider what you first did swear unto:
> To fast, to study, and to see no woman –
> Flat treason 'gainst the kingly state of youth. . . .
> Now, for not looking on a woman's face,
> You have in that forsworn the use of eyes,
> And study too, the causer of your vow;
> For where is any author in the world
> Teaches such beauty as a woman's eye? . . .
> Then fools you were these women to forswear,
> Or, keeping what is sworn, you will prove fools. . . .
> Let us once lose our oaths to find ourselves,
> Or else we lose ourselves to keep our oaths.
> It is religion to be thus forsworn.
>
> (IV, iii, 286–358, passim)

It remains to be seen how the women will take this about-face. Having analysed the love letters mercilessly both for style and hypocritical content, they wait for the courtiers, who come masking, ready to 'swear themselves out of all suit', and be sent off 'dry-beaten with pure scoff'. When the men appear in their own likenesses, however, a note of seriousness again intrudes and for a moment replaces the wit. The King would lead the Princess into the court, but she rebukes him: 'This field shall hold me, and so hold your vow./ Nor God nor I delights in perjured men' (V, ii, 346–7). Ferdinand's attempt to shift the blame draws from her a more lengthy reproof.

King: Rebuke me not for that which you provoke.
The virtue of your eye must break my oath.
Princess: You nickname virtue. 'Vice' you should have spoke;
For virtue's office never breaks men's troth.
Now, by my maiden honour, yet as pure

As the unsullied lily, I protest,
A world of torments though I should endure,
I would not yield to be your house's guest,
So much I hate a breaking cause to be
Of heavenly oaths, vowed with integrity.
                                        (V, ii, 348–57)

Sincerity and straightforwardness are called for at this point, and
Berowne is characteristically the leader in admitting his earlier
foolishness, both in his actions and in using 'Taffeta phrases . . ./
Three-piled hyperboles . . ./Figures pedantical'. He now forswears all
things that lead to 'maggot ostentation'. We know that he is making
the transition to the values of the ladies when he declares mildly,
'and I here protest/By this white glove . . ./Henceforth my wooing
mind shall be expressed/In russet yeas and honest kersey noes'
(V, ii, 411–14).

The ladies had involved the 'Russians' in oaths sworn to the
wrong people, however, and when the tokens and errors are revealed
the men realise that they have again been rash. They have confused appearance and reality or, as Berowne says, they have 'wooed
but the sign of she', and are perforce forsworn again.

This is one of Shakespeare's longest scenes, and it is lengthened
still farther by episodes in sharply contrasting moods: the intellectually pretentious masque of the Nine Worthies, and the
solemn news of the French King's death. The play has focused
on the amusing discovery of perjury, the romantic protestations
of courtiers, the posturings of Armado, and other comic byplay.
The Nine Worthies represent an exaggerated form of this aspect,
which Berowne is already rejecting. But behind the comedy, almost
forgotten, is the serious business of the property claims, which the
Princess negotiates successfully, and the sickness of her father.
Properly staged, the appearance of Marcade with his message can
be very sombring, a visual presentation of the contrasting mood
that runs beneath the surface of the play. The last 150 lines of
dialogue proper combine this same sense of joy and sadness, of
hopeful courtship and conscious reproof, of eagerness and
resignation that is echoed in the closing song of Spring and Winter.
The men's impetuous desire to rush into love or academe has been
balanced throughout by the more considered comments of the
ladies, although Shakespeare is careful to give the men a Berowne,
and with him a share of the wit, understanding, reservations and
experience. He is overstating a bit when he concludes, 'Thus pour
the stars down plagues for perjury' (V, ii, 395). The ruling powers
may not approve, but the punishments are meted out by the women
in a very down-to-earth fashion. They may believe that the men

have 'played foul play with oaths' because of them; it is a flattering excuse. But they need assurance that other distractions will not make the vows of love as soon 'neglected'.

If the men are as serious as they say, they will face a test of constancy. As the Princess said in her earlier sombre interlude: 'Nor God nor I delights in perjured men.' Each of the offenders, so fortuitously matched to one of the ladies, will now be assigned a suitable year-long task. The King, who thought up the academe with all its ascetic rules, will be bound to a more extreme form of privation in 'some forlorn and naked hermitage' with 'frosts and fasts, hard lodging and thin weeds', to test the endurance of his proclaimed love. And she, who takes oaths so seriously, makes one for the future that we can assume is binding. If the King endures, 'by this virgin palm now kissing thine,/I will be thine'.

The others take their cues from her. Berowne, for his 'faults and perjury' must visit and amuse the sick for a year; Dumaine is warned not to swear his lasting faith, lest he be 'forsworn again', as he and Longaville are put off for twelve months. Berowne comments correctly that it 'doth not end like an old play'. Despite the feeling of lightness he has provided by language, wit and potential romance, Shakespeare has resisted the comic pressures to march couples to the altar. Later, in *A Midsummer Night's Dream* and *As You Like It*, he will use fairy magic or sudden, child-like changes of affection to find necessary partners and pair off his young people. Here, he has four couples that seem suited from the first. But he has chosen to bring in news of a death that will be properly mourned. In addition to this awareness of good taste that a Hamlet would have approved of, there is the more heavily weighted idea of perjury. Where oaths should be taken carefully and kept honourably, these men have spoken carelessly and rationalised a quick lapse. Working with the play, one finds one's self making lists of instances where 'perjury' or 'oath' is repeated. Shakespeare is, in fact, reiterating to make more obvious the structural importance of the broken vows. It would be far less interesting, given this emphasis, if the women did not impose tests. If their constancy can endure, it will then be time to trust the men anew and accept the vows of love and marriage that are so counter to the oath of abstemious scholarship that opened the play.

One could cite numerous parallels to some of the scenes we have just examined. History plays other than *Henry IV, Part One*, or *King John* have shown shifts of allegiance or oath-breaking rebels. After all, Hotspur and his cohorts are referring to something Shakespeare dramatised in *Richard II*. A brief sequence of scenes in *Henry VI, Part One*, might have been a precursor of much of *King John*. Talbot, the English hero, presents Burgundy with the honourable course of action as they move toward Rouen:

> Vow, Burgundy, by honour of thy house . . .
> Either to get the town again or die;
> And I, as sure as English Henry lives
> And as his father here was conqueror,
> As sure as in this late betrayèd town
> Great Coeur-de-lion's heart was burièd,
> So sure I swear to get the town or die.
>   (III, ii, 77–84)

Burgundy assures him, 'My vows are equal partners with thy vows,' but is immediately and easily persuaded by Joan La Pucelle to forsake the English. She comments, 'Done like a Frenchman,' adding an aside that would be appreciated by the English audience: '– turn and turn again'.

Romantic stories frequently use vows pivotally in some part of the action. Proteus, in *The Two Gentlemen of Verona*, forsakes Julia, engineers his friend Valentine's banishment, and pays court to Sylvia. Her response, as he reports it, might have come from the French princess. It momentarily dismays this man whose name is a clue to his faithlessness.

> When I protest true loyalty to her,
> She twits me with my falsehood to my friend.
> When to her beauty I commend my vows,
> She bids me think how I have been forsworn
> In breaking faith with Julia whom I loved.
>   (IV, ii, 7–11)

Bertram, urged on by the untruthful Parolles, tries to escape from his marriage vows to Helena, and writes to his mother that he will not bed her, and that he has 'sworn to make the "not" eternal' (*All's Well that Ends Well*, III, ii, 21–2). The former vow-breaking seems more important for what it tells us about Proteus than for its structural influence. Bertram's vow not to consummate his marriage to Helena, on the other hand, does provide the mainspring for much of the ensuing action in *All's Well that Ends Well*. But, as Helena follows him and passes the test he has set for her, we are more aware of her careful planning than of his oath. The list could be extended, and we will see more examples as we look at fashionable swearing and at oaths of air and honour. But it is in the group of plays analysed here that Shakespeare makes emphatic structural use of vows. There may be the careful recall of one particular example, or the repeated acts of swearing that become a series of springboards for further action and character development but also often function on their own as a leitmotif to emphasise the meaning of the play.

Chapter 3

Fashionable Swearing

Bragging soldiers and young gallants are the types most apt to follow fashion among the swearers in Shakespeare's plays. Other soldiers swear, of course. Hotspur, proven in battle, is no *miles gloriosus*, but his vocabulary and form of delivery at times have much in common with the studied explosiveness of the braggart who creates deeds by words alone. And many young men who could be called gallants are moved by more than mere modishness. Fenton in *The Merry Wives of Windsor*, Laertes and Horatio swear seriously for a variety of reasons.

Here, however, we are concerned with those oaths uttered predominantly for the same reasons that a person would have worn a particular gold chain, a fancy pair of gloves, or a strikingly elaborate doublet – to help create an outward appearance. This does not preclude the fact that in some instances there is another purpose. Petruchio's words are part of his shrew-taming method. Lovers and husbands often express true faith with an exaggerated string of phrases or a trite expression. In these instances, there may be a woman ready to interject a sharp comment. Portia and Nerissa in *The Merchant of Venice* comment scornfully on Bassanio and Gratiano's last-act protestations, while the ladies in *Love's Labour's Lost* are justifiably sceptical of some of the vows they hear. Cleopatra quickly recognises the trite phrase.

There is a brief exchange in the third scene of *Antony and Cleopatra* that demonstrates how far Shakespeare goes beyond satire while at the same time commenting on the vocabulary of soldiers. Antony has not yet told her the news of Fulvia's death, but Cleopatra castigates him:

> Why should I think you can be mine, and true,
> (Though you in swearing shake the thronèd gods)
> Who have been false to Fulvia? Riotous madness,
> To be entangled with those mouth-made vows
> Which break themselves in swearing.

> (I, iii, 27–31)

He insists, 'By the fire/That quickens Nilus' slime, I go from hence/Thy soldier, servant . . .' (I, iii, 68–70). She answers scornfully, commanding him to 'play one scene/Of excellent dissembling, and let it look,/Like perfect honour', and he complies, 'Now by my sword—' She immediately interjects, 'And target,' undercutting him and showing us how conventional his soldierly vocabulary is. He may be sincere, but with her characteristic quickness of mind she seems to be recalling a phrase she has heard many times before and implying that in fact he is merely acting the role of faithful soldier.

Lovers' vows are more explicitly satirised in *A Midsummer Night's Dream*, where Hermia calls to mind other often-used phrases. Even under the pressure of her father's intransigence and the necessity of eloping, she retains her spirit. She might simply have promised Lysander, 'tomorrow truly will I meet thee', but she prefaces this with the exaggerated

> I swear to thee by Cupid's strongest bow,
> By his best arrow, with the golden head,
> By the simplicity of Venus' doves,
> By that which knitteth souls and prospers loves,
> And by that fire which burned the Carthage queen
> When the false Troyan under sail was seen,
> By all the vows that ever men have broke
> (In number more than ever women spoke).
>
> (I, i, 169–76)

At first Shakespeare seems to be making fun of her, but the last two lines shift the thrust of the satire toward young bloods like Lysander. The criticism is reinforced a few minutes later by the unhappy Helena, who cites a specific example of forswearing:

> ere Demetrius looked on Hermia's eyne,
> He hailed down oaths that he was only mine;
> And when this hail some heat from Hermia felt,
> So he dissolved, and show'rs of oaths did melt.
>
> (I, i, 242–5)

Puck, too, has opinions about young men, and is amazed that there should be one true lover, when 'A million fail, confounding oath on oath'. Ultimately even Demetrius will return to his initial love, but in the meantime Shakespeare has shown the fragility of lovers' vows.

Despite their occasional excesses in oaths or poetry-writing, the truly romantic lovers remain essentially admirable. They are not so sharply satirised as the foolish men aspiring to be gentlemen and lovers, whose hollow characters reverberate with a great spate of words. Shakespeare, and contemporaries who were sometimes even more caustic in their treatment of these foolish figures, make sure the audience perceives immediately that these men, like the braggart soldiers, should be laughed at. The would-be gallants, forerunners of the fops in Restoration comedy, strive to create what they think are suitable impressions. Osric appears with the news of the wager, and Hamlet comments on this 'waterfly' and his hat and elaborate language. Osric provides a comic counterpoint to a deadly serious business, and seems a personification of all that Polonius earlier warned Laertes against. He could have been made much of in a play satirising court manners, and one feels that he probably could have been allowed more oaths had not Shakespeare been focusing on the expression of Hamlet's tension, as we will see later. In the same way, the swaggering soldier will appear bedecked in scarves, as Parolles does, while the better soldier goes more quietly about his business or is respected for his prowess, as is the explosive Hotspur.

There is great variety within these two types and, furthermore, the line between braggart and gallant sometimes blurs. Emphasising his bravery, the gallant may come close to the *miles gloriosus*. Or, like Don Armado in *Love's Labour's Lost*, he may adopt a fantastic appearance. Most frequently, he is the suitor, his object ranging from Armado's Jaquenetta to Aguecheek's Olivia. Trying to impress others, he swears in order to give weight to otherwise empty statements. A psychologist might speak of overcompensation for basic feelings of inadequacy on battlefield or in parlour, but the dramatists and audiences of four centuries ago were less interested in underlying causes than in laughing at pretensions.[1] We feel no sympathy when others ridicule Slender, when Aguecheek is pushed into a duel, or when the braggart Pistol is cudgelled. Occasionally, of course, we will realise how despicable some of the braggarts are. Parolles reveals military secrets to his 'captors', and Pistol participates in a fatal beating (*Henry IV, Part Two*, V, iv), while Cloten plans a particularly tasteless revenge on Posthumus and Imogen in *Cymbeline*.

Shakespeare's most complex swearing braggart, of course, is the Falstaff of the history plays, speaking of his gentlemanly youth, trying to convince others of his battlefield prowess despite his soliloquy on honour, and inhabiting the taverns where gentlemen and soldiers often came together. Countless critics have argued about him. It would be interesting, though, to note the reaction to *The Merry Wives of Windsor* by a person with no prior knowledge about the fat knight. Falstaff might be regarded simply as an older Ralph Royster Doyster, a silly pretender physically beaten, finally disabused of his self-satisfied belief that he can win a virtuous English woman away from her husband or fiancé, and worthy only of derisive laughter.

Before we concentrate on Shakespeare's fashionable swearers, we need to extend the frame of reference of the opening chapter, looking at a few non-Shakespearian characters and at some of the comments Renaissance Englishmen were making about gentry and swashbucklers. There is a long tradition in English drama, reaching an apex in the Restoration and eighteenth century, of the young man who seeks a life that he thinks is exciting, fashionable or apt to impress others. Like Sheridan's Bob Acres, he usually has some money, a willingness to be led, and an inability to recognise a bad advisor. Sir Lucius O'Trigger is antedated by Sir Toby Belch, Bobadil and Autolycus, and a number of tempters in the earlier moralities and interludes. These men may lead their gulls into embarrassing situations, take advantage of their wealth, or merely advise them on behaviour or swearing. Likes may attract, as when a braggart becomes the advisor to a would-be gallant. Of course, at times the young man does not need to be led; placed in certain situations, he reveals his native foolishness and pretence.

Hick Scorner is an early sixteenth-century example of the young man who falls into bad company and must undergo a beating before he realises that the attractive life is actually corrupt.[2] Still in the first quarter of the century, Riot swears and misleads Youth, who tries to imitate him until Charity and Humility finally effect a conversion.[3] As the plays became increasingly secular, of course, this sometimes innocent and always gullible young man, so anxious to gain or pretend a panache he lacked, was not seen as eventually discovering the right path to heaven. Instead, he might be made physically uncomfortable, might become reconciled to some whom he had been disturbing, and might even gain some temporal wisdom. Upon occasion, if he proved too vicious, he might be punished.

Udall's Plautine *Ralph Royster Doyster*, delighting English schoolboys a couple of decades before Shakespeare's birth, contains elements that will be repeated in later plays. Ralph, less a soldier than his literary ancestor, Pyrgopolynices, but equally foolish, is bent on love; Custance has as little interest in him as Olivia has in Sir Andrew Aguecheek. A swaggerer who can declare 'By His armes' he will not be far from an attacker, 'nor runne behinde' (I, ii, 61–2), he fights ineffectually. Merrygreek's opening soliloquy tells us about Ralph, and we can watch his eagerness for praise, his willingness to be led, and his inability to face facts that others see plainly.[4] He dismisses Widow Custance's betrothal to Gawyn Goodlucke: 'by sweete Sainct Anne./. . . I will have hir myne owne selfe I make God a vow' (I, ii, 96–8). His only real prowess lies in his voice, and Udall does allow him a wider range of oaths than any of his fellows. Pyrgopolynices, in fact, would have been no match for him![5]

Ralph could swear when the play opened, as can Sir Andrew. Shakespeare, in fact, seldom shows a comic figure learning how, and does not indulge in the kind of training programme Jonson enjoyed creating for Stephen, striving 'to swear as well as' Bobadil,[6] or for Sogliardo in *Every Man Out of His Humour*. This young man learns from Buffone, another tutor, that upon entering an ordinary gentleman should 'Only (now and then) give fire, discharge a good full oath, and offer a great wager'.[7] All these, however, would subscribe to the sentiments so disapproved of by Barnaby Rich:

> he that hath not for every word an oath, and can swear voluntarily without any cause, is holden to be but of weak spirit, and he that should reprove him in his blasphemies, they say he is a *puritan*, a precise foole, not fitte to hold a gentleman company.[8]

Stubbes, in a supplication to Henry VIII, had spoken of vice and noted that men deprecated oaths 'by all parts of Christes bodye' by 'callynge them in scorne huntinge othes'.[9] Roger Ascham was aware of the pressure to coin 'some new othe, that is not stale, but will rin [run] round in the mouth';[10] and Boyle, although writing later, describes most explicitly a quality that had remained current since Jonson's time, and was occasionally apparent in Shakespeare's characters:

> many of our Gallants, who not content with the received forms of dishonouring their Maker's name, do as much affect Novelty in their Oaths, as in the Fashion; and if they have a gift of Singularity in Swearing, are as proud of it, as of their Mistress' favour; Such people are as Nice as Impious in their Oaths, they will never use any till it be stale and threadbare, but (ever like their cloaths) leave them off before they have been worn long enough to grow old.[11]

At first Ralph uses such common phrases as 'By cocke', 'by the Masse', or 'Gog's armes', and he never makes a point of his originality. He never employs what Bob Acres would call the 'oath referential', but he does sound cosmopolitan with 'By the Armes of Calyes', and is perhaps unconsciously apposite as he vows 'By cock's precious potsticke' to destroy Custance, house and all. Soon he will hear only the noise of broom, distaff and skimmer on his cooking-pot helmet as the women drive him away.

It is important to note that in *Ralph Royster Doyster* oaths are not in themselves the object of satire that they will be in *Every Man In His Humour* or in many Shakespearian scenes, where hollowness, exaggeration or inappropriateness are explicitly pointed out. But it is even more important to recognise that they are necessary building-blocks for a character such as Ralph's. They will continue to be a necessity to far more polished craftsmen than Udall. Stubbes wrote with dismay of the regard both gentlemen and soldiers had for oaths, and the scorn they showed for those who would not use them:

> swearing in private and familiar talke . . . is used and taken there for a vertue. So that he that can lashe out the bloudiest othes, is coumpted the bravest fellowe: For (saie thei) it is a signe of a coragious harte, of a valiaunt stomacke, & of a generoseous, heroicall, and puissant mynde. And who, either for feare of Gods Judgementes will not, or for want of practice cannot, rappe out othes at every word, he is counted a Dastard, a Cowarde, an Asse, a Pesant, a Clowne, a Patche, an effeminate person, and what not that is evill. By continuall use whereof, it is growne to this perfection, that at every other worde, you shal heare either woundes, bloud, sides, harte, nailes, foote, or some other parte of Christes blessed bodie, yea, sometymes no parte thereof shalbe left untorne of these bloudie Villaines.[12]

Richard Brathwaite describes the habitual verbal fierceness of soldiers home from the wars with their moustaches and weapons: 'They're blustering boyes . . ./They have a mint of oaths, yet when they sweare,/Of death and murder, there's small danger there.'[13] Decades earlier, Ferrarius had been even more voluble about the offences of soldiers and their camp followers,

> which in every light talke upon everie small occasion, do sweare continually not only by heven, but also by God him selfe, and the verie blessed woundes of our saviour Christ, beside those that they use, by the elementes, by every creature, by the most holy Sainctes: hereunto doe they coyne filthie talke, and gyve them selves to the devill. . . . Whiche detestable blasphemie, although moste men do impute to those Ruffians and unshamefast Villaines, which followe the campes, as a speciall fruite of warre, yet it is certaine that childre which can scarcelie speake do heare such othes of their mothers, nurses, and parentes, and so learn that while they be younge.[14]

Unfortunately, as Rich points out, it is the surface that most impresses in the English society of 1604: 'It is enough . . . if he

can sweare *Sblood* and *Sownes*, take a pipe of Tabacco, and bring
my Ladies letter to my Lord, it is Experience enough, and he
shall be preferred before another that hath served 20 yeares in the
Campe.'[15]

There were many points of contact between soldiers and young
gentry. Rich mentions one. We think of Bertram in *All's Well that
Ends Well*, or Claudio in *Much Ado about Nothing* going off to
fight, or of Poins accompanying Prince Hal to the tavern. Gentlemen, hunting excitement, would frequent places where soldiers and
cony-catchers were trying to win a few shillings or at least a few
drinks, and Ben Jonson portrays the gullible young man led by a
bragging 'captain'. It will be helpful to look at *Every Man In His
Humour* in some detail before we concentrate again on Shakespeare.
In a single work we find an exceptionally wide range of the sort
of swearing we are interested in, for Jonson, unlike Shakespeare,
or even Udall, allowed more general swearing. The true gentry,
Young Knowell and Wellbred; the country gull, Stephen, and
water-carrier Cob with their tutor Bobadil; Brainworm disguised as
a returned soldier; even the Elder Knowell – all combine to provide
a wonderful catalogue. Despite the Italian setting of the 1598
version, as Hazelton Spencer says, 'Jonson weaves a racy tapestry
of contemporary London life'.[16]

Stephen believes that 'by gadslid . . . 'Slid . . . a gentleman
mun show himself like a gentleman'.[17] The Elder Knowell,
realising that his nephew is a 'prodigal, absurd coxcomb', tries to
give advice. Although Jonson often lets his audience draw their
own conclusions about human folly and vice, here he combines
in the older gentleman a thread of moral strictness with an
experienced understanding that would have been absent from a
Puritan commentator. Knowell accidentally opens a letter intended
for his son and reacts much as Ferrarius might to this invitation
to reprehensible amusement, lamenting the bad example set for
children who 'suck'd our ill customs with their milk!' He adds,
'We make their palates cunning! . . . A witty child! – Can't swear?
The father's darling!/Give it two plums'.[18] The reaction seems
overly strong in the 1616 Folio, where the oaths have been cut.
Originally, young Prospero had written Lorenzo, Junior, a letter
sprinkled with ' 'Sblood', 'by Phoebus', and other exclamations that
lacked even the justification of anger.

One might expect this collection of young men to fall in love
and have some object for their massive oaths. But Jonson supplies
only one young woman, Bridget, who is free to marry; and
although Matthew, the town gull, does pay court with some
plagiarised verse, Young Knowell's successful wooing takes place
clandestinely while our attention is focused on the antics of others.

In the earlier version, most of the oaths are conventional phrases, and the inventiveness comes from Bobadil and his pupil, Cob, who brags:

> Ild forsweare them all, by the life of Pharoah, there's an oath; how many waterbearers shall you hear sweare such an oath? Oh I have a guest (he teacheth me) he doth swear the best of any man christned: By Phoebus, By the life of Pharoah, by the body of me, As I am a gentleman, and a soldier: such daintie oathes.[19]

So strong is the compulsion to swear that a character will feel inadequate if he cannot think of a suitable phrase. On one serious occasion Wellbręd stutters, 'Why, by – what shall I swear by? Thou shalt have her, as I am—' (Folio, IV, v, 38–9). Stephen wavers between overloading his own speeches to prove his ability and raptly admiring Bobadil's most mundane utterances, including 'as I am a gentleman and soldier'. When he has real cause for anger, after being cheated on a sword, he tries in vain to remember his mentor's words: 'but by – I ha' forgot the Captain's oath; I thought to ha' sworn by it – an e'er I meet him—' (Folio, III, i, 218–20). Later still, he listens and comments with a hopeless envy:

Bobadil:	By Pharoah's foot, I would have done it.
Stephen	
[*aside*]:	Oh, he swears admirably! 'By Pharoah's foot!' 'Body of Caesar!' I shall never do it, sure. – Upon mine honour, and by St George! – No, I ha' not the right grace.
Matthew:	Master Stephen, will you any? By this air, the most divine Tobacco that ever I drunk!
Stephen:	None, I thank you, sir. – [*aside*] Oh, this gentleman does it rarely too! But nothing like the other. By this air! As I am a gentleman! By—

(Folio, III, v, 155–68)

Stephen will never have the easy confidence of Young Knowell, and none of the young men or their real-life counterparts will be able to forget fashion and share the casualness of Sir John Hazelwood, who wrote, 'If ever I should betake myself to swearing, I shall give very little concern to the fashion of the oath. Odd's bodikins will do well enough for me, and lack-a-daisy for my wife.'[20]

When we turn to *Twelfth Night*, we see Sir Andrew under some of the same compulsions that characterise these Jonsonian gallants. A phrase from *The Poetaster* would have been suitable for him and Sir Toby – Crispinus' 'as I am a Gentleman and reveller'. *Twelfth Night*, available only in the Folio text, may have been censored, for Sir Toby seems mild in comparison with Falstaff. But Sir Andrew is allowed some remarkably strong phrases, and the play as a whole provides many instances of swearing attuned to fashion.

There is, first, the *pro forma* verbal violence of the sort Sir Toby urges upon Sir Andrew before the duel with the disguised Viola.

> So soon as ever thou seest him, draw; and as thou draw'st, swear horrible; for it comes to pass oft that a terrible oath, with a swaggering accent sharply twanged off, gives manhood more approbation than ever proof itself would have earned him.
>
> (III, iv, 164–8)

Sir Andrew assures him, 'Nay, let me alone for swearing.' Sir Toby continues leading Sir Andrew on, speaking not merely of noise, but of honour. The lank, flaxen-haired knight would prefer to give up a horse and go home, but is told that the youth 'will fight you for's oath's sake'. Sir Andrew is scarcely comforted by the assurances that Cesario has decided the quarrel is worthless and must be carried on merely 'for the supportance of his vow'. Sir Toby continues, 'He protests he will not hurt you . . . he has promised me, as he is a gentleman and a soldier, he will not hurt you' (III, iv, 277–88).

From Maria's opening report to Sir Toby that Olivia has spoken of 'a foolish knight that you brought in one night to be her wooer', we are left in no doubt about Sir Andrew's status. His three thousand pounds cannot counteract the fact that 'He's a very fool and a prodigal . . . besides . . . he's a great quarreller' (I, iii, 22–7). When Sir Toby protests, 'By this hand, they are scoundrels and substractors that say so of him,' she adds, 'he's drunk nightly in your company'. When Sir Andrew enters, misunderstanding 'accost', and clumsily capering on command, he is patently one with Stephen and Royster Doyster, and with Shakespeare's own inept Slender. Initially he swears only the same mild 'By my troth' or 'marry' that Feste and Maria often use, and Sir Toby's 'by this hand' sounds forceful by comparison.

Frequency of swearing can carry weight, however, in creating the sense of thoughtless habit rather than frightening seriousness. When we see Sir Andrew in II, ii, he is trying to give his speech life and emphasis by appending 'i' faith' or 'by my troth' to the most mundane statements. When the clown sings, he feels compelled to comment, 'A mellifluous voice, as I am true knight' (II, iii, 50), a joke that Shakespeare had earlier elaborated on in *As You Like It*. There Touchstone interjects a bit of repartee that has nothing to do with the play's action. Sent from Celia's father, he characteristically rises to Rosalind's question.

Touchstone: . . . by mine honour . . . I was bid to come for you.
Rosalind: Where learned you that oath, fool?
Touchstone: Of a certain knight that swore by his honour they were good pancakes, and swore by his honour the mustard was naught. Now I'll stand to it, the pancakes were naught, and the mustard was good, and yet was not the knight forsworn.
Celia: How prove you that in the great heap of your knowledge? . . .
Touchstone: . . . Stroke your chins, and swear by your beards that I am a knave.
Celia: By our beards, if we had them, thou art. .
Touchstone: By my knavery, if I had it, then I were; but if you swear by that that is not, you are not forsworn; no more was this knight, swearing by his honour, for he never had any; or if he had, he had sworn it away before ever he saw those pancakes or that mustard.

(I, ii, 57–74)

Similarly, Sir Andrew's oath puts a comic twist on the appraisal of the song, although Feste may, indeed, have sung well.

Feste had interjected the common 'By'r Lady' and later used 'by Saint Anne' to the sanctimonious Malvolio, but his swearing soon pales beside Sir Andrew's. The foolish knight's oaths, in no way inventive, grow in sharpness as his excitement mounts. ''Slight, I could so beat the rogue,' he blusters as they watch Malvolio pick up the letter. He will use this, the strongest oath in the play, several more times. ''Slight! will you make an ass o' me?' he inquires when Fabian insists 'upon the oaths of judgement and reason' that Olivia's favours to Cesario are only intended to arouse Sir Andrew's jealousy. He is made an ass indeed when he believes Fabian and is led to challenge Cesario. After the quivering attempt at a duel, Viola's twin beats him in earnest. A change comes into his swearing. No longer is he merely trying to sound fashionable or to give substance to hollow utterances. He shifts to the diminutive 'Od's lifelings', a form used by many mild or ineffectual figures, to express his genuine dismay at his bloody coxcomb.

While Sir Toby's group is engaged in revelry and practical jokes, the romantic figures are engaged in wooing and frustration. John Russell Brown, H. B. Charlton and others have commented on the values of Orsino at the beginning of the play, when his grand feeling for Olivia seems actually to be a romanticised infatuation with the idea of love, its music and its missives.[21] There is pretence in Olivia's mourning for her dead brother, too, for she immediately doffs both veil and attitude upon seeing the disguised Viola.

In the exchanges between these two women Shakespeare finds a subtle source of amusement, as he shows the conventions of wooing, with their attendant vows. Viola has some of the wittiness under stress that we have already noted in Hermia in *A Midsummer Night's Dream*. Shipwrecked, apparently also bereft of a brother, she takes disguised service with the love-lorn Duke as a way of surviving in a strange land. Soon she is messenger to a lady who will see no one. Her arrival at Olivia's gate had been underscored with an oath that she would come in (I, v). A deeper seriousness enters at line 175, for her '(by the very fangs of malice I swear) I am not that I play' seems a strange and threatening parenthesis. Its starkness may recall the hardships she has endured. Furness, early in this century, pointed out that the fangs seemed the worst part of the monster.[22] Viola may be thinking of all she must endure as she pays futile court for her master. Very probably there is, too, a hint of her own tearing anguish that she cannot declare her love for Orsino without revealing her identity.

Wit takes over again, at least on the surface, as she plays the good page reciting a 'poetical' message rather similar to one of Shakespeare's 'procreation' sonnets. Were *she* courting Olivia, she would engage in other conventional displays of love: building a willow cabin by the gate, writing 'loyal cantons of contemnéd love' and singing them all night, crying Olivia's name for all the elements to hear. Her course would be more active than Orsino's languishing, and Olivia responds, eventually herself swearing the sort of lover's vows generally reserved for a man.

In the meantime, Viola creates for Orsino a story of her father's daughter pining for a concealed love. Her comments on the truth of women remind us of Hermia's remarks, although here the disguise and an undertone of 'smiling at grief' temper what she says.

> Was not this love indeed?
> We men may say more, swear more; but indeed
> Our shows are more than will; for still we prove
> Much in our vows but little in our love.
>
> (II, iv, 114–17)

Another aspect of love and oaths appears as Olivia begins to take the initiative, filling a traditional man's role. Here, Cesario ought to be uttering vows of devotion, in keeping with the first-act description of wooing. But 'he' is, of course, not interested. Furthermore, a page, despite parentage 'above my fortunes', is not in a position to court a lady. In the same situation, the Duchess of Malfi takes the initiative with Antonio, even to managing the marriage. Olivia here must do the courting, and she adds to her stock of womanly phrases one that was usually reserved for men – 'honour' – although certainly women were concerned about it, and the Princess in *Love's Labour's Lost*, again a person of high rank, swears by it (V, ii, 352). Suddenly Olivia approaches the 'youth':

> Cesario, by the roses of the spring,
> By maidhood, honour, truth, and everything,
> I love thee so that, maugre all they pride,
> Nor wit nor reason can my passion hide.
>
> (III, i, 146–9)

Viola's appropriate and truthful 'By innocence I swear, and by my youth,/I have one heart, one bosom, and one truth,/And that no woman has' seems a heartless answer, since it carries a meaning Olivia is not able to comprehend.

Ultimately, of course, Olivia's attention shifts unwittingly to Sebastian. Formal marriage vows that we do not hear replace fashionable courtship phrases which, although deeply meant, are amusing to us because they are uttered so hurriedly, with so little knowledge of their object. Shakespeare cannot resist the temptation to have one final confusion, when Viola is accused of perjury as she swears she knew nothing about the wedding. Fortunately there is a timely explanation just before she is banished by the incensed Orsino, and her penultimate speech can be a formal declaration of the love she has so long concealed.

> And all those sayings will I over swear,
> And all those swearings keep as true in soul
> As doth that orbèd continent the fire
> That severs day from night.
>
> (V, i, 261–4)

After his gentle criticism of the oaths and other pretensions of lovers and gallants, Shakespeare follows a pattern he will use in other comedies, focusing finally on the binding oaths of sincere lovers. Characteristically, to avoid detracting from these vows, he has muted the *pro forma* swearing late in the play.

Other foolish Shakespearian gentlemen are less developed than Sir Andrew: Thurio in *The Two Gentlemen of Verona* deserves only a passing glance, and Slender in *The Merry Wives of Windsor* can be easily dealt with. Cloten, the Queen's son in *Cymbeline*, is somewhat more complex. In the opening scenes he is apparently another of the young men who by virtue of birth or wealth might exhibit true honour, but instead seems to show only exaggerated surface characteristics that earn him widespread scorn. Robert Heilman has pointed out that he has a degree of patriotism, lacks the cowardice usually found in the type, and even has some pathos. Despite this complexity, he is predominantly an 'oafish courtier of dubious principles'.²³ It is only later, as he defies the Romans and tries to carry out his revenge for Imogen's insult, that we feel mixed emotions. When the play opens, we laugh at this sweaty, unskilled and ungracious dueller. The Second Lord's asides help to classify him as a fool, and his own complaints inform us that he is an unsuccessful suitor (I, ii). As with Falstaff in *The Merry Wives of Windsor*, so with Cloten there is limited on-stage swearing. But early in the second act he describes an argument, and we learn more of this bad loser, a swearing gambler with a very good opinion of himself and his rank.

Cloten: Was there ever man had such luck? When I kissed the jack upon an upcast, to be hit away! I had a hundred pound on't. And then a whoreson jackanapes must take me up for swearing, as if I borrowed mine oaths of him and might not spend them at my pleasure.

1 Lord: What got he by that? You have broke his pate with your bowl. . . .

Cloten: When a gentleman is disposed to swear, it is not for any standers-by to curtail his oaths. Ha?

(II, i, 1–11)

We are reminded again that young men had individual oaths which they guarded jealously, a point emphasised by a similar character in Nat Field's *Amends for Ladies*. Lord Feesimple appropriated profanity belonging to Tearchaps, and was chastised: 'Use your own words, damn me is mine, I am known by it all the town o'er. D'ye hear?'²⁴

Cloten's frustration continues as he presses his suit for Imogen. Like Thurio, he has arranged for music under his lady's window. His 'Still I swear I love you', however, brings only her scathing 'If you but said so, 'twere as deep with me./If you swear still, your recompense is still/That I regard it not' (II, iii, 90–3).²⁵ Later his role darkens, as he threatens Posthumus' servant, Pisanio, while planning his revenge. In the meantime, we learn of other despicable human actions, including a perjury that years ago led to Belarius' banishment, and the lies that lead to Posthumus' suspicion of Imogen's faith. We shall return to this aspect of the vows in *Cymbeline* when we concentrate on the post-1606 plays. Here we need only note that, although Cloten does not rise to a formal vow of revenge, he does not stoop to the hollow bombast of a bragging coward before his fight with Guiderius. Later, when Belarius worries about the consequences of killing the Queen's son, Guiderius does say he 'swore/With his own single hand he'ld take us in./. . . Why, worthy father, what have we to lose/But that he swore to take, our lives?' (IV, ii, 120–5).

This shift from the portrayal of Cloten the oaf to Cloten the threat is essential to the larger pattern of the play, where an innately noble prince must not be shown killing a mere man of straw. Shakespeare, of course, has to be careful not to overdo the shift from an apparently harmless gamester and spoiled brat to a heroic fighter. The feeling of misguided honour that Hotspur elicits as Hal defeats him would be inappropriate here, and Shakespeare avoids this partially by carefully eliminating the use of oaths that could make Cloten seem more honourable.

Slender in *The Merry Wives of Windsor* is a much simpler character, with oaths as appropriate as any of Jonson's referential ones. In this mixture of farce and romantic love there are many other conventional figures: Fenton the suitor, Anne Page, Ford the jealous husband, to name a few. Some of these, as well as Falstaff and his rogues, should have provided a richer panoply of oaths than the text shows. But the Folio edition, perhaps again because of the censor, presents a muted Falstaff. He is reputedly 'one that is as slanderous as Satan . . . given to fornications, and to taverns . . . and to drinkings and swearings and starings' (V, v, 150–5). The corrupt Quarto does provide ''Sblood', 'by the lord', and 'by the masse' often enough to make the descriptions seem accurate, but we must be wary of basing critical conclusions on this version.[26] Even in the Quarto Nym, Bardolph and Pistol are far less profane than contemporary descriptions of such types would lead us to believe. Again, comments by others suggest words we never hear. Falstaff complains when Pistol attempts to borrow money:

> Not a penny. . . . I am damned in hell for swearing to gentle-men my friends, you were good soldiers and tall fellows . . . and yet you, rogue, will ensconce . . . your red-lattice phrases, and your bold-beating oaths, under the shelter of your honour!
> (II, ii, 5–27)

The actual oaths are concentrated in the farcical parts of the Anne Page courtship, with the excitable Frenchman, Dr Caius, and the whey-faced, yellow-bearded, strutting-gaited Slender.

A characteristic would-be gallant, Slender has been learning to fence, wants to marry well enough to quarter a coat of arms, would like to buy a fallow greyhound, and seems interested in clothes. His first oath is on an article of fashion, and the Quarto transcriber, although he changed much of the phraseology, recognised this concern with outward habiliments and wrote, 'By this handkerchief' (p. 4). The phrase is 'By these gloves' in the Folio, where it is repeated several times over ten lines as Slender accuses Pistol of picking his pocket, then declares with equal assurance that it was Nym, and finally decides, 'By this hat, then he in the red face had it; for though I cannot remember what I did when you made me drunk, yet I am not altogether an ass' (I, i, 135–52).

As he did with Sir Andrew, Shakespeare swiftly establishes the contrast between what this positive-sounding man is and what he is trying to be. The verbal certainty, coupled with the shifting accusations, makes him seem inept, and his foolishness is furthered by his malapropisms as he talks of a 'decreasing' love for Anne Page. By the third act, despite her father and his uncle's urging, he has made little progress with the courtship, and seems emotionally detached: ''Slid, 'tis but venturing.' From the opening scene, where he effetely declared to Anne that since bruising his shin at swordplay he could not abide the smell of hot meat, he has shown a willingness to be led by others. There, Page's 'By cock and pie, you shall not choose sir! Come, come' moves him to the table. At the end of the play, relatively unchanged, he will do as he is directed during the revels at Herne's Oak. Remarkably, in this last scene he forgoes oaths and recounts angrily but straightforwardly his discovery that the 'maid' in white is a postmaster's son.

One feels that Shakespeare is saving the final explosion for Dr Caius, who immediately roars in using the one oath that Shakespeare has made exclusively his: 'Vere is Mistress Page? By gar, I am cozened – I ha' married un garçon . . . by gar, a boy. . . . By gar, I am cozened. . . . by gar, and 'tis a boy. By gar, I'll raise all Windsor' (V, v, 194–9). He rushes out, leaving the way clear for Fenton's triumphal entry with Anne. Like some other romantic lovers, he might have been expected to swear his devotion. But Shakespeare heightens the contrast between him and the others by giving him a sincerity that needs no exaggeration.

This has been true of Fenton throughout the play. Described by the Host as one who capers, dances, 'has the eyes of youth', writes verses and 'speaks holiday' (III, ii, 59–61), and by his own admission one with debts and a wild past who was first attracted by Anne's money, he certainly seems to fit the pattern of the swearing gentleman. But with Anne he has taken on the same kind of simplicity that Berowne intends to assume. And she accepts the strongest words he utters – 'heaven so speed me in my time to come!' – as a truthful declaration that it is now herself alone, not her dowry, that attracts him (III, iv, 12). One might suggest that the Folio has been cut, but Fenton's pledge is atypical of what we find when we compare original oaths and Folio substitutions in other plays. It seems more as if Shakespeare has controlled Fenton's swearing to heighten the contrast between him and the two less desirable suitors.

We need to return briefly to Dr Caius, for he is not only one of the few who swear in dialect, but also one of those to whom Shakespeare gives a special speech rhythm. Falstaff has the short phrases, with many breathing-places, that might characterise a fat, wheezing old man; Othello has long, rolling lines. Dr Caius, with his great impatience, speaks in staccato bursts, and his oaths tend to punctuate his utterances. There are many questions and many exclamations. One of his longest unbroken phrases is 'and I vill teach a scurvy jackanape priest to meddle or make', where most of the words are single syllables (I, iv, 98–9). 'By gar' fits into the monosyllabic pattern, as well as being a conventional part of a stage French accent. Shakespeare had not used this mincing of 'by God' for the French in *Henry VI, Part One*, or *King John*, or while making fun of the enemy in *Henry V*. There 'Dieu' and 'Ma Foi' served. Here the Frenchman is speaking a mongrel English like that of Monsieur in *Jack Drum's Entertainment*, who cries, 'By gor,/Hee, by gor I smell a rat . . . by gor,'[27] or Jonson's Pache in *The Case Is Altered*, who declares, 'By gar, me shall be hang for tell dis same.'[28] Dr Caius' torrents of words, including this oath that escaped the censor, as he whips out his rapier, utters challenges and waits impatiently to duel with Sir Hugh, make him sound a bit like a comic French Hotspur.

The primary use of oaths in the play, we find as we examine either the reputable or the bad text, is to give a fashionable emphasis to the speech of two unsuccessful suitors who never have the opportunity to swear lovers' vows. It seems far less a matter of fashion as Sir Hugh, the Welsh parson, uses 'By Jeshu' or 'py'r lady'. Suffolk, in *Sir John Oldcastle*, chided Sir John, Parson of Wrotham, for blurting out "sblood': 'you must not swear, it ill becomes One of your coate, to rap out bloody Oathes.'[29] But, if we recall some of the comments quoted in the first chapter, we realise that there were exceptions. Furthermore, Sir Hugh's dialect makes him a Welshman first; and his concerns about coats of arms and duelling-sites push his priesthood farther into the background. Characteristic is his discussion with Dr Caius: 'As I am a Christians soul, now, look you, this is the place appointed. I'll be judgment by mine Host of the Garter' (III, i, 85–7). His swearing is not particularly strong, but it adds a bit of explosiveness to another character caught up in the swirling farce of the courtship plots.

One other swearing gentleman should catch our attention before we turn to the more military braggarts. Again, there is only a Folio text, and we might suspect some cutting. But there also seems to be an artistic principle operating in *The Taming of the Shrew*, where gentry and beggar alike say less than we would expect, and our attention is focused on the oaths of Petruchio. Despite the amount of time given to Lucentio, Hortensio, the pantaloon Gremio, and the rather conventional Bianca plot, the play is, after all, carried by the taming of Kate. Petruchio's careful use of oaths in that taming process must not be submerged in a plethora of other protestations.

In the textually problematic *The Taming of a Shrew*, Christoper Sly is allowed 'jesus', 'by the mass', and a ringing 'Souns',[30] but in *The Taming of the Shrew* his ejection from the tavern elicits only 'in faith', and at first we wonder why this drunken beggar should be so unprofane. Then Shakespeare's purpose becomes apparent. As Richard Hosley points out, the whip-cracking, wife-beating tamer of today's productions is not called for in the text.[31] Petruchio's method is subtler: expectation built then denied, a demonstration of Kate's scolding technique while she watches helplessly, a honeymoon filled with turmoil, profanity and complaint. About one-third of the swearing or references to it involves Petruchio, while the lengthy exchange between Hortensio and Tranio counts in terms of mere numbers but holds our attention only fleetingly. We watch with momentary amusement as Tranio's decoy-vows never to see Bianca again are matched by Hortensio's serious ones, thus clearing the way for Lucentio (IV, ii). Our interest, however, immediately reverts to the taming plot, while in *The Taming of a Shrew* attention was drawn from Ferando, the tamer, by general bustle and swearing servants.

Petruchio fits the pattern of the young gentleman who swaggers a bit, commenting that he has 'heard great ordnance in the field', and that Kate's reputation for a chiding tongue cannot daunt him (I, ii, 67–207 passim). We are not surprised that he swears, but we do notice a calculation in his use of oaths that differs from the bluster of many of his dramatic counterparts. Within a few hundred lines, Kate is threatened with a cuffing if she strikes again, hears him state insultingly, 'Now, by Saint George, I am too young for you' (II, i, 238), and finally is thrown completely off balance as he declares, 'by this light, whereby I see thy beauty/. . . Thou must be married to no man but me' (II, i, 275–7). When she complains to her father about this 'half lunatic,/. . . madcap ruffian and . . . swearing Jack,/That thinks with oaths to face the matter out' (II, i, 289–91), she hears her future husband utter praises and lie baldly that she has protested 'oath on oath' and won him 'to her love'.

Gremio's description of the off-stage wedding indicates that the performance has continued with refinements. Petruchio startled the priest who inquired if Kate would be his wife: ' "Ay, by gogs-wouns," quoth he, and swore so loud/That, all amazed, the priest let fall the book' (III, ii, 156–7). A trembling Kate can only ask why he is stamping and swearing (for this is a moment when even the most voluble gentleman should curb his tongue). Immediately we join Curtis in wonderment as Grumio reports that Petruchio continues his oaths while she has turned to prayer. Starving and helplessly angry, she will later remark that she is being kept awake by his swearing (IV, iii, 9–10). We may remember the scenes with the meat and the tailor more vividly, but these reports show that Petruchio's language is as much a part of his plan to tame Kate as the other tricks.

When we turn from men like Petruchio, who have had some military experience, to those whose emphasis is on military prowess, Pistol and Parolles come immediately to mind. Contemporary descriptions of taverns and city life frequently mention the type, Jonson's Brainworm adopts the disguise easily as he turns to cony-catching, and Bobadil trades on his rank of captain. Shakespeare's braggarts are less apt to evoke the sense of the far-away or the classical than Bobadil, who calls upon 'the life of Pharoah', 'the host of Egypt', 'Hercules' or the 'body of Caesar', objects that would be more appropriate to Antony or Cleopatra.[32] Once Stephen is meticulous in drawing the line between himself and the military man, using 'as I am a gentleman, but no soldier indeed'. He is delighted to be told that he need not make the distinction, and immediately calls himself a soldier as he praises some 'divine Tobacco'.[33] To the gullible young man, this sounds brave; Touchstone's technicality about forswearing would apply well, too! The gallant suitors court women who, like Diana reacting to Bertram, can remember a warning and declare, 'all men/Have the like oaths'. Similarly, the braggarts meet those who are not impressed. Musco (Brainworm) in disguise is reprimanded by the elder Lorenzo (Knowell): 'Nay, nay, I like not these affected othes; Speake plainly man.'[34] Yet, had he not interlarded his speech with stock phrases like 'by the place and honour of a souldier', one wonders whether Stephen would have been so intent on buying the sword.

'Affectation' is the key word for all these men who assume a manner in keeping with the deeds they say they have done, living by 'oaths and big-mouth'd menaces'.[35] One can imagine Pistol impressing the more gullible in the taverns of London or Windsor with tales of Agincourt. Left with the taste of leek in his mouth, lumps on his head, and the warning, 'If I owe you anything, I will pay you in cudgels', after his argument with Fluellen, he is further chastised by Gower: 'You are a counterfeit cowardly knave. Will you mock at an ancient tradition . . . and dare not avouch in your deeds any of your words?' (*Henry V*, V, i, 62–6). Seemingly at his nadir, Pistol takes stock and announces a plan.

Old I do wax, and from my weary limbs
Honour is cudgelled. Well, bawd I'll turn . . .
To England will I steal, and there I'll steal;
And patches will I get unto these cudgelled scars
And swear I got them in the Gallia Wars.

(V, i, 76–81)

Contemporary authors add background to the few examples we find in Shakespeare. Barry, writing *Ram Alley* a few years after the censorship law, provides a contrast between the non-swearing Captain Puff and blustering Captain Face, whose typical speech is filled with threats: 'Zounes. . . . By Dis I will be Knight. . . . Zounes Ile first be damn'd, shall sport bee laught at; by *Dis*, by Pluto, and great Proserpine,/My fatall blade once drawne, falls but with death.'[36]

Sometimes good fighters were impressed by this kind of language. Fluellen, himself given to rather explosive talk, at first praises Pistol, who has uttered brave words by the 'pridge', although Gower immediately calls him a counterfeit (*Henry V*, III vi), and the boy is not fooled: 'I have observed these three swashers. I am boy to them all three; but all they . . . could not be man to me. . . . For Bardolph, he is white-livered and red-faced . . . 'a faces it out, but fights not. For Pistol, he hath a killing tongue and a quiet sword' (III, ii, 25–31).

Bertram, a young nobleman without the experience that has made the baggage boy so perceptive, is deceived by Parolles through the first half of *All's Well that Ends Well*. Probably he would have followed anyone to get away from Helena, but he seems genuinely nonplussed when he sees the depth of Parolles' cowardice. As the 'interrogation' of the 'captive' progresses, he becomes increasingly disgusted by 'this counterfeit module [who] has deceived me like a double-meaning prophesier' (IV, iii, 92–4).

In *All's Well that Ends Well*, the plays *Henry IV* and *Henry V*, however, the braggarts are less profane than pamphleteers and other dramatic portrayals would lead us to expect. With *All's Well that Ends Well*, of course, there is the problem of having only the Folio text. With the *Henry IV* plays, where there are early Quarto editions, we sense that Falstaff's cronies must not be allowed to detract from his own bluster. *All's Well that Ends Well*, too, seems to present a conscious artistic pattern. There is a noticeable alternation between scenes with serious avowals as Helena cures the King, chooses a husband, is denied the consummation of her marriage, and finally meets Bertram's conditions, and scenes where Parolles brags and exclaims and even moves others to swear. And Parolles' oaths or the references of others to them virtually equal all other instances of swearing in the play.

Helena immediately characterises him as a coward and a fool, with 'some stain of soldier', a strangely pejorative word. She adds that he goes backward when he fights. Perfectly at ease among the gentry, he ventures a sophistic and slightly risqué argument about virginity and, although his asseverations are mild in this opening scene, they appear in his speech alone. There follow several scenes with such seriously used and appropriate phrases as Helena's 'by grace itself I swear' and Lafew's 'Now by my faith and honour,' when the King is persuaded to try her remedies. Parolles' bluster provides comic relief, and Lafew's acidulous comments about his scarf and bannerets prompt the boast, 'I'll beat him, by my life, if I can meet him with any convenience'. This man who has made Lafew's age a convenient excuse for not fighting becomes predictably mild when the old gentleman returns.

Camp and battle scenes, of course, show a braggart in the least congenial setting, for there he may be required to perform the great deeds he recounts in civilian life. The French know that under stress Parolles will 'deliver all the intelligence in his power . . . and that with the divine forfeit of his soul upon oath' (III, vi, 27–8). Although we laugh at Shakespeare's satire of the man, we are also slightly dismayed by Parolles' smallness. Tricked into volunteering to recapture the drum, he declares, 'By the hand of a soldier, I will undertake it,' although he qualifies this immediately: 'I know not what the success will be, my lord, but the attempt I vow.' The lords wait for him, knowing that, rather than risk his life, he will 'beguile two hours in a sleep, and then . . . return and swear the lies he forges' (IV, i, 21–3). Overheard by the Second Lord, Parolles contemplates the tale he will tell:

Parolles: Though I swore I leapt from the window of the citadel—
2 Lord: How deep?
Parolles: Thirty fathom.
2 Lord: Three great oaths would scarce make that be believed.
Parolles: I would I had any drum of the enemy's; I would swear I recovered it.

(IV, i, 52–9)

When he is 'captured', his protestations for once underline the truth as he tells the numbers of horse and foot. His warnings about the other officers almost amount to a transference of his own characteristics, as he calls Dumain one who 'professes not keeping of oaths; in breaking 'em he is stronger than Hercules' (IV, iii, 236–8). His letter to Diana, advising her to ask for gold when the Count swears oaths, is closer to the truth, but it implies an insensitivity to her virtuous principles. And principles, of course, are what Parolles lacks. The scene ends with a soliloquy akin to Pistol's that shows the resilience of the unheroic opportunist: 'Yet am I thankful. If my heart were great,/'Twould burst at this.' Recognising that 'every braggart shall be found an ass', he decides to give up his sword, a step that may mark the end of his career as braggart warrior. Still his reform is only partial, for he declares: 'Being fooled, by foolery thrive!/There's place and means for every man alive.'

With a few exceptions, Shakespeare uses the same oaths for fashionable swearers and for the most serious characters. This conventionality might add a bit of credibility to the hollow words, although actual word-choice is less amusing than some of Jonson's inventions. It also ensures that we will evaluate the oaths in context, a factor especially important in the history plays. In the *Henry IV* plays, as we noted earlier, any rodomontade that Nym, Bardolph or Pistol might indulge in is kept subordinate to that of Falstaff. In a relatively recent book on Renaissance comedy braggarts, Daniel Boughner makes frequent references to Sir John.[37] We might also have looked at Falstaff as an example of the fashionable gentleman grown old, or as a thief and a rogue, another stock type with a fashion in swearing. However, when he brags of his exploits with the sword, even hacking it as proof of a hard-fought battle, runs or plays dead on the battlefield, and carries off Hotspur, he has more than a touch of the *miles gloriosus*. But, by being so much more than the braggart warrior, he provides us with the most interesting study of the sometimes thoughtless, sometimes calculating swearer.

Falstaff's profane utterances resemble the vocabulary of Hotspur, serving, as does much of his role, to put the historical scenes into a new perspective. The two are the most prolific swearers in *Henry IV, Part One*; they are also the most frequent users of 'Zounds' and ''Sblood'. The second and third scenes establish this similarity between two men who would think themselves diametrically opposed at all points, and who represent extremes that Hal will ultimately reject. Others swear too, using some of the same oaths Falstaff employs, and the key to differentiation lies in the occasion, sincerity and frequency, rather than in the actual words. Vernon, one of the most upright of the rebels, will call his life to account as he denies Douglas' allegations of cowardice (IV, iii, 8–9). Later, he avouches with equal sincerity, 'by my soul, I never in my life/Did hear a challenge urged more modestly,' as he describes Hal's words (V, ii, 51–2). One could provide a long catalogue of similar restrained examples, all different in effect from Hotspur's exclamations or Falstaff's frequent outbursts.

Like Hotspur, Sir John does not always use his strongest oaths in moments of great stress. He can answer Hal's question about where they will take a purse with 'Zounds, where thou wilt, lad!' then register dismay after Hal has rifled his pockets with a simple 'I'll be sworn my pocket was picked.' His profanity covers the entire range noted in the opening chapter, and one might postulate that the milder and less exclamatory he sounds, the more seriously he is taking his swearing. But even this is not a consistent evaluation. If he uses 'By the Lord' early in the scene, he may repeat that several times before turning to another phrase, perhaps with the repetitiveness characteristic of some older people. Despite his awareness of himself as a character, and his cleverness, he does not cultivate distinctive oaths. And, with his rank, he is not subject to 'one of the gravest charges brought against the Hectors and Bobadils . . . that they dare assume acquaintance with courtly oaths'.[38] Occasionally his phrases seem closely tied to the situation. The soldier's stock 'by these hilts' as he shows his hacked sword helps underline his version of Gadshill (II, iv, 195). During an argument, Bardolph's complexion provokes 'If thou were any way given to virtue, I would swear by thy face; my oath should be "By this fire, that's God's angel"' (III, iii, 31–3). In *Henry IV, Part Two*, there are more frequent examples as he moves through a series of episodes where this kind of wittiness in part makes up for the absence of many interchanges with the Prince.

Boughner says, 'The safety of flight is proverbial with the *miles gloriosus*'.[39] Equally proverbial is making the flight look heroic, pretending there has been no retreat, or shifting the blame to someone else. After Gadshill, Falstaff takes the offensive, complaining of the cowardice of others. When accused of inconsistencies, he becomes increasingly explosive and evasive, using 'Zounds' and ''Sblood' to emphasise his fierce words. When finally confronted with the truth, his masterful excuse has an oath to give it added weight: 'By the Lord, I knew ye. . . . Was it for me to kill the heir apparent?' (*Henry IV, Part One*, II, iv, 253–5).

Swearing is so much a habit that, when he is role-playing with the Prince, he retains his vocabulary and is immediately chastised. Hal as the King questions Falstaff as Prince: 'The complaints I hear of thee are grievous'; and is met with ''Sblood, my lord, they are false.' Nay, I'll tickle ye for a young prince, i' faith' (II, iv, 420–2). Neither King nor Prince ever swears so strongly, and Hal responds immediately with what seems a mixture of good acting and genuine disapproval. (The cut of the oath from the Folio, incidentally, makes Hal's 'Swearest thou' virtually meaningless.)

Falstaff is most the *miles gloriosus* in the last act, at Shrewsbury. Some have argued that he is no coward, for he has led his tropps into the thick of battle. But what we see is a practical behaviour sharply contrasting to that of Hal, Hotspur, Walter Blunt and others. After he has played dead, he muses on his act, emphasising statements to himself with his habitual oaths.

'Sblood, 'twas time to counterfeit, or that hot termagant Scot
had paid me scot and lot too. . . . The better part of valour
is discretion. . . . Zounds, I am afraid of this gunpowder Percy,
though he be dead. How if he should counterfeit too, and rise?
By my faith, I am afraid he would prove the better counterfeit.
Therefore I'll make him sure; yea, and I'll swear I killed him.
Why may not he rise as well as I?

(V, iv, 112–24)

Here is the braggart-coward in thought and action. Feeling perfectly
justified in his pretence of death, he must still try to appear the
hero. But, just as he failed to imitate the Prince's vocabulary in the
play scene, so here he either misunderstands or studiously ignores
Hotspur's way of thinking. He assumes young Percy would counterfeit, and prepares to swear to it.

As the lords understood Parolles, so the Prince comprehends. He
has heard from Bardolph and Peto that Falstaff hacked his own sword
at Gadshill and 'said he would swear truth out of England but he
would make you believe it was done in fight', and that he instructed
them to tickle their noses and swear the blood on their garments
was 'of true men' (II, iv, 290–5). Now, when Falstaff says emphatically
that, if anyone dares deny he and Hotspur fought, 'zounds!
I would make him eat a piece of my sword', Hal exhibits a
generosity no braggart could have and promises to gild the lie
(V, iv, 148–53).

In *Henry IV, Part Two*, the words are milder. As yet there was no
thought of complying with a law. But there was not an explosive
Hotspur for contrast, either. Although Falstaff and the comic
characters have a larger share of the total lines, the beating of
Pistol and capture of Coleville of the Dale cannot compare with
the Gadshill story or the lie about Hotspur. And the oaths, which
for Shakespeare are surprisingly referential, are also less concentrated in Falstaff. The Hostess and Doll Tearsheet have numerous
and occasionally strong phrases. Justice Shallow tries to recapture a
past Falstaff says is invented, and exclaims an oath from time to
time to give a sense of his vitality.

As if subconsciously aware that he is gradually separating from the
security of association with the Prince, Falstaff places increasing
emphasis on his rank. First there is his knightly disgust at Dombledon, the tailor. Then, parrying the commands delivered by the Lord
Chief Justice's servant, he mentions both knighthood and soldier-
ship. Repetitively he declares 'As I am a gentleman', while talking
with the Chief Justice and distracting the Hostess from her attempt
to collect a debt (II, i). With Hal, he will call his honour into account
as he tries to transform some rather insulting remarks in a pallid

reminder of his escape from the Gadshill denouement. There is nothing exceptional in all this, save that his rank is higher than that of most braggarts.

Two instances, however, are particularly interesting because they contrast to Falstaff's more conventional swearing. As he welcomes the Prince back to London, his somewhat subdued 'by this light flesh and corrupt blood' (II, iv, 276) seems remarkably apposite in view of the Prince and Poins' comments that his desires have outlived his performance, and that he is a 'withered elder'. He has just referred to his age, and the oath fits into the larger pattern of remarks on age and sickness that helps darken the tone of this play. More puzzling is the phrase in a letter purporting to warn Hal against Poins, where he prefaces his signature with words he had disparaged a few scenes earlier: 'Thine, by yea and no'. The Bible had instructed men, 'Let your communication be yea, yea; Nay, nay: for whatsoever is more than these cometh of evil';[40] and, as R. P. Cowl has pointed out, the phrase was considered a 'Puritan expletive'.[41] Is Falstaff here parodying Puritanism as he warns the Prince to repent? We laugh at the letter's excesses, but he sounds serious. Furthermore, there is even more pretension in the address and signature of the letter than in his missives to the merry wives. It seems possible that Falstaff is trying to reaffirm his putative role as mentor to the Prince, this time deciding that a pose of virtue, even in the closing asseveration, is the surest way (II, ii, 121).

It is not until Falstaff is in Gloucestershire that he has something of his old bluster. As he calls up the recruits, his speech becomes a bit more emphatic, yet there is still restraint until he sees Bullcalf and delightedly declares, "Fore God, a likely fellow!' (III, ii, 166). Again, he is in a dominant position. In one instance there is even a remarkable similarity between the quibbling way we might expect him to use an oath, and what happens in the historical portion of the play. Prince John, having spoken of the 'honour' of his blood and sworn by his soul that 'griefs shall be . . . redressed', arrests the rebel leaders and then denies that he has broken a vow (IV, ii).

When we see Falstaff again, in the following scene, the line between braggart and honourable noble seems further blurred. Earlier, we had assumed that most military men would see through his bluster. Now we find Coleville of the Dale surrendering without a fight, ostensibly because of Falstaff's reputation, although Prince John says slightingly, 'It was more of his courtesy than your deserving.' Sir John, however, sees it as material for further boasting. If the Prince will not have it 'booked with the rest of this day's deeds', he avers, 'by the Lord, I will have it in a particular ballad else, with mine own picture on the top on't, Coleville kissing my foot' (IV, iii,

44–7). This, of course, is the picture the *miles gloriosus* would like all to have of him. Even better, Falstaff has honestly achieved a victory without any risk – for which he remembers to thank Coleville.

Although most braggart warriors do not consciously play the clown, they share the clown's ability to bounce back from beatings and embarrassments. But Falstaff sees himself as a cause of laughter: 'The brain of this foolish compounded clay – man is not able to invent anything that intends to laughter more than I invent or is invented in me.' He plans the way he will use his experiences to amuse Hal when they meet in London, and his method will be akin to Pistol's in *Henry V* – 'a lie with a slight oath'.

Falstaff has sworn more than any other single character in the two plays. Shakespeare has not made him unique in his oaths – there is more to be gained artistically by having parallels where they might not be expected, such as Hotspur's outbursts, or contrasts, such as Vernon's sincerity. After all, as Sir Thomas Elyot said in *The Governour*, years before, comedies were 'a mirrour of man's life',[42] and certainly the Falstaff scenes are comedy that also holds up a distorting mirror to the more serious side of life where others, too, are trying to steal or build reputations. Despite his lapse in the *Henry IV, Part One*, playlet, Falstaff is aware of the oaths and swearing of others, from that tailor to Poins, who 'swears with a good grace'. His own speech includes oaths, apparently now often unconsciously, as part of the dominance, camaraderie and social pose he has cultivated for years.

If one compares the Quarto text with the Folio, where oath after oath is either omitted or cut to a very mild 'marry' or 'in troth', one feels the loss. The phrases are still short and a bit breathy. The actions are the same. But there is none of the added richness that contributes to the picture of decay and helps to justify Hal's final rejection of the old man. As Elyot said, decay seldom happens without 'horrible oaths', and Hal speaks of one 'So surfeit-swelled, so old, and so profane'. Henry IV, on his deathbed, had feared for his kingdom, and the speech quoted more fully in the opening chapter does not flatter the 'ruffian that will swear, drink, dance . . .'. Hal must reject these practices just as Falstaff, years ago, rejected the sober path and gave himself, despite his knighthood and early service as a page, to the string of villainies that in moralistic texts of the time invariably included swearing.

The tavern followers, braggarts on the battlefield and common rogues in peacetime, add to the impression of corruption with their quarrelling. Pistol, a distillation of one aspect of Sir John, is criticised by Doll Tearsheet more scurrilously than the Hostess ever attacked Falstaff:

Captain! . . . cheater . . . An captains were of my mind, they
would truncheon you out for taking their names upon you before
you have earned them. You a captain! You slave, for what?
For tearing a poor whore's ruff in a bawdy-house? He a captain!
. . . God's light . . . .

(Henry IV, Part Two, II, iv, 126–33)

Pistol's response has the classical terms that characterise a Bobadil,
but that Falstaff generally avoids: 'I'll see her damned first, to
Pluto's damned lake, by this hand, to the infernal deep, with
Erebus and tortures vile also.' Shakespeare is careful to show that it is
Falstaff who commands, however, and, when swords are drawn, can
very easily drive Pistol out. With his modicum of bravery, more
varied use of oaths, and all the other facets noted by so many critics,
Falstaff becomes the culmination of what a dramatist can make of
the swearing rogue whose part is more than comic relief.

Only in *Henry V*, with the fat knight dead, do Pistol and
Bardolph come more into their own as swearers. They represent, in a
compressed way, the dishonourable bluster of rogues in comparison
with the true, if amusing, patriotism of the regional types. Fluellen
and Henry actually swear more, but in the former case the utterances
seem more heartfelt, and in the latter are generally honourable
vows. It is instructive to compare Pistol and Bardolph with Fluellen,
who at first glance seems to be a fashionably hot-headed soldier
with a laughable accent. The Folio text, remarkably uncensored,
gives him an additional "Sblood!' (IV, viii, 8), while matching his
dialectal 'by Cheshu' with MacMorris' 'By Crish'.[43]

Many of Fluellen's exclamations come at tense moments, although
he will add 'By Jesus' or 'By this day and this light' to a relatively
unimportant observation (Quarto and Folio at IV, viii, 57). We
remember him, however, reacting to the news of the baggage boys,
urging others to the attack, or defending his nationality as well as his
leek, rather than merely blustering. In the glove sequence Williams,
unaware of his night-time challenger's identity, recalls: 'I have sworn
to take him a box o' th' ear. . . .' The King questions the
obligation: 'What think you, Captain Fluellen? Is it fit this soldier
keep his oath?' The Welshman pronounces, 'it is necessary . . . that
he keep his vow and his oath. If he be perjured . . . his reputation
is as arrant a villain . . .' (IV, vii, 120–34). Henry recognises the
level of seriousness in both men, and sends Warwick and Gloucester
to make sure that the two do not come to 'some sudden mischief'.
Unlike the braggarts, these men will fight for a principle, and
their oaths have substance.

We have seen the coward's approach earlier, before the English
left for France. Nym had admitted he 'dare not fight', and Bardolph

hoped, by providing breakfast, to make them 'all three sworn brothers'. When Pistol arrives with his new wife, who had been 'troth-plight' to Nym, however, tempers flare anew. Bardolph addresses him as 'host', and he reacts: 'Now by this hand I swear I scorn the term. . . .' The oath is another stock one for a soldier. Pistol and Nym then challenge each other, and Bardolph in turn draws his sword, declaring, 'He that strikes the first stroke, I'll run him up to the hilts, as I am a soldier' (II, i, 61–3).

The Elder Knowell might have called it an affectation and paid little attention, but Pistol, attuned to what swearers hoped such language would mean, uses it as an excuse to back away – 'An oath of mickle might, and fury shall abate.' It is a good sequence, and Shakespeare repeats it, with Bardolph again intervening: 'By this sword, he that makes the first thrust, I'll kill him! By this sword, I will.' The expert, Pistol, declares, ' "Sword" is an oath, and oaths must have their course' (II, i, 95–7). Finally hands are shaken. Bardolph has known how to make a blustering show to enforce a peace, where sword-rattling is expected, but swordplay is avoided. The exchange shows exceptionally well the braggart's ability to find a seemingly honourable reason for avoiding a fight. Later, it will take a king's intervention to stop the more serious-minded Fluellen and Williams, where another vow is a spur to action.

Just before going to France, Pistol will express the rogue's attitude in a broad statement that Shakespeare will be at pains to show inaccurate: 'Trust none;/For oaths are straws, man's faiths are wafercakes' (II, iii, 45–6). We will see more of his innate ability to make an oath work for him, however, as he blusters a French soldier into surrender. The Boy must interpret, but Pistol instinctively grasps 'Permafoy' and adds it to his shouting.

The final interchange with Fluellen, already noted, shows the two aspects of the braggart: the swaggering in camp, 'swelling like a turkey cock', with the ensuing deflation akin to Parolles'; and the lying at home, gulling a peacetime society with oaths to lend credibility to fabrications. In a wider selection of Shakespeare's works than we have sampled here, aspects of the braggart and of the would-be dandy are repeated. Lovers' vows are embroidered far more elaborately than they need be; promises of action are sworn when there is no intention of following through; people toss in oaths to impress their auditors. A tedious catalogue of minor instances could be compiled, but we have examined the more important examples.

Oaths and the larger patterns of action work together, of course, as we have already seen. In Shakespeare's own time, the recognition of various types of swearers would have been facilitated by acquaintance with other writers and by actual observation. Edward VI, when he became king, swore because he had been told such language was 'dignified and becoming in the person of a sovereign', although his advisor was soon punished for misinforming him![44] Brathwaite, epigrammatising a cashiered courtier, says he 'Could sweare an oath, could fome at mouth, could set/His words in fustian'. For soldiers generally, he states, 'and what-soere they speak they sweare its good'.[45] Chapman's *May-Day* has the swaggering Lodovico and his military counterpart, Captain Quintiliano, who is accompanied by Innocentio, another vigorous swearer.[46] There is even a slightly later satirical piece, *The Swearing-Master*, that has a Londoner with a patent from 'Sancha Pancha' essaying to educate country folk in a school. Ned, one of the 'Bumkinly', is unlike many we meet in plays, for he feels no need of tutelage in oaths, and is not impressed by the chance to polish his technique and create an impression.[47]

The important point is that Shakespeare takes these stock bits – the oaths, and other details and even some elements of the action – and touches them with individuality. The oaths, in fact, may become an invariable, while other aspects are transmuted. Sometimes he makes a phrase particularly appropriate to a scene. More often the swearing is a rote performance – the 'gentleman and soldier' or 'by this hand' that suits a military man – with the circumstances helping to determine the effect. Once we know that the character is following a fashion at variance with his inner nature, we appreciate what this added richness can tell us. We quickly see the similarities between Sir Andrew and Slender. They will move through very different plays, but their oaths are a constant factor in their reactions. With the economy of a good caricaturist, Shakespeare can restrain himself, and can focus on the oaths of a few, giving his sketches of them an added clarity that would disappear were he to use the same lavishness that the early Jonson practised.

Chapter 4

Oaths of Air and of Honour

Many times in this chapter we will find ourselves saying, 'This is really part of fashion, where oaths are uttered *pro forma* and any thought is about the style, not the reliability of a turn of phrase.' Obviously Beatrice, Benedick and many others in *Much Ado about Nothing* are members of a fashionable group, and Beatrice remarks disparagingly, 'He hath every month a new sworn brother. . . . He wears his faith but as the fashion of his hat' (I, i, 63–7). Yet farther into the play there is a real concern about honour and the breaking of oaths.

Frequently, as we noted in the chapter on structure, an oath will reveal something about a character and simultaneously influence the plot. Even Celia's devotion to Rosalind and her promise on her honour to return the Duke's usurped property bespeak the dedication that will lead her to forsake comfort and safety for exile in the forest (*As You Like It*, I, ii, 17–20). And certainly many of the natural contrasts of honour and dishonour that lead to disaster in the tragedies could well fit here, but should be treated from a different perspective.

We do, however, need to focus briefly on a few of the plays where there is an emphasis on perjury in contrast to honourable behaviour, where people remark on the emptiness of a particular vow, or where we recognise a hollowness that the characters do not suspect. Shakespeare is, in these instances, echoing the concern of many of his contemporaries, including some of those whose views we sampled in the opening chapter.

There are a few tantalising moments when we are uncertain who is lying. The Marshal ceremoniously commands both Bolingbroke and Mowbray: 'Speak truly on thy knighthood and thy oath. . . .' Mowbray readily declares himself 'engagèd by my oath/(Which God defend a knight should violate!)' (*Richard II*, I, iii, 14–18). But we can only guess the merits of the mutual accusations! More frequently we know how we are expected to react. We must prefer the other young people to the shifting Proteus, or the Bastard Faulconbridge to the opportunists. We have already seen Hotspur, late in his life, becoming quite concerned with what he calls perjury, and Hal choosing an upright course that has no place for the rampant dishonour of Falstaff. This set of brief reminders points out the range; an empty oath can affect an entire country or merely a pair of lovers.

Things said in one play may help to elucidate actions we question in another, although this is not a totally reliable way of drawing conclusions. Shakespeare, however, could expect his audience to understand a great deal without detailed explanations, and at times we are dependent on philosophising passages in tracts or in some of the early plays for that same understanding.

We must remember, for a start, that 'perjury' was defined far more widely than it is for most of us today. In the opening chapter, we glanced at some of the commentaries on it. Ferrarius admitted that oaths taken religiously, not rashly, were necessary to civil government,[1] and we are used to thinking of perjury in official cases. The 'Ballad of the distressed Virgin' moves toward a wider definition in describing a young man who had forsworn a woman:

> O faithless wretch consider well
>   that heaven abborath perjury.
> Great torments are prepared in hell
>   for them that thus will swear and lie.[2]

'Perjury' meant breaking any vow or promise, or proving false in any way after even a private oath.[3] The sin and future retribution, as well as the civil crime with its temporal punishment, should be in people's minds. We find Adams admiring the plain dealer who will not break a vow even though he suffers for his honesty.[4] Bernard's allegorical True Holiness was busily investigating 'Blasphemy, rash swearing, false swearing',[5] while Throte, a lawyer in Barry's *Ram Alley*, flouted justice by talking about the serious swearing at court while he knew that in the case at hand a man would be forswearing. In *The Swearing-Master*, incidentally, characters consider the possibility of making a bit of money by saying the proper things while under oath![6] In a more private sector, the 'civill Devill', a woman of ill repute, is epigrammatised by Brathwaite as swearing all sorts of oaths he knows she will not keep.[7]

The oath of air might be perjury, or it might be the slightly less reprehensible declaration about something as unimportant as Touchstone's knight's mustard. Gervaise Babington, despite all his moralising, has the redeeming frankness to admit that at times he has gone far beyond the yeas and nays he should have spoken, for he has 'sought to get and keepe my credite with mortall man by swearing', just as Milo thinks 'a man esteemes his oath,/

Whom otherwise to credit would be loath'. Parrott finishes that little verse, though, with 'The more he swears, the lesse he is believ'd'.[8] Most people instinctively doubted the *miles gloriosus*, and only the gulls of satire or someone like Bertram, a poor judge of character, could be fooled for long. In addition to all these airy swearers, we should note those cited by Nowell who are not even aware of what they have said.[9]

The gradient of Shakespearian swearers runs the gamut from Othello, the man of honour misguided into an oath, down to a Cressida, Proteus or Iago. It encompasses men who break oaths from weakness or ambition, even if they initially had good intentions, and of course includes the villains consciously swearing falsely to cause disaster. The ambitious often rationalise their perjury quite cleverly; the weaker men will frequently accept the rationalising or excuse-making of others. Where rationalisation takes place, there are numerous technicalities. Can an oath by something non-existent be broken? Would prior allegiance nullify a vow? Can a person be held to something sworn by a deity he does not believe in?[10]

We have already noted the fashionable selection of an appropriate oath, and we will see more of Shakespeare's ability as author to choose a word that seems to grow organically out of the context in which it is used. A third kind of choice turns upon the meaning the object has for the person doing the swearing, and this is the most basic to the honourable oath that will be kept. Jonson has a sample of this in his satire, *The Poetaster*, where Crispinus and Demetrius have a trial of sorts. Virgil instructs his judges:

> You shall sweare,
> By Thunder-darting Jove, the king of Gods,
> And by the Genius of Augustus Caesar,
> By your own white, and uncorrupted Soules;
> And the deepe reverence of our Romane Iustice;
> To judge thee this Case, with Truth and Equitie:
> As bound, by your Religion, and your Lawes.[11]

Shakespeare ranges from the amusing, where there is often a fleeting reference, to the sombre where, especially in the earlier plays, the discussion may be longer. Portia insists in the ring scene that only Bassanio's 'double self' would be 'an oath of credit', and we laugh as he hunts for something to prove his sincerity. There is even a touch of lightness at the end of the balcony scene, when Juliet rejects Romeo's attempt to swear his fealty by the moon, although she touches on points that should be of concern to anyone prescribing an oath: 'swear by thy gracious self,/Which is the god of my idolatry' (II, ii, 113–14). The moon is too changeable; she knows there must be a conscious religious focus. It is interesting to compare this with Aaron the Moor's knowledge about oaths, and her suggestion that Romeo not swear with the attitude of Brutus as he talks to the conspirators.

Titus Andronicus shows how early in his career Shakespeare was realising the possibilities of this aspect of the language. There are a few protestations of dubious value from Tamora when Saturninus, rebuffed by Lavinia and Bassianus, pretends more insult than he feels. He avers 'by all the Roman gods' he will marry the captive Tamora, and she returns the promise, 'in sight of heaven and Rome I swear', saying she will be a good wife. Soon this self-seeking Goth is promising on her honour to try to reconcile things, but immediately revealing in an aside that this is an empty oath. We recognise that a clever manipulator may sound conveniently honourable; it will take some time for the sincere Andronici to realise how evil she and her sons are. But how often is she forsworn? What does Rome or even honour mean to her? The vows may compare in meaningfulness with Aaron's later oath by the Gothic gods.

The clever Aaron is perceptive about the way oaths work. He had revealed his feeling for his son with the play's strongest expletive – 'Zounds' – when the nurse spoke slightingly of Tamora's black child. At the end of the play, he is willing to bargain for the boy's life – a final example of a parent pleading for a child in a cruel play where he had seen similar pleas ignored. Lucius worries in the same way that Hall would about the profane man who has no god 'unless perhaps himselfe bee his owne deitie'.[12] Aaron, however, realises that only Lucius' faith is at issue, for he is the one with the power to save the boy in return for the confession.

Lucius: Who should I swear by? thou believest no god.
          That granted, how canst thou believe an oath?
Aaron: What if I do not? as indeed I do not.
          Yet, for I know thou art religious
          And hast a thing within thee callèd conscience,
          With twenty popish tricks and ceremonies
          Which I have seen thee careful to observe,
          Therefore I urge thy oath; for that I know
          An idiot holds his bauble for a god
          And keeps the oath which by that god he swears . . .
                  therefore thou shalt vow
          By that same god, what god soe'er it be,
          That thou adorest and hast in reverence.
                                          (V, i, 71–83)

Conscience, which even checked the swearing of the Second Murderer in *Richard III*, is useful, and so is religiosity, to a villain who knows how the minds of men work. Iago won't delineate things so carefully, but he, too, obviously knows how others regard oaths.

One of the fullest discussions of this problem in the entire Shakespeare canon comes from the fourth act of *Richard III*. Here it is the auditor who must believe, and the swearer who is apt to prove false. Queen Elizabeth will soon offer her daughter in marriage to Richmond, an honourable man who does not need to swear while so many of the dishonourable utter oaths. Richard himself tries to convince her that he would be suitable for the Princess, but she parries his every statement, interrupting his 'Now, by my George, my garter, and my crown' with 'Profaned, dishonoured, and the third usurped'. The passage is long, but it shows unequivocally how a person's actions may make usually valid objects part of oaths of mere air.

Richard:	I swear—
Elizabeth:	By nothing, for this is no oath:
	Thy George, profaned, hath lost his lordly honour;
	Thy garter, blemished, pawned his knightly virtue;
	Thy crown, usurped, disgraced his kingly glory.
	If something thou would swear to be believed,
	Swear by something that thou has not wronged.
Richard:	Then by myself—
Elizabeth:	Thyself is self-misused.
Richard:	Now by the world—
Elizabeth:	'Tis full of thy foul wrongs.
Richard:	My father's death—
Elizabeth:	Thy life hath it dishonoured.
Richard:	Why then, by God—
Elizabeth:	God's wrong is most of all:
	If thou didst fear to break an oath with him,
	The unity the king my husband made
	Thou hadst not broken, nor my brothers died. . . .
	Thy broken faith hath made the prey for worms.
	What canst thou swear by now?
Richard:	The time to come.
Elizabeth:	That thou hast wrongèd in the time o'erpast. . . .
	Swear not by time to come, for that thou hast
	Misused ere used, by times ill-used o'erpast.

(IV, iv, 368–96)

The only thing he can use, finally, is a sort of self-curse, common in this play and destined, like the others, to be fulfilled.

It is not that Richard misunderstands the distinction between proper and improper swearing. At this moment, he is trying to use oaths for his own ends as consciously as an Iago or Parolles. Both this sort of bad swearing, if another believes it, and the perfectly honourable variety can lead to tragedy. Lear thinks he is absolutely correct when he refuses to reverse his sworn decree to banish Cordelia. Othello believes Iago's oaths, swears his own for vengeance, and speaks of the sin of perjury as Desdemona denies his accusations. We can understand the adherence to principle that drives these heroes – in a horrifying way it is more positive than Shylock's sudden turn as he forgets his great oath and asks for his money.

Antony may twist the word 'honourable' as he speaks of the conspirators, and Cassius is certainly a clever manipulator. But Cassius always yields to Brutus' superior moral stances, and Antony finally lauds Brutus' motives. *Julius Caesar*, not a play with many specific oaths, has frequent Roman references to swearing. One very revealing interchange occurs on that pivotal night when the muffled conspirators are breaking any last allegiances they may have had to Caesar. Brutus, who habitually tries to make the deed seem far better than the bloody butchery it really is, rejects Cassius' proposed oath and attempts to raise the conspirators above a need for such things.

> Swear priests and cowards and men cautelous . . .
>   unto bad causes swear
> Such creatures as men doubt; but do not stain
> The even virtue of our enterprise,
> Nor th' insuppressive mettle of our spirits,
> To think that or our cause or our performance
> Did need an oath.
>
> (II, i, 129–36)

Brutus had evidently sworn marriage vows to Portia (II, i, 272–3), and he will not hesitate to pledge his honour that Antony can safely come to the conspirators (III, i, 141–2). Obviously he will use an oath to reassure. But he would like, where possible, to rely on other bonds, as many of the moralists of Shakespeare's time were suggesting.[13] Incidentally, it is only at Sardis, under the combined military and personal pressures that Octavius' pursuit and Portia's death have engendered, that he turns to the more exclamatory oath, while again assuming moral superiority.

Many tragedies by Shakespeare's contemporaries place a similar emphasis on honour and on vows that must be kept. There is generally a pivotal scene where a course of action is set, frequently for vengeance.[14] The technique can spill over into comedy, as most of the plays we will consider in this chapter demonstrate. *Much Ado about*

Nothing contains a scene that might well lead to disaster, but the whole structure of the play is so carefully controlled that we do not expect the potential to be realised.

Shakespeare may keep us from getting too tense about the impending duel, but he also, characteristically, puts much of his more casual swearing in the first three acts, and then emphasises honour and the vow extracted from Benedick. Some of the earlier examples are important, such as Don John and Borachio's report that the Prince has sworn his affection for Hero, a mistake that leads to the first of Claudio's errors about Hero's love (II, i, 150–2). Less important for the moment, but essential in preparing us for Benedick's capitulation, is his sincere 'by this day, she's a fair lady!' Obviously, he is not woman-proof, and when he does finally admit, 'I will not be sworn but love may transform me to an oyster', we realise the change is taking place much to his amazement (II, iii, 21–2). Later, Borachio will relate that Claudio swore to disgrace Hero (III, iii, 147–50). By the time this disgrace takes place, however, and Benedick is being led to a very serious vow, we have been shown Dogberry and Verges muddling toward the truth, and our attention is to be caught quickly by the Friar's concealment plan. Add to this the tone of asperity that has so long characterised Beatrice's dialogue with Benedick, and it is no wonder that 'Kill Claudio' lacks some of the impact of a 'Kill Claudius'. Not that honour is less important to these people than to Hamlet. After all, Benedick is a proper soldier returned from the wars, and Leonato, foreshadowing Othello's worry about Desdemona, hopes his daughter will not deny the accusation and thus 'add to her damnation/A sin of perjury' (IV, i, 170–1).

But there is also a planned lack of focus in this scene, for while Beatrice has wept at Hero's disgrace Benedick has kept declaring his love in terms in keeping with some of his earlier fashionable language. His oath, natural for a soldier, is also unconsciously apposite for the ensuing conversation: 'By my sword, Beatrice, thou lovest me' (IV, i, 270). She suggests that under stress he will eat his words, and like a knight of old he demands some test of his sincerity. Her 'Kill Claudio' is not what he expected, but she is completely serious, for Hero has been 'slandered, scorned, and dishonoured'. Her spate of words swirls scornfully around him, and she accuses him of swearing a lie. Her final rebuff to his 'By this hand, I love thee' is a single-minded 'Use it for my love some other way than swearing by it' (IV, i, 319–22). The timing, with the vow rather close to the end of the play, and the challenge delivered as the truth about Don John's villainy is being brought out, takes away from the potential suspense, as Shakespeare of course intended. In the ensuing rush to resolve so much, we witness a series of events that lack the impact of this scene, and contain a few oaths conventionally used. We are even reminded of *Love's Labour's Lost* as Benedick's dreadful verse is produced and Claudio swears the two are in love (V, iv, 85–8).

Dogberry and Verges have saved Claudio from a disastrous duel, and people accept his speedy declaration of contrition. As in other comedies, where vengeance has been vowed because daughters have disobeyed or lesser figures are deemed responsible for a daughter's flight, we feel that the swearer can somehow make an honourable retraction.[15] The threatener may be absolutely serious, but a ruler's decree, some new information, or even a mood of forgiveness can cause a reversal. Both Claudio and Benedick are free to act as circumstances now dictate.

Other examples of honour throughout the comedies not only reveal details of character but influence the conduct of succeeding scenes. Rulers sometimes show a sense of position that is lacking in their history-play counterparts. There is no doubt in Solinus' mind that he must abide by the laws he has sworn to uphold, despite his sympathy for the aged Egeon.

> Now trust me, were it not against our laws,
> Against my crown, my oath, my dignity,
> Which princes, would they, may not disannul,
> My soul should sue as advocate for thee.
>
> (I, i, 142–5)

The scene is so early in *The Comedy of Errors* that, were it not for the title and the highly romantic nature of the old man's tale, we might expect a tense story of a search for the necessary bail. It seems strange to make any comparisons of Solinus with King Lear, but the two men, on their different levels, show the firm belief that a ruler's oath must be kept. Showing a person in power breaking vows, in fact, is one of the most effective ways of casting doubts on his fitness to rule. We have already noted Melun's revelation that Lewis intends to trick the English barons, and Prince John's dealing with the rebels. Henry V's care in keeping vows and in pointing out their importance is part of his depiction as the paragon of rulers.

While a king's oath-keeping can tell us much about him, the allegiance of others can reflect his concept of himself and give a very good indication of his strength. *Richard II*, short on profanity, is thick with mention of the relation of subject and king. Hotspur and the rebels try to make Henry IV seem an oath-breaker. The *Henry VI* trilogy is rich with examples of almost all sorts of perfidy where oaths become mere air, and vanish without a trace except perhaps in the wronged person's memory, as armourers and earls alike perjure themselves.

As Shakespeare and the history books portray him, Henry VI is too weak a ruler to inspire or command much allegiance despite his long stay on the throne. He was reputed not to have sworn, even under extreme provocation, and Shakespeare does not vary tradition.[16] Furthermore, we seldom see Henry making use of the more formalised pledges. He misses the opportunity that Richard II, with his love of panoply, was able to employ easily as he made the newly banished Bolingbroke and Mowbray swear never to join in league against him.

We can watch Henry learning from various sources how men's allegiance evaporates, sometimes with a legalistic rationalisation, sometimes with a very simple explanation. At the end of *Part Two* he retains enough power to command Buckingham to ask York 'why thou, being a subject as I am,/Against thy oath and true allegiance sworn/Should raise so great a power without his leave' (V, i, 19–21). For a moment the steadfast few like Iden and Buckingham give Henry authority over the Cades and the Yorks. However, nothing can overcome the effect of a more binding oath scene, invented to show the men in the Temple Garden swearing by symbolic roses and aligning themselves for civil strife. No sooner has York left than Henry is forced to repeat his question to Richard, Edward and the restive earls of Warwick and Salisbury. 'Hast thou not sworn allegiance unto me? . . ./Canst thou dispense with heaven for such an oath?' (V, i, 179–81). Salisbury's rationalisation points ahead to arguments in later plays:

> It is great sin to swear unto a sin,
> But greater sin to keep a sinful oath.
> Who can be bound by any solemn vow
> To do a murd'rous deed, to rob a man . . .
> And have no other reason for this wrong
> But that he was bound by a solemn oath?
>
> (V, i, 182–90)

By the third part of the trilogy Henry is bargaining to keep his crown at the expense of his heirs. He will consign the crown to York and his posterity when he dies 'Conditionally that here thou take an oath/To cease this civil war', a variant on the vow found in Holinshed. At the end of nearly a century when the legitimacy of the royal claim has been a cause of rebellion after rebellion, there would be an advantage to this type of legality, and York is quite willing to take and perform the meaningful oath that Henry wants (I, i, 196–201).

Richard II, we recall, was still very much the king when he made Mowbray and Bolingbroke swear on a sword in front of the assembled court. In Henry's case, however, York is sitting on the throne, and the scene is more informal. When York later comes upon his sons in discussion, they seem dutiful, merely wanting their father to have his rightful crown. York's honourable intent is soon undercut as Edward declares, 'But for a kingdom any oath may be broken./I would break a thousand oaths to reign one year' (I, ii, 16–17). We realise with shock that England will soon have a ruler to whom greed and expediency mean far more than principle. It is a surprise when Richard, whom we have heard castigated, seems to agree with his father: 'No. God forbid your grace should be forsworn.' But he continues with a Machiavellian cleverness we will see more of later:

> An oath is of no moment, being not took
> Before a true and lawful magistrate
> That hath authority over him that swears.
> Henry had none, but did usurp the place.
> Then, seeing 'twas he that made you to depose,
> Your oath, my lord, is vain and frivolous.
>
> (I, ii, 22–7)

Here, again, there is expected verbiage: every regicide, every friend-turned-rival, finds excuses for his actions. There will be dramatic value in forswearing allegiances and yielding to ambition throughout the Shakespeare canon, and even in *The Tempest* usurpations and murders are planned for a mere island.

So far, we have been looking at the way oaths are turned to air by men of some power. Henry must also learn about the common man, and the lesson is taught by two keepers who capture him as he wanders alone near the Scottish border. He is 'the king King Edward hath deposed', and they respond to his logical question about their loyalty. They have broken no oath, though they call themselves 'subjects sworn' to Edward, and explain quite simply that they 'were subjects but while you were king' (III, i, 69–81). Even the old Duke of York in *Richard II* made a similar, whole-hearted shift to Henry IV after the deposition.

Farther down the scale, the same sorts of contrast between the honourable and the wavering also are found. This is, of course, the natural dramatic stuff of history, and without it there would be far less tension in the plays. We must remember that there is always a commentary of some sort on the forswearing – either a king or a subject questioning the conduct, or a man like Talbot demonstrating to the death what true allegiance is, after remarking on Burgundy.

In the histories, and generally in the tragedies, more than individual happiness hangs on honour, although individual reactions are certainly important and there is seldom the thematic emphasis that we found in *King John*. With the comedies, we tend to get into a more private world. There could be larger consequences for swearing, as the perjury of Parolles shows. There is also more of the inconsequential swearing of the sort that laced the comic scenes of the *Henry IV* plays and occasionally crops up in the tragedies. We are not surprised by the Host's 'By my halidom, I was fast asleep', after he has dozed through Proteus' wooing (*The Two Gentlemen of Verona*, IV, ii, 135), or by Dr Caius' habitual 'by gar'. But there is sometimes a startling reaction to a casual comment. When Speed greets Launce, 'by mine honesty, welcome to Padua,' Launce carefully rejoins, 'Forswear not thyself, sweet youth, for I am not welcome' (II, v, 1–3). It is appropriate in a play that will make much of the contrast between empty vows and true faith.

A few young men in the comedies are titled, like Count Rossillion, and should be exhibiting the qualities that will make them honourable rulers as well as true lovers. The opening scene of *All's Well that Ends Well*, in fact, emphasises not only the honesty of Helena's father, but also the hope that Bertram will take after the honourable old count. We know that this will somehow become a theme of the play. Both *All's Well that Ends Well* and *Measure for Measure* dwell on the contrasts between what men are and what they should be or what they pretend to be, and of all the comedies these two most frequently refer to 'honour'. Before we come to these dark comedies, and to that other problem play, *Troilus and Cressida*, we should again glance quickly at *A Midsummer Night's Dream*, and look more thoroughly at *The Two Gentlemen of Verona*, where Shakespeare did some of his earliest comic work with oaths of honour and those of mere air.

In a world where, as Puck points out, 'truth, reason and love keep little company together nowadays' (III, i, 130–1) Helena has first faced the melting of Demetrius' oaths, then heard both men passionately declare their love. Experienced, she questions such protestations, and when Lysander points out that his vows are accompanied by tears, 'and vows so born,/In their nativity all truth appears' (III, ii, 124–5), she rejoins:

> These vows are Hermia's. Will you give her o'er?
> Weigh oath with oath, and you will nothing weigh.
> Your vows to her and me, put in two scales,
> Will even weigh; and both as light as tales.
>
> (III, ii, 130–3)

In this play where dream and reality, imagination and reason are complexly intermingled, and magic suffuses so much of the action, we must remember that the first shift, with Demetrius breaking his vows of love, occurred before Puck ever squeezed a magic flower. Theseus had intended to look into the matter, and both Helena and Hermia made the comments on men's faith which we have already noted. The magical influence must, in fact, carry into the real world in Demetrius' instance if the original faith is to be re-established. Once properly reunited, however, the young people, like those in *Love's Labour's Lost*, merely state their feelings, leaving the great hollow phrases to Pyramus and Thisbe.

There is no magic in *The Two Gentlemen of Verona* to excuse or reform Proteus when he pursues his friend's beloved, and it is human action that must in the end effect the proper pairing. Though oaths and their breaking are not structurally basic, they are important in the contrasting of character and in the comment the play makes on human behaviour. Earlier, Proteus had seemed sincere, and 'heavenly Julia' had, in return, sent a letter which he clasped: 'Sweet love, sweet lines, sweet life!/. . . Here is her oath for love, her honour's pawn' (I, iii, 45–7). Julia, starting in pursuit, refers to his 'thousand oaths' and tears of parting (II, vii, 69).

In Milan and informing on Valentine, Proteus finds the Duke steadfast in his announced plans to marry Silvia to Thurio. Blind to his daughter's feelings about this ineffectual man, he declares 'By heaven' his wrath at Valentine is greater than his love for her. Silvia, with the independence and perception that many of Shakespeare's comic heroines share, rejects Thurio and delineates Proteus' character as he in turn declares his love. We feel even more dislike for this turncoat and informer because in his rationalising soliloquy he is so aware of the amount of perjury he is committing.

> To leave my Julia, shall I be forsworn;
> To love fair Silvia, shall I be forsworn;
> To wrong my friend, I shall be much forsworn;
> And ev'n that pow'r which gave me first my oath
> Provokes me to this threefold perjury.
> Love bade me swear, and Love bids me forswear. . . .
> Unheedful vows may heedfully be broken.
>
> (II, vi, 1–11)

It is ironic that Julia, only a scene later, will be recalling his 'thousand oaths', which are to her like oracles.

We are delighted to hear how poorly he has succeeded with Silvia, who continues to scorn his treachery. And at least he recognises that she is 'too fair, too true, too holy,/To be corrupted with my worthless gifts'. What he does not seem to realise is that his person has now been rendered equally worthless, for he continues his pursuit. His description suggests that Silvia's reply was similar to Elizabeth's summary of Richard III's past falsehoods, another indication of the way the same words or responses fit into different contexts.

All Valentine's doubts about Silvia would be allayed could he but hear Proteus' complaint, or the interchange that follows the serenade. From her window, she reminds Proteus that he is 'subtle, perjured, false, disloyal', a man who has 'deceived so many with . . . vows'. In the Folio text, the Duke's 'By heaven' is the strongest oath, and there may never have been much more, for this is a work about honour and perjury, not casual swearing. The emphasis is on oaths past and now broken, rathèr than on the bluster or anger that could lead to sworn exclamations. The outlaws have few lines; Julia remains as mild as Shakespeare's other disguised heroines;[17] Silvia, rejecting Proteus, uses not a stock phrase, but 'by this pale queen of night', which fits organically with the time and subject (IV, ii, 100). Here, not the moon's changeability, but the relation to the chaste Diana inspires the words flung at the besotted man. Later she will tear up his letter without reading it, for it will be 'stuffed with protestations/And full of new-found oaths, which he will break' (IV, iv, 127–8).

The contrast between Proteus and others is emphasised even in the cameo sketch of Sir Eglamore, whose name recalls his gallant forerunner in Arthurian legend, just as 'Proteus' suggests Greek myth. Silvia points to his vow of 'pure chastity' taken on his lady's grave, and trusts herself to his 'faith and honour' in her escape from her father's court. Meanwhile Julia, watching Proteus' pursuit of another, invents an appropriate tale that is a forerunner of Viola's. She speaks of being dressed to play Ariadne's 'passioning/For Theseus' perjury and unjust flight' (IV, iv, 165–6). The classical turn of reference is still in her mind when she declares that 'By Jove' she would scratch the eyes out of the picture Proteus now worships, were it not for Silvia's faith and goodness.

Less than two hundred lines from the end, Proteus tries to make his rescue of Silvia from the outlaws sound chivalric. She returns scant thanks, still detesting 'false perjured Proteus', reminding him a final time that for Julia's

> dear sake thou didst then rend thy faith
> Into a thousand oaths, and all those oaths
> Descended into perjury, to love me.
> Thou hast no faith left now.
>
> (V, iv, 47–50)

Valentine, rescuing Silvia in turn, adds his own expression of dismay, and Julia finally reveals her identity and bemoans the perjury that has 'cleft the root' of her heart.

Today we are inclined to suspect sudden conversions, and Proteus' new-found conscience and return to Julia with a 'Bear witness, heaven, I have my wish for ever' is not convincing. But Elizabethans evidently accepted these shifts, as sudden as reforms at an evangelist's meeting, and would have considered this final vow a lasting one. It remains only for the story of Valentine and Silvia to be resolved, and again honour enters. When the Duke realises that Thurio is unwilling to risk anything for Silvia, he relents with a better grace than some of Shakespeare's older men. Calling to witness 'the honour of my ancestry', he cancels his grudges. Presumably we see these characters moving into a more perfect world that will no longer be upset by perjury or by vows of those whose plans are inflicted on others.

To many who admire Helena, Bertram in *All's Well that Ends Well* is even more despicable than Proteus, and a series of confrontations emphasises his self-centredness and a dishonour that is more important than Parolles'. Bertram's initial reluctance to marry is understandable, even though other young men are all willing to have Helena for their bride. But, while the Countess Rossillion, insisting that Helena is a paragon, overlooks the class distinction that Helena herself has noted, Bertram puts this in the foreground. He is, of course, trapped by the King's promise of a reward if Helena can effect a cure. The King had called his 'sceptre and . . . hopes of heaven' to witness his promise, and with his own honour at stake he delivers an appropriate lecture to Bertram. In the face of the decree, Bertram yields, and by doing so loses more ground with us, for he goes through the marriage ceremony only to forswear immediately what the ceremony implies. For this love plot there are two pivotal oaths – the King's to reward Helena and Bertram's not to bed her. Both stipulate certain action on Helena's part, the second one containing conditions that motivate her manipulation of events.[18] The Countess comments that her son has lost more honour by his refusal to consummate his marriage than he can ever win in the wars (III, ii, 91–2), and at the end of the play, when he is caught in a series of lies, he seems irredeemable. Yet the spirit of forgiveness, so much more obviously treated in *Measure for Measure*, reigns here as Helena remains in love with him after witnessing his faithless behaviour.

Again we are asked to accept a last-minute conversion, but it is difficult to understand why Helena has gone to such pains to win him. Bertram may have inherited something good from his father; certainly he serves honourably in battle; he is appropriately distressed when he learns about Parolles. As a secondary lover, like Claudio or Oliver, he would be all right, but as a husband of the heroine he is made unacceptably weak by his lapses at the end of the play. A hero should not need this much help to see what steadfast virtue is.

The group of people who support Helena and finally entrap Bertram are not the great swearers of the play. Lafew may make occasional sarcastic use of an oath, such as his 'By mine honour, if I were but two hours younger, I'd beat thee' (II, iii, 247–8). But Lafew is not a hollow swearer, the King means to keep his vows, and Mariana warns against the 'promises, enticements, oaths, tokens' that young soldiers such as Bertram employ to tempt the Dianas of the world (III, v, 17–18). It is fortunate for Helena that the Capilets are so attuned to honour, and that Diana will brush Bertram's protestations aside with another analytical and moral speech that applies not only to her scene, but also to the one immediately following, where Parolles answers his 'captors'.

> 'Tis not the many oaths that makes the truth,
> But the plain single vow that is vowed true.
> What is not holy, that we swear not by,
> But take the High'st to witness; then pray you tell me,
> If I should swear by Jove's great attributes
> I loved you dearly, would you believe my oaths
> When I did love you ill? This has no holding,
> To swear by Him whom I protest to love,
> That I will work against Him. Therefore your oaths
> Are words, and poor conditions but unsealed.
>
> (IV, ii, 20–30)

Bertram may have been calling Jove to witness his love for her. She is certainly pointing out the sin in any vows between her and a married man, and emphasising the quality an oath should have. The whole interchange focuses on virtue, although of course at the end she prepares him for the bed trick with a seeming yielding.

The last scene of the play draws the threads of honour and perjury together once again in something resembling a trial with various witnesses and accusations. The opening notes are of forgiveness and forgetting, rather than the revenge the King had originally planned, but Bertram is soon in difficulty and a harsher justice seems appropriate when Lafew recognises the ring. 'By my old beard/And every hair that's on't', he exclaims, 'Helen that's dead/Was a sweet creature' (V, iii, 76–8). The Countess joins the chorus, averring on her life that the ring was Helena's, and Bertram compounds his trouble by lying that it was thrown to him and painting a very honourable picture of his behaviour to the donor. But the King remains suspicious, for he remembers that Helena had 'called the saints to surety/That she would never put it from her finger/Unless she gave it to yourself in bed' (V, iii, 108–10). Diana's letter, narrating what Bertram in fact thinks he has done, dishonours him further, and the confrontation again turns on vows:

> If you shall marry . . .
> You give away heaven's vows, and those are mine . . .
> For I by vow am so embodied yours
> That she which marries you must marry me.
>
> (V, iii, 169–74)

Bertram may pretend that he is too honourable to have done what Diana accuses, but he ducks the suggestion that he be asked 'upon his oath if he does think/He had not my virginity'. When she seems to have won her case, however, Diana arouses the King's impatience by becoming very ambiguous. Again, she uses oaths or references to them in her ambiguity, first declaring 'By Jove, if ever I knew man, 'twas you' (V, iii, 284), and then adding a set of riddling statements:

> he's guilty, and he is not guilty.
> He knows I am no maid, and he'll swear to't;
> I'll swear I am a maid and he knows not.
> Great king, I am no strumpet, by my life;
> I am either maid, or else this old man's wife.
>
> (V, iii, 286–90)

When the full truth is revealed, Bertram suddenly promises that, if Helena can tell clearly how she fulfilled the conditions of his earlier angry vow, he will 'love her dearly – ever, ever dearly'. With his recent lies, this is hard to believe. Yet we can accept it intellectually if we assume that in fact his early vow was as sincerely meant as the King's promise. He had never expected her to fulfil the conditions, but she has done so, and in a play that turns so heavily on honour and dishonour it is possible that he will have the good faith to love this woman who has been able to achieve something that seemed so improbable.

The other of Shakespeare's dark comedies, *Measure for Measure*, provides us with many of the same problems, including the devotion of a girl for a man who will lie to save his reputation. Again, we have a play with more references to swearing than actual instances. Lucio, with his coarseness, has only the mildest examples, and here we expect Folio censorship. He and the seething low life of Vienna ought to say more than 'marry', 'faith' and 'In good sooth'! Pompey does manage 'By this hand', but the unregenerate Barnardine simply states, 'I swear I will not die today' (IV, iii, 56). We don't want the play filled with exclamatory oaths, but there seems to be a problem when the Duke, for all his virtue, says essentially the same things, and in fact has more varied oaths than Lucio.

What we learn about character from oaths must come, again, from the way people regard them. We hear from Vincentio that

Angelo is disregarding vows made to Mariana. Lucio swears casually that he has wronged a woman. The kindly Provost firmly announces that it is 'against my oath' to disobey orders (IV, ii, 175). And Escalus shows his dislike of profanity by exclaiming that the Bawd and her followers 'would make mercy swear'.

There is an apparent dichotomy in the fact that Angelo is to be criticised for his perjuries, while the Duke can swear lies and presumably remain admirable. We might comment that technically Vincentio's 'By the vow of mine order' is meaningless, although he uses it to convince the Provost (IV, ii, 164). The 'sacred vow' that covers his 'disappearance' is, of course, a fabrication (IV, iii). Both might have been expected in these situations, and the Duke, playing a role, would want to provide the expected. Harder to take is his harsh 'By heaven, fond wretch', when Isabella is so desperately making her charges in the last scene. We can only conclude that his intent is good, and that these otherwise reprehensible instances must be forgiven as part of his plan to test and help people. In that testing process, more important patterns of honour and dishonour stand out.

There are essentially three pairs of sworn lovers in the play, although they differ greatly. Isabella has not yet taken her formal vows, though surely she envisions herself betrothed to the Church (I, iv). Claudio and Juliet consider themselves betrothed, although there has been no formal announcement. Angelo and Mariana have sworn the contract that she and the Duke still regard as valid. Their reactions to these vows fit perfectly with other aspects of character that are gradually revealed: Isabella's steadfast morality; Claudio's impetuous weakness; Angelo's callous self-centredness.

A relief from this, but part of the endemic immorality of Vienna, is the frank corruption of Mistress Overdone and her followers, and of Lucio, who, despite moments of sincerity, can cheerfully admit to perjuring himself to escape marriage to a pregnant bawd (IV, iii, 168–9). As he cavalierly makes his allegations about the Duke's morality, and unknowingly assures the punishment he had earlier escaped, he is characteristic of those who spend their time 'swearing . . . braving, scoffing'.[19] When the Duke/Friar once suggested Lucio would forswear all he said, he proclaimed, 'I'll be hanged first' (III, ii, 156–7), a line the Duke may remember when he threatens a sentence in the last act.

Despite much excellent modern writing about this play, however, more can be said concerning the particular emphasis placed on Angelo as perjurer, with his past history, his pretence of goodness, and his newly acquired power. In the play, he is not a swearer, and the one oath we hear is, so far as he knows, true. But by the time he denies, upon his 'faith and honour', that he has had any recent contact with Mariana we know that, like Touchstone's knight, he is mentioning non-existent qualities (V, i, 222). While Angelo continues to exude moral superiority, Mariana speaks of past oaths. Here, although the Duke pretends disbelief, we know the truth, and wonder how long Angelo will be allowed to think that his 'unsoiled name' and 'place i' th' state' are overweighing the accusations. (See II, iv, 154–7.) The Duke seems angry at Mariana: 'think'st thou thy oaths,/Though they would swear down each particular saint/Were testimonies against his worth and credit?' (V, i, 240–2).

Part of Vincentio's ability to solve the problem of the midnight assignation rests on his knowledge that, well before Claudio's arrest, Angelo had 'swallowed his vows whole, pretending in [Mariana] discoveries of dishonour' (III, i, 221–2). Angelo is morally as well as legally vulnerable, and one wonders whether Isabella would have agreed to the bed trick if there had not been that sense of righting an old wrong. The time lapse since that first breach of faith has served to test Mariana's constancy, and to demonstrate further Angelo's habit of behaving despicably while pretending great goodness. In the accusation scene, Mariana must catalogue her anguish, recalling publicly that Angelo had once sworn her face was worth looking on, once clasped her hand with a sworn contract (V, i, 205–8). Her participation in the Tuesday night assignation is, like the Duke's perjuries, no reflection on her morality, for she has agreed to the plan as the only way of assuring Isabella's, Claudio's and her own happiness.

Finally, of course, the Duke reveals that he knows of Angelo's mere façade of honour, under which there is no truth regarding oaths and promises. We sense the full irony of the overdone compliment to Angelo at the beginning of the act. Escalus is genuinely amazed at the dishonour when Angelo finally crumbles in confession, but Vincentio continues to play a role, this time as the implacable justice. We know that ironically there is truth in part of Angelo's claim of innocence, for he has not been allowed to commit the crimes he intended. On the other hand, like those young men in *Love's Labour's Lost*, he has broken vows and must be made an example of. While he at least has the legalistic constancy to ask that he, too, be sentenced to death, we hear Mariana's plea that 'best men are moulded out of faults' and Isabella's extenuating support. The way is open to reinstitute the contract that had been broken off, reversing the old forswearing. Presumably no lasting harm has been done, and there can be forgiveness now that the dangers of pretended honour have been exposed. The tables have been turned and Angelo's invented discoveries about Mariana are far outweighed by the real discoveries about him.

In the last moments of the play, the Duke institutes two more actions related to vows. The perjuring Lucio is given a suitable punishment, and another wronged woman and miscarriage of justice taken care of. Although we may wonder how much of the corruption in Vienna will be ended with the Duke back in office and dispensing mercy rather than strict justice, we do realise that he is making certain that vows may not be violated, and that perjury will not be an avenue of escape. He is aware, too, that Isabella has not yet taken her conventual vows, and that she may still be invited to join the march to the altar. If she accepts, she will do so with a far greater understanding about oaths, trustworthiness and human weakness than she had a week before.

All the examples of broken faith that we have seen so far, and all the satiric references to unkept vows between men and women, have placed the blame on the men. In fact, when Shakespeare's women do forswear, they are usually politically motivated. Lady Macbeth's ambition for her husband outweighs her allegiance to Duncan; Queen Margaret wants power at all costs. There may be accusations of infidelity, but in most instances they are groundless. Desdemona, Hermione and Mistress Ford are all accused by jealous husbands who later discover their innocence. *Troilus and Cressida* presents a departure from the norm in this as in many other ways. There is no doubt about the reaction we are supposed to have as Cressida's lust overcomes any prior commitments, and she begs Diomedes to return, giving him the token Troilus had lovingly presented to her. The ending of the play, with its human weaknesses not suddenly removed by repentance and reversal, seems more believable than some we have just examined. It seems in keeping, too, with other elements of the story, where Cressida's lack of honour is echoed in the attitudes and actions of people that Homer had taught us were generally admirable despite their occasional wiliness or wilfulness. The play is Shakespeare at his most blatantly satiric, and has already provided scholars with much material, although often they overlook the heavy irony of the oaths.[20]

Even Thersites' 'By Pluto' seems to dovetail with his hellish vision of men's ideals as he reduces all to a squabble over a whore and a placket. The Prologue speaks of the grand Greek vows to retrieve Helen, and then suddenly lapses into doubts about the chance of war. Frequently, where one might expect firm allegiances and set courses of action, characters display divided loyalties or waver – very human failings, but not conducive to raising our opinion of them. The Greeks come off worst, as 'crafty-swearing' rather than straightforward men, but both Greeks and Trojans change course often enough to make many vows seem as empty as the oaths in *King John*. There, at least, English loyalty finally triumphed over French treachery. In *Troilus and Cressida* vows only serve to emphasise the vacillations. Cressida, Achilles, even Hector, are part of a longer list of waverers. And all the while the concept of honour, which had been viewed from different vantage points in *Henry IV, Part One*, is here undercut by comments and actions. For most of Shakespeare's serious or romantic characters, 'honour' is not, as Falstaff said, mere air. But in this play it tends to be omitted, or opposed to reason, or treated as a mere commodity. The concept is not even mentioned until Hector delivers his challenge in the third scene. Before this, we have seen a parade of Trojan heroes and heard a discussion of Greek problems that turns on the much more mechanical concept of degree. The Trojan counterpart of this discussion is the debate about keeping Helen. In legend we hear that she fell in love with Paris and willingly cuckolded her husband. Here we see her relaxed, bantering, with her inconsequential conversation detached from the grimness of the battles fought in her name. Troilus and Paris try to ennoble the situation. They have a psychological point when they argue that she must be kept to give value to the lives already lost and eventually to wipe off the 'soil of her fair rape'.

Hector is rational in arguing for her return to her husband, but suddenly reverses his position. It is as if only half of him had argued for the 'way of truth', the other half embracing the concept of honour that is based on a dishonourable deed. To excuse his shift, we must remember that Hector would be unable to withdraw unilaterally from the war without falling into Achilles' position, just as later his vow to fight will prevent his listening to Andromache or Cassandra when the other Trojans go to battle. It is characteristic of the way Shakespeare intertwines themes in this play that Hector's challenge to personal combat, sent before the discussion in Troy, not only talked of the sort of honour Troilus supports, but also turned on the wisdom, truth and fairness of his own lady in comparison with the 'Grecian dames' (I, iii, 264–83).

Another reversal occurs when the challenge is finally answered. We have heard of Hesione, Helen's older Trojan counterpart, as well as of the plans to fix the lottery so that Ajax will meet Hector. As the single combat is about to begin, we hear that Hector will fight to any length the Greeks want. 'He cares not; he'll obey conditions,' announces Aeneas (IV, v, 72). But 'This Ajax is half made of Hector's blood,/In love whereof half Hector stays at home' (IV, v, 83–4), and the fight has scarcely begun when Hector stops it. The stronger bonds of family have outweighed the current obligations of honour carried in his challenge to combat. It is anti-climactic, but shows a sense of something deeper than a regard for the number of battles won. By contrast, Achilles will later forget his bond to Polyxena and kill her brother in a shameful fashion.

Shakespeare has a purpose in moving the attachment to Polyxena to a spot ahead of the death of Hector. Achilles will use it as an excuse for abstaining from battle, making his sudden change more despicable by mentioning the vow that was apparently formally made to the Trojan Queen.[21]

> My sweet Patroclus, I am thwarted quite
> From my great purpose in to-morrow's battle.
> Here is a letter from Queen Hecuba,
> A token from her daughter, my fair love,
> Both taxing me and gaging me to keep
> An oath that I have sworn. I will not break it.
> Fall Greeks, fail fame, honour or go or stay,
> My major vow lies here; this I'll obey.
> (V, i, 36–43)

In fewer than four hundred lines, this vow, which he had apparently forgotten until reminded by the letter, will again be pushed aside. He will swear vengeance for his minion and set off to find Hector. This second vow is carried out without any semblance of the honour one would expect from so great a fighter, however, and even the blockish Ajax recognises it as a hollow victory.

We may be shocked at the way Shakespeare portrays this conquest, but we must remember that Achilles had earlier thought of honour and reputation as equal to 'place, riches, favour', surface manifestations rather than intrinsic qualities. He cynically believes this sort of honour comes as much by accident as by merit (III, iii, 83), and when he chances upon the unarmed Hector it is an opportunity he can accept without question.

Against this kind of background, it is small wonder that Cressida behaves as she does. Her early soliloquy bespeaking a worried love reveals calculation rather than innocence. She recognises her uncle as a bawd. She knows that her father is a turncoat now living in the Greek camp. She will later experience the distress of being taken from her native city and dispatched like a piece of merchandise as a return for Antenor. Diomedes, sent to convey her to the Greeks, already has a low opinion of Helen, with her 'soilure' and 'dishonour', and sounds like a trader discrediting the merchandise he wishes to buy, while Paris in turn prides himself on not commending what he intends 'to sell'. Cressida adapts quickly to the Greek camp and soon bears little resemblance to the idealised portrait Troilus carries in his mind as he watches her with Diomedes and cries in anguish to Ulysses:

> If beauty have a soul, this is not she;
> If souls guide vows, if vows be sanctimonies,

If sanctimony be the gods' delight . . .
This was not she.

(V, ii, 134–8)

This emphasis on Cressida's soul and the sanctified nature of the vows she has made fits perfectly with the attitudes summarised briefly by Adams in his study of the homiletic drama of the period.[22] There is none of the toying with the possibility of such sinning that slips out in *Romeo and Juliet*, where we are told that Jove himself laughs at lovers' perjuries, none of the amazement expressed by Puck at the discovery that two lovers have remained true (*Romeo and Juliet*, II, ii, 92–3; *A Midsummer Night's Dream*, III, ii, 92–3). Cressida's swearing could never be used as a comforting cordial, either, in the way postulated by Humphrey in *The Knight of the Burning Pestle*.[23]

If we look back at those scenes Troilus is recalling, however, we see a forecast that Cressida's behaviour will form a counterpoint to Troilus' conduct. The most concentrated use of swearing comes in the disillusionment scene, and three earlier scenes serving as a prelude to this gives us the impression that the lovers have made more vows than we ever hear. Occasionally Shakespeare will use this technique, talking around oaths in such a way that we are sure we have heard people swear their feelings as well as their abiding love.

In the third act, Troilus has doubts about a woman who shows 'more craft than love'. Pandarus urges him to 'swear the oaths now to her that you have sworn to me' (III, ii, 39–40), but Troilus shows another restraint. He is wary of insincerity on either side, and scorns the monstrous undertakings of lovers who 'vow to weep seas, live in fire, eat rocks, tame tigers'. He realistically admits 'the desire is boundless and the act a slave to limit' (III, ii, 71–7). Cressida is unconsciously, ironically apposite when she responds, 'They say all lovers swear more performance than they are able, and yet reserve an ability that they never perform, vowing more than the perfection of ten and discharging less than the tenth part of one' (III, ii, 78–81). Hypothetical doubts are entirely different from the visual proof that Troilus is so unprepared for, however, and despite their awareness of possible pitfalls the lovers indulge in a kind of epic exaggeration about their faithfulness. They set themselves up as archetypes, balancing his 'As true as Troilus' with her ironically correct 'As false as Cressid'. Before her forced departure for the Greek camp, she echoes these earlier lines, adding a self-curse: 'O you gods divine,/Make Cressid's name the very crown of falsehood/If ever she leave Troilus!' (IV, ii, 98–100).

Chaucer carried farther the overdone protestations of fidelity, and included not her name, but her very life in the self-damnation:

And this on every god celestial
I swere it yow, and ek on ech goddesse,
On every nymphe and deite infernal,
On satiry and fawny more and lesse,
That halve goddes ben of wildernesse;
And Attropos my thred of life tobreste,
If I be fals! now trowe me if yow leste![24]

Shakespeare seemed to feel he had exaggerated enough with her empty refusals to be expatriated, and waited until the actual parting to continue her immoderate expression of grief. Troilus, seeing chance strangling their 'dear vows', repeats his worries about her, warning her against the temptations she will soon meet. Here, again, there is evidence of the mind divided – half of Troilus afraid of what she may become, and half of him sure of their great love.

When we actually hear oaths in the fourth scene, however, they are tangentially related to this theme. Initially, Troilus shows Diomedes a courtesy he could have learned from Hector, declaring 'by my soul, fair Greek,/If e'er thou stand at mercy of my sword,/Name Cressid, and thy life shall be . . . safe' (IV, iv, 112–14). He foreshadows another of the reversals so common in the play by appending a more threatening promise after Diomedes' courtly address to Cressida. He called his own soul to witness the cordial vow, but here he seems to feel a need for supernatural reinforcement:

I charge thee use her well, even for my charge;
For, by the dreadful Pluto, if thou dost not,
Though the great bulk Achilles be thy guard,
I'll cut thy throat.

(IV, iv, 125–8)

Diomedes' defiant rejoinder that he will do as he pleases and as Cressida deserves should prepare the audience for some lapse from the faith so heavily emphasised in these two scenes (IV, ii and iv). Her oaths will vanish into air, while for Troilus they will remain as tangible as that sleeve he gave her.

At the beginning of the play, Troilus had wavered between refusing to battle for Helen and then championing the 'honour and renown' of keeping her (I, i, 89; II, ii, 199). But he is also one of the few positive elements in the play, hypothesising about honourable constancy to a wife which should override one's shifting will (II, ii, 66–8). Later he carries out his vow to pursue Diomedes, but also fights more generally in the rescue of Aeneas. His oath, 'by the flame of yonder glorious heaven', as he vows Ajax shall not keep Aeneas, has a wide-ranging brightness that is in sharp contrast to the unpleasant imagery and actions of the next quick scenes with Thersites, Achilles and Hector.

Between the parting and these battle scenes there is that contrapuntal episode which is part of the artificiality of Elizabethan drama and lets us see actions and reactions in simultaneous conversations. After the broken-off duel and the courtesies of the truce, Ulysses takes Troilus to watch his love. Each speech of Cressida engenders anguished comment from Troilus, with a heavy concentration of oaths helping attest his frame of mind while her wheedling and vowing diminish her further. There has been very little other exclamatory swearing in the play, so again the oaths function most effectively: The others in this scene – Thersites, Ulysses and Diomedes – seldom swear. But their comments elicit more oaths from Troilus as Shakespeare again uses his technique of focus. Despite his promise, 'By Jove, I will not speak a word' (V, ii, 50), he must repeatedly be quieted. 'By hell, and all hell's torments' strikes us as the most appropriate of the series of ejaculations that punctuate every few lines. The unusual outpouring of a stream of exclamatory oaths from a man at the height of disgust and disillusionment is a technique that Shakespeare used even more effectively in *Hamlet*.

The other outstanding voice in this counterpoint is Cressida's, as she responds to Diomedes. His comment that she is forsworn is appropriate to her relationship with Troilus, but we learn that it refers to some recent promise that she is trying to break: 'I prithee, do not hold me to mine oath;/Bid me do anything but that, sweet Greek' (V, ii, 25–6). He has only to turn away, as she had earlier done with Troilus, to make her coax with an 'In faith' that he knows is meaningless. Words are air, and tokens are at least tangible. Cressida may actually be torn at this point, but she soon gives him the sleeve. There is much less of the rationalisation about oath-breaking than we see in some of the history plays. Instead, at this point we have a romanticised little speech about Troilus sighing in his bed, and soon he will receive a letter that he might have clasped to his breast had he not witnessed this scene. Ulysses had warned that 'She will sing any man at first sight', and Cressida seems to accept her weakness quite easily, making it a general rather than a personal flaw.

> Ah, poor our sex! this fault in us I find,
> The error of our eye directs our mind.
> What error leads must err. O, then conclude
> Minds swayed by eyes are full of turpitude.
>
> (V, ii, 105–8)

Shakespeare has been most satiric in having her declare

inappropriately 'By all Diana's waiting-women yond,/And by herself, that she will not reveal the donor of the sleeve she is unchastely giving away. By the end of the scene, Troilus sounds almost like Thersites as he declares:

> The bonds of heaven are slipped, dissolved, and loosed;
> And with another knot, five-finger-tied,
> The fractions of her faith, orts of her love,
> The fragments, scraps, the bits, and greasy relics
> Of her o'er-eaten faith, are bound to Diomed.
> (V, ii, 152–6)

Despite having a share of the turncoats who people this play, the Trojans generally use oaths with a sense of their import. The Greeks, on the other hand, are much less likely to emphasise them. Thersites may toss out the anachronous "Sfoot' when his railings produce only beatings; Achilles does vow vengeance for Patroclus. But we do not hear the oaths of honour that we might expect from this concentration of military men. There are half a dozen that we should examine, though, for they are not employed merely to make the soldiers sound fierce. A tone of irony suffuses some of these, while in others there is a consciousness of the loves that cause so much trouble.

Ajax declares 'by my head' that Achilles is proud, little realising that his own head is becoming swelled (II, iii, 83–4). On the night of the Cressida exchange, Aeneas and Diomedes spar verbally, with Diomedes averring that when this truce is over, 'By Jove, I'll play the hunter for thy life' (IV, i, 17). Aeneas, welcoming him to Troy, expresses the same attitude in more original and revealing terms.

> Now, by Anchises' life,
> Welcome indeed! By Venus' hand I swear,
> No man alive can love in such a sort
> That thing he means to kill more excellently.
> (IV, i, 21–4)

Aeneas, expressing his admiring hatred, is linking the aspects Hector will later place in their more traditional opposition when he acknowledges Menelaus' welcome with 'By Mars his gauntlet, thanks!/Mock not that I affect th' untraded oath; Your quondam wife swears still by Venus' glove' (IV, v, 176–8). Even the references to hands and gloves show these aspects, for the hand was not only part of a soldier's oath, but was also extended in marriage, while the glove could be a token of love or of challenge. The contrast of the gauntlet and glove further underlines the difference between the warriors and the object of their battles.

There are a few examples when something mortal is sworn by –

Nestor calls attention to his white beard, Ajax refers to his head, Aeneas thinks of his father. In a play with so many cynical over-tones, the mention of Anchises is completely reverent. It is appro-priate, too, for it underlines the reverence warriors may have for a worthy opponent in time of truce, although they fully intend to fight to the death when the battle resumes.

More frequently, gods are called upon. Hector swears 'by Jove multipotent' that Ajax' left cheek bounds in his father's blood. His final praise for this man known more for his strength than his wit is an appropriate affirmation: 'By him that thunders, thou hast lusty arms' (IV, v, 135). He is much less flattering as he defies Achilles, promising, 'I'll not kill thee there, nor there, nor there;/But, by the forge that stithied Mars his helm,/I'll kill thee everywhere' (IV, v, 253–5). It is a grimly ironic foreshadowing of the way the swarming Myrmidons will stab him. One wonders, too, if Shakespeare was thinking of Hector without his armour as he wrote the phrase about Mars' helmet.

This series of references to the gods, coupled with the earlier note of Diana and Pluto, brings to mind an important detail about Shakespeare's use of oaths to suggest a pagan cosmology. He has an array of gods, including Mars, Venus, one that forges armour, and another who thunders. But they are almost all Roman and, although a modern footnote might equate the thunderer with Zeus, one suspects Shakespeare would have said Jove. Nowhere, in any of his plays, does a Greek call on Zeus or, for that matter, on Artemis, although her brother Apollo, also important to the Romans, is noted. Aphrodite and Ares are ignored in favour of Venus and Mars, and only Pluto merits a few inclusions. Unless we are terribly sensitive to anachronisms, we feel a sense of classical divinity. Presumably the Elizabethans were also satisfied. Certainly Chaucer and other writers set Shakespeare no precedent for mythological accuracy.[25] The important points are two: these Greeks and Trojans are shown with a different frame of reference from later Christians; and they are shown swearing hollowly or completely sincerely by their pagan deities.

In all the plays we have been examining, and especially those treated in this chapter, contrasting attitudes are strongly felt. There may be shock as a character learns of the emptiness of a vow, as do Talbot and Troilus. There may be direct accusations of the sort one finds early in *Richard II* and again when Surrey challenges Fitzwater (IV, i, 64). We often see the irony of a character's trust because we have learned earlier of a breach of faith. Othello's references to Iago come immediately to mind. And at times we share the recognition that some people or types use oaths so carelessly or profusely that all meaning has been lost. Mercutio thinks automatically of the stock instance of the soldier who awakens, 'swears a prayer or two/And sleeps again' (*Romeo and Juliet*, I, iv, 87–8).

At the risk of oversimplifying, perhaps even of being simplistic, one looks at the multitude of examples and generalises. If the oaths of honour triumph over those of air, the results will usually be happy. If villains who swear, or even fashionable swearers to whom too much attention is paid, are identified in time, there can be appropriate punishment or laughter. But the hollowness of an Iago's vows is suspected too late, and his air triumphs over Othello's honour. In *Richard III* people like Clarence recognise their own unfaithfulness, and even damn themselves with self-curses as Buckingham does during Edward's peace-making. Curses, perjury and death are all closely related.

Obviously there will be major exceptions. King Lear's honourable but misguided vows, and others like them, can bring tragedy. And there is much more in a play than swearing to account for the direction a story takes. Higher standards, however, prevail in *The Two Gentlemen of Verona* and lead to Proteus' reform, while the baser values dominate in *Troilus and Cressida*, bringing Troilus his anguish and Hector his unfair death. The more elaborate a vow, the more suspect it may be. Northumberland told Richard of Henry Bolingbroke's overdone disclaimer of any ambition beyond his own inheritance, but almost immediately opportunity and opportunism lead him to the crown, and the rebels will call this a forsworn oath.[26]

There are standards for good and bad vows, too, that can be cited as forswearing is contemplated. Cassandra touches on the spirit of Hector's words when she tries to hold him back from battle and he insists the gods have heard him swear:

> The gods are deaf to hot and peevish vows.
> They are polluted off'rings. . . .
> It is the purpose that makes strong the vow;
> But vows to every purpose must not hold.
> (V, iii, 16–24)

Her description seems more suited to Hotspur than to the Hector we see, but she is emphasising that vows alone do not make honour. One's attitude is all-important. But this sort of argument is the exception, and the predominant opinion was that one did not break a vow. Prince Hal may mislead the rogues, but he never forswears. As Fluellen would say in *Henry V,* 'If he be perjured . . . his reputation is as arrant a villain and a jack sauce as ever his plack shoe trod upon God's ground . . . in my conscience' (IV,

vii, 133–5). Henry, paying court to Kate, will declare, 'before God
. . . I have no cunning in protestation, only downright oaths which
I never use till urged, nor never break for urging' (V, ii, 141–4).
If we remember that Henry V was to the Elizabethans a model king,
we have even more assurance that these two excerpts point the place
of the oath of honour. A soldier must keep his word – this Henry
recognises, although he will not speak of it so explosively as
Fluellen. And a person, even a lover, should not overdo the
swearing. Oaths must be used carefully, not unconsciously, and,
once uttered, must not be allowed to evaporate into thin air.[27]

Chapter 5

Oaths and Tragic Tension

Shakespeare began early to show the effects of tension on a person's oaths: In *Richard III*, where Richard dominates the swearing, we see him calculating the effect of his words in the first four acts. Mock concern mingles with moralising as he exclaims over King Edward's health, 'Now, by Saint John, that news is bad indeed' (I, i, 138). Posing as good though misshapen, he comments on Clarence's perjury and, with the occasional exception of 'By Saint Paul', uses only 'marry'. His public virtue increases as his private plotting worsens, and he finally appears to the populace with Bible in hand and clergy at elbow to hear Buckingham's 'persuasion' speech. We are not told how much of the dialogue is planned, but Buckingham ends in apparent exasperation, 'Zounds, I'll entreat no more!' and Richard immediately reproves him: 'O, do not swear, my lord of Buckingham.'[1] It demonstrates Richard's consummate acting ability – a seemingly involuntary reaction to an oath that had previously been used only by Clarence's murderers. His control here contrasts sharply with his fears at the end of the play, when forces living and ghostly gather against him. Like those murderers, he has a moment of conscience, asks, 'Zounds, who is there?' and admits to Ratcliff, 'By the apostle Paul', the dream has terrified him.[2] Richard's range of oaths is not broad, but until this moment his use of them marks determination and control. Now his exclamation, using a word that he earlier criticised, marks a succumbing to tension and irrationality which of course he will soon overcome. In *The True Tragedy of Richard Duke of York*, 'zounds' is used by page and servant, and this detracts from its impact in a way Shakespeare will not allow.

The use of oaths in moments of tension will continue through *Coriolanus* and even occasionally into the romances. But no plays demonstrate the effective use of swearing as well as *Hamlet* and *Othello*, where oaths are among the most telling signs of changes in attitude in very fully developed characters. Both plays are set in Christian worlds. Othello, despite memories of pagan magic, seems to have adopted the religion of his Venetian employers that is shared, of course, by Cassio and Desdemona. Hamlet's Ghost talks of purgatory, and the Danish priests administer truncated Christian burial rites over Ophelia. For many in the audience, no matter how familiar they might be with the theoretical fact that a Roman should not swear lightly by his ranking deity, Jupiter, the doctrinal details of these two plays would still make a somewhat swifter impact. Shakespeare would need to spend no time explaining the concern about killing a soul, although both plays may today need a footnote on that point. The details about the anguish of an unprepared soul in purgatory may strike a chord in the audience's minds as other characters die unshriven, but the Ghost's description is designed to shock Hamlet as much as to enlighten the public. The point is that, without using anachronisms, Shakespeare can, in these two plays, get instant reactions on spiritual matters, including profanity.

The techniques in the two works are not identical. In *Hamlet*, with a wider emphasis on swearing, the Prince uses his words without tutelage. In *Othello* one finds that people are led by Iago to expletives and vows. In both there is a cohesiveness that is lacking, for example, in *Antony and Cleopatra*. Shakespeare is to some extent again demonstrating principles developed earlier. Hotspur, as we noted, ceased his casual swearing as he carried more and more of the weight of the doomed rebellion and emphasised a formal oath. Romeo, a decade before Hamlet, swore little and took his vows seriously in the early part of the play. But in the last act, with tension at a peak, he became 'savage-wild' and intent on suicide, and suddenly swore 'By heaven' to tear Balthazar apart, or announced to Paris that 'By heaven' he loved him 'better than myself' (V, iii, 35–7, 64). By the fifth act, the coarse ribaldry of Mercutio is almost forgotten, and even the Nurse's frequent but milder exclamations are in the past. In mid-play, Juliet had reached the same acme of tension, angrily refusing Paris, 'Now by Saint Peter's Church, and Peter too,/He shall not make me there a joyful bride!', adding that, if she does marry, she swears 'It shall be Romeo' (III, v, 117–23). The argument leads Old Capulet to a series of outbursts a bit suggestive of Lear's displeasure with Cordelia. 'God's bread! It makes me mad,' he exclaims as his care to plan for his daughter seems senselessly rebuffed. His twenty-line speech ends in a climactic threat that unless she yields, 'by my soul, I'll ne'er acknowledge thee,/Nor what is mine shall never do thee good./Trust to't . . . I'll not be forsworn' (III, v, 195–7). Yet, in this early tragedy, we do not feel the continuing sense of focus, for swearing honours are divided, and the Nurse and Mercutio capture their scenes with their vitality and verbosity. Mercutio, in fact, begins as a fashionable and mild swearer, and himself reaches a peak of tension with 'Zounds' in his anger at Tybalt and his realisation that he is a sacrifice to the feuding houses (III, i).

The diversity of swearing patterns in the play seems designed to serve another artistic function, with even the mild expletives helping to create a sense of hot tempers in servants and masters alike. Restraint and rationality might counter the stars' influence. But the testiness of the older generations and the quarrelsomeness of the young Veronese are established before the lovers meet with their controlled sonnet of love. The exclamatory oaths even extend to Friar Lawrence, who will later declare to John, 'By my brother-hood,/The letter was not nice, but full of charge' (V, ii, 17–18). Earlier, he had prefaced a reaction to Romeo's change of loves with 'Holy Saint Francis' (II, iii, 65).

In contrast to the scattering of oaths among so many in *Romeo and Juliet*, *Hamlet* exhibits focus. The Prince does almost half of the swearing, and the oaths of others are frequently at his command or tied to patterns he is establishing. The Prince's own use ranges from the formal to the wildly explosive. The situation is far different in *Othello*, where Iago is the most frequent swearer. There, we can measure the tensions to which he subjects others by watching them be moved, one by one, to stronger oaths. There are other keys to the states of mind of these men, of course, but swearing is a very reliable way to measure the success of this devilish puppeteer. When we compare the Quarto and Folio texts, the latter's obvious censorings make us even more thankful that the *Othello* Quarto of 1622 was fortuitously printed without the expurgations that should have taken place. In both plays, comparison of passages where nothing else was changed makes more strikingly obvious the added richness oaths can give to character delineation; even the 1603 *Hamlet* Quarto retains most of them in some form, despite other mutilations.

As *Hamlet* opens, Horatio, the rational scholar, scoffs slightly at the frightened guards. But he is also a religious man, and his learning extends to the folk belief surrounding a ghost, and the distinct possibility that this may be some evil spirit tempting Hamlet to death or madness (I, iv, 69–74).[3] Confronted by the apparition, he carefully couches his command: 'By heaven I charge thee, speak.' When the Ghost stalks away, he admits to Bernardo that his rational doubts have vanished, for the Ghost has satisfied his empiricism: 'Before my God, I might not this believe/Without the sensible and true avouch/Of mine own eyes' (I, i, 56–8). The second silent appearance of the mysterious figure and the approach of dawn breed an urge to get further support, and Horatio suggests they go to 'young Hamlet, for upon my life/This spirit, dumb to us, will speak to him' (I, i, 170–1). He has turned from references to heaven to assertions by his own existence and, when Hamlet later remarks on the strangeness of the tale, he will earnestly affirm, 'As I do live, my honoured lord, 'tis true' (I, ii, 221). The phrases fit with his insistence that he see the Ghost before believing in it – his own life may be the thing he feels most certain of at this moment.

Later, enjoying the prospect of the play, Hamlet will indulge in some almost casual swearing, with a jocular 'By'r Lady' to the young boy who plays women's parts as he avers that 'your ladyship' has grown, and an exclamation of 'God's bodkin' to Polonius as he tells the old man to treat the players better than their deserts (II, ii, 415, 516–17). In the first act, however, he responds to the news and to the experience of the Ghost first with some low-key but serious oaths, and then with the very formal binding of the witnesses.

Like Horatio, Hamlet is well acquainted with the threat this figure presents if it should be a 'goblin damned' bringing 'blasts from hell' rather than wholesome 'airs from heaven'. The Prince exclaims a precautionary 'Angels and ministers of grace defend us!' when he first sees the Ghost. Like Horatio, he seems to feel the need to mention heaven, first as he asserts his determination to follow the Ghost, and then in affirming the injunction to remember:

> Yea, from the table of my memory
> I'll wipe away all trivial fond records . . .
> And thy commandment all alone shall live
> Within the book and volume of my brain,
> Unmixed with baser matter. Yes, by heaven!
>   (I, v, 98–104)

Here the Folio has its first censorship cut, with the oath replaced by 'yes, yes'. We must imagine when the swearing that Hamlet notes in line 112 might have taken place. (It is not the only time that inconsistency results when the reference is kept but the example cut in the Folio!)

Despite his shock, the Prince realises that news of the Ghost must not become common gossip trotted to Claudius by the bustling Polonius. There is a grotesquery in Hamlet's comments as the Ghost echoes 'Swear', and a great deal of movement around the stage that some producers try to make into laughable bustle. But there is no doubt that under his wildness Hamlet is desperately serious. In lieu of Bible or proper cross, he extends his cruciform sword hilts and makes an elaborate proposal that hints at his course of action and carries a threat of spiritual disaster should the witnesses forget.

> Here as before, never, so help you mercy,
> How strange or odd some'er I bear myself . . .

> That you, at such times seeing me, never shall,
> With arms encumb'red thus, or this head-shake,
> Or by pronouncing of some doubtful phrase . . .
> Or such ambiguous giving out, to note
> That you know aught of me – this do swear,
> So grace and mercy at your most need help you.
>   (I, v, 169–80)

The men who at first demurred and preferred their simple vows yield to the importunacy of Prince and Ghost, and never do we hear that they have forsworn themselves. This is essential, for it means that Hamlet can parry the thrusts of Rosencrantz, Guildenstern and Polonius without fear that the watchers will eagerly volunteer the solution to Hamlet's 'mystery'. The scene, with its grotesqueness, also has the immediate effect, for the audience if not for the Prince, of relieving the tension after the interview with the Ghost and the news of the murder. It has produced more critical commentary than most oaths, from the rather obvious remark that the sword was 'very soldier-like' to a series of observations on the custom with both its pagan and Christian significances.[4]

Notes gathered in the New Variorum Edition also try at length to elucidate the one oath in the play that seems out of keeping – Hamlet's reply, 'Yes, by Saint Patrick, but there is, Horatio,/And much offence, too,' uttered amidst this concern with secrecy. Tschischwitz, with characteristic Germanic historical accuracy, points out that Shakespeare should 'have made a Dane swear by Saint Ansgarius', surely not a name familiar to Englishmen. But he adds that Saint Patrick kept a purgatory, which seems particularly appropriate to the revelation of an unpunished crime by a soul being purged.[5] Warburton's observation that Ireland was at this time the source of much northern culture, coupled with his conclusion that it was probably a random usage, and Caldecott's opinion that Shakespeare 'would little hesitate to make any stranger invoke the name of a saint popular in his own [country]' show the range of speculation.[6] But Shakespeare was not prone to casualness with saints' names after he had created that patently Catholic clown in *Titus Andronicus* (IV, iv, 42, 47). Hamlet's is the unique instance in all the plays when the Irish saint is invoked,[7] and might be said to demonstrate the breadth of the Prince's learning. For Shakespeare's audience, however, I suspect the immediate reaction would be the recognition of a Catholic saint who was also noted in *The Honest Whore* as keeping a purgatory.[8]

Polonius is very much a part of the convivial, ceremonial world of Claudius' court that contrasts so sharply to the chill midnight horror of the Ghost scenes. The old man bustles about, occasionally trying to lend weight to his statements by interjecting a rather exclamatory oath with very little show of tension, although on principle he seems opposed to swearing. At least, as he sends Reynaldo to spy on Laertes, he includes it among the 'wanton, wild, and usual slips'. His commonplace list of 'drinking, fencing, swearing, quarrelling,/Drabbing' need not show, as he carefully points out, things that will really dishonour a person, but 'the taints of liberty' (II, i, 22–32). One wonders if he still retains a few oaths as last remnants of the fashionable peccadilloes of youth. Only a few lines later, he loses his train of thought, exclaiming, 'By the mass, I was about to say something' (II, i, 50–1), a phrase strong enough to be omitted from the Folio and, in another instance, to be slipped past the censor as 'by the Misse' (III, ii, 363).

In II, i, Polonius waxes a bit stronger, declaring 'By heaven' how common it is for older people to read too much into an action. It is a unique admission of error, and he seems to feel the need to excuse his reaction as characteristic of many when he reappraises the seriousness of Hamlet's love. (Later, needing more assurance, he will ask Claudius to affirm that, when he has said a thing is so, it has indeed proved so.) Although his oath is mechanical, lacking the tension that accompanied the same phrase on the ramparts, something is lost besides rhythm by the Folio substitution of 'it seems', for Polonius needs the emphasis of the oath to impress on others the positiveness of his statements. The same emphasis becomes ironic in the next scene when he insists the players are 'Upon my honour . . . The best actors in the world' (II, ii, 385–7). We have seen this man becoming less and less honourable as he spies and pries, and his appraisal of the players might therefore be questionable! Of course, we might even doubt his critical faculties as he continues his habit of speech in praising Hamlet's attempt at the 'Pyrrhus' lines. His 'Fore God, my lord, well spoken' is a forerunner of the drunken Cassio's repeated reactions to Iago's drinking-songs.

By contrast, Hamlet is trying to cover his increasing tension and excitement over the players with jocular remarks and with gibes at Polonius. His 'by my fay' (II, ii, 262) may echo Guildenstern's 'faith' in the interchange where his distrust of his erstwhile friends is somewhat despairingly shown. He is soon moved from the minced oaths that he occasionally uses in moments of relatively good humour to a "Sblood, there is something in this more than natural' as he contemplates the fickleness of popular favour, both for the players and for a king such as Claudius, whose picture now commands a hundred ducats (II, ii, 358–9). His mind is also responding to the players and to the chance to make a corrective comment to the advice-filled old courtier, as we noted earlier.

No sooner have the players been led off to their lodgings, however, than he lapses into a self-excoriating soliloquy, with "swounds,

I should take it', marking the extent of his anger at the indignities he suffers as he imagines himself passive and 'pigeon-livered'. (The Folio cuts both ''Sblood' and ''swounds', as we might expect, and replaces the latter with 'Why', which at least fits the metre.) Hamlet is the only person in the play who swears this strongly. Laertes, briefly seen under comparable pressure to revenge, and equally angry, is much more verbally restrained. Of course, we see relatively little of his anguish. But Shakespeare allows him a 'By heaven' only when he vows that Ophelia's madness 'shall be paid by weight' (IV, v, 156), and not a single oath as Claudius works out the details of revenge two scenes later. At the graveside, he is kept relatively mute, so that Hamlet's tension can explode verbally as well as physically with more shocking emphasis.

It becomes even more apparent that Shakespeare wished to reserve this method of stressing feelings for Hamlet alone when we examine the words of soldiers, gravediggers and the other young men – Rosencrantz, Guildenstern or the fashionable Osric – none of whom exclaims more than the occasional 'marry' or 'faith'. There would have been conventional grounds for having them swear, and the soldiers on the ramparts have emotional cause, but they utter 'by heaven' only at Hamlet's urging to secrecy. The Folio text is weakened by the absence of even unexceptionable classical substitutes which a university student might have been expected to exclaim. In his self-criticism after the departure of Rosencrantz and Guildenstern, when he compares himself, 'dull and muddy-mettled', with the actor mourning Hecuba, ''swounds' helps attest the fact that, after a series of short exclamations, he has reached a similar level of emotion (II, ii).

It is with a different, anticipatory excitement that he awaits the acting of his 'mousetrap' play, envying the balance of blood and judgment in Horatio. With forced jocularity and a strain of cynicism he cleverly confuses the straightforward Ophelia. Has it been two months and more since his father died? Then memory may last half a year. After that, 'by'r Lady', a man must build churches if he would be remembered. To Hamlet, who had recently been thinking about reputation and man's fickle mind, this is a patent truth. To Ophelia, however, it barely makes sense. Again, but with a different, more serious inspiration, Hamlet swears by the Virgin. He is talking of churches to a woman who is probably nowhere nearly so bad as he has suggested. As in the scene with the boy actor, one can almost see his mind making an unconscious connection, picking the oath organically related to the subject and object of his talk. .

Immediately, we have a different kind of vow as the Player Queen rejects the idea of a temptation toward a second marriage with the sort of protestation and self-curse Hamlet feels Gertrude had forgotten. While Gertrude fidgets, the Player Queen declares, 'Both here and hence pursue me lasting strife,/If, once a widow, ever I be wife!' (III, ii, 214–15) and the Player King responds, ''Tis deeply sworn.' Led by Hamlet's thinking, we feel we are seeing a retelling of a real-life exchange in the Danish court, although Gertrude may not even recognise herself or feel the prick of conscience. Certainly she does not respond to Hamlet's ironic 'O, but she'll keep her word' a few moments before the Player King is expected to win the Queen's love.

Swearing has often been characterised as a verbal crutch for those unable to express their feelings in non-profane terms or needing to flesh out their short sentences.[9] This may be true of some Shakespearian characters, such as the two gravediggers who to some extent rely on 'faith', 'marry' or a 'mass', or Juliet's Nurse, who uses more oaths than any other character in that play, and rattles out many of them in the third scene, where she is under no particular tension. But verbal limitation certainly does not characterise Hamlet, and his oaths often are heavy with overtones. I have already noted the way he mentions the Virgin. After the play, Rosencrantz and Guildenstern bring the command to visit his mother, and he rather tartly asks, 'Have you any further trade with us?' Rosencrantz tries to push deeper into the mystery of Hamlet's behaviour, plaintively asserting, 'My lord, you once did love me.' Hamlet's answering 'And do still, by these pickers and stealers' leads into the brief exchange on Hamlet's lack of 'advancement' (III, ii, 321–30). 'By these hands' would be the normal phrase, and one Hamlet will use seriously when he later denies he is mocking Laertes by praising his sword-play. With the spying Rosencrantz and Guildenstern, however, there is less of respect. Strachey comments:

> the last gleam of Hamlet's old regard for his schoolfellows shines out here for a moment; but it fades again instantly, and he ends with a jesting allusion to the catechism, – intending to avow, rather than conceal, his feeling that he is using his tongue in a way forbidden, as much as picking and stealing are to his hands.[10]

Whether it is quite as Strachey interprets it or whether Hamlet is making the reference because he feels there is guilt on the part of the two is a moot point. With an audience trained in the catechism, there would be an instantaneous recognition of the words from the 'duty to neighbours' section, which reads in full: 'To keep my hands from picking and stealing, and my tongue from evil speaking, lying, and slaundering'.[11] Hamlet is seeing all parts of the body tinged with dishonesty; thieving hands are a fitting object when he is vowing a love he does not feel. After all, the messages of both the Ghost and the 'mousetrap' have been about stealing, with hands pouring poison, grasping crowns, and joining in illicit love.

In a minute, Hamlet will cry out that these men want to play him as they cannot play a recorder, using figurative hands to 'pluck out the heart of my mystery' (III, ii, 351–2). The Folio strips much of the feeling from "Sblood, do you think I am easier to be played on than a pipe?' (III, ii, 355–6) by substituting the feeble 'Why'. From doggerel verse with its minced French 'perdy', in his joy that the King dislikes the play, through an oblique reference to the rules of conduct, and on to intense anger, Hamlet's oaths have paralleled the movement of his emotions and helped to delineate it.

He goes to his mother's closet determined to rebuke but not to harm her, and his puzzling opening words lead her to ask, 'Have you forgot me?' 'By the rood' is used only five times in the plays, but here it seems a suitable choice as the Prince assures her he has not, and unflatteringly describes who she is. He has used the cruciform sword hilts earlier, has recently referred to Christian teachings, and has just abstained from killing Claudius, who may have been kneeling before a cross in his attempt to pray. The symbol would be in his mind, ready to become an oath.

Hamlet, who has perhaps seemed a bit prudish in his comments on Danish drinking, also joins the seventeenth-century tract-writers in linking swearing and other sins. He thinks of his mother's marriage vows, made 'false as dicers' oaths'. Wanting to make sure Claudius' soul is damned, he emphasises the need to catch him in some sinful activitiy:

> drunk asleep, or in his rage,
> Or in th'incestuous pleasure of his bed,
> At game a-swearing, or about some act
> That has no relish of salvation in't.
>   (III, iii, 89–92)

In the play, and in later critical writing, men have raised doubts about Hamlet's sincerity with Ophelia. Laertes and Polonius have both warned her; Hamlet's own treatment of her seems unnecessarily cruel at times. Yet the regard for broken vows, the insistence on a formal oath from the guards, and even the odd affirmation of his lie to Rosencrantz and Guildenstern could well indicate that he was quite serious in his reported vows of love. We are not sure when those vows took place – perhaps before his father's death and Gertrude's remarriage, although Ophelia's report makes them sound more recent. To Polonius' suggestion that it is only fashion, she replies he 'hath given countenance to his speech, my lord,/With almost all the holy vows of heaven' (I, iii, 113–14). She realises that Hamlet was once 'the glass of fashion', and her father insists his words are mere fashionable surface, or 'springes to catch woodcocks'. The vows should be regarded as 'brokers,/... Breathing like sanctified and pious bawds,/The better to beguile' (I, iii, 127–31). But Polonius is not a spokesman whom we trust, and Hamlet's thoughtfulness as well as his annoyance at the fashionable Osric indicate a possible sincerity at the earlier moment. Certainly Ophelia's part in the spying, and of course the examples of his mother and of Gonzago's queen, could turn him against his vows, no matter how sincerely they were made.

Were he not sincere, his behaviour in the last act would be even more tasteless and shocking. There he may be overstating his desire to have his devotion tested against Laertes', but his wildness cannot be discounted as acting, or as mere madness, despite reactions to it. The scene had begun quietly, with Hamlet fitting his exclamations to the 'marry' and 'faith' used by the gravediggers, and making his observations about the universality of death and its levelling effects. The funeral procession interrupts him, though, and the tension increases as he realises whose corpse is being followed. Laertes' leap into the grave for a macabre final kiss leads Hamlet to declare himself, answering Laertes' 'The devil take thy soul' with an avowal that he is not 'splenetive and rash' but still has 'something dangerous' in him. Passion again rules, and his expletive signals his impatience as he makes his hopelessly wild challenges.

> I loved Ophelia. Forty thousand brothers
> Could not with all their quantity of love
> Make up my sum. What wilt thou do for her?...
> 'Swounds, show me what thou't do.
> (V, i, 256–61)

As the play ends, he has accepted the 'divinity that shapes our ends'. He is sorry for nothing except that he forgot himself with Laertes, whose cause he recognises as so like his own. Despite the illness around his heart, he is again in control of himself outwardly, even echoing Osric's 'in faith'. But the oaths in the play come full circle as the poison begins to take effect and Hamlet summons his last strength to oppose the will of Horatio. Once he had vowed 'by heaven' to make a ghost of any who tried to hinder him. Now he seizes the poisoned cup with the same assertion of his determination. In that early scene there was a need to discover the truth from the Ghost. Here, he is desperate that all the truth be told. The phrase may seem mild in comparison with ''swounds' or ''sblood', but we remember that it has generally been used under stress in this play. Even Polonius is very much in earnest as he admits error, and Laertes is in great anguish as he first sees his sister mad, vows revenge, and compares the mortality of her wits and his father's life (II, i, 114–15; IV, v, 156–60).

Although Hamlet himself sees the parallel between his and Laertes' situations, and although the play presents us with many young men whom we can compare in some ways with Hamlet, there is in no other instance the patterning of oaths that one finds with the Prince. In him we see the variety ranging from the formal vow through the gently gibing phrase that underlines a bit of conversation to the exclamatory oath accompanying a strong emotion. Almost instinctively, and certainly without Iago's calculation, he may utter a phrase on the same level as the characters he is conversing with, providing almost an echo in the conversation. But the oaths are his, coming from his own mind and depending on the stimulus of the moment. He provides the incentive for Horatio and Marcellus to pledge secrecy; he will wait to catch Claudius sinning, perhaps swearing. We never feel he is manipulated as are Iago's victims when they are moved to swear and behave in unexpected ways.

For a play of this length, the list of oaths is relatively short, even when broadened to include 'marry' and a couple like Ophelia's 'By Cock', couched within a song. But there is the focus on Hamlet's words that I have already noted, the periodic emphasis on how bad swearing can be, and the criticism of the broken oath of fidelity. Othello and Cassio share this dismay at oaths tossed off casually or in temper, while they too attach great significance to the seriously made vow. Cassio is ashamed of his drunken behaviour; Othello affirms his intent of revenge on Desdemona in a formalised way. Time and again in the earlier chapters we have seen how familiar these attitudes would have been to Shakespeare's audience, not only because of plays but because of the strictures of laws, sermons and pamphlets that emphasised the difference between careful and casual swearing. Iago, the puppeteer, knows well these points of view, which are held by his honourable victims. He manipulates men, and the oaths become part of a barometer registering changes in emotional pressure. In fact, he makes people what he says they are, for his opening conversation with Roderigo describes Othello's speech as 'Horribly stuffed with epithets of war' (I, i, 14), although Othello scarcely resembles the kind of pseudo-soldier typically satirised by Marston and others as 'naught but huge blaspheming othes'.[12] Iago also makes people use the sort of language he alone has employed in the opening scenes when, in his calculating way, he is the most profane of characters.

Marvin Rosenberg, while looking at the theatre history of the play, has noticed something of this nature, for he points out that Iago thinks of the sex act, and seeks 'to fasten similar thoughts on his companions'.[13] In his close textual study, Robert Heilman comments several times on this manipulation, as when Iago reduces Othello to prose rhythms, transforms quiet into unnecessary fury, reduces people to the bestial, or soothes his own jealousies by arousing jealousy in others.[14] Heilman does not, however, concentrate on the way that oaths contribute to the patterns of excitement that keep recurring with variations until one has the climactic vow from Othello, a ceremony lacking in the sources.

The Quarto text fortuitously seems to have been printed in a haste that ignored the blasphemy laws. Alice Walker, in her study of the Folio, points out that there was a break in the printing, and in the interim Buck resigned. She adds, 'it looks as if whoever prepared the copy for Jaggard anticipated a more rigorous attitude towards profanity from Buck's successor'. The break is roughly between the comedies and the histories; as a result, *Othello* is 'rigorously purged of its oaths and most of the milder asseverations'.[15] On the other hand, she is sure that some of the phrases in the Quarto are interpolations that had crept into an acting edition: 'Othello's "Zouns" (Q) to Desdemona at III, iv, 99, replaced by "Away" in the folio, is as objectionable as his oath at III, iii, 158 [a milder "By heaven"]. So too is Emilia's "O Lord" ("Alas" F) at V, ii, 120 and, worst of all, Othello's undignified "ud's death" at V, ii, 73.'[16] What seems to be missing here, even if we ignore some inaccuracy, is any consideration of whether the words that seem so objectionable coming from Othello are in fact any worse than some of the other things he has been moved to do, things that would not be believed if reported back in Venice. The phrases would seem characteristic coming from Iago, although "ud's" is a kind of mincing that Shakespeare seldom uses; but that word actually is spoken by Emilia. (I find an earlier 'Zouns' more questionable.) Iago has succeeded so well in reducing Othello to his level that the oaths seem horribly appropriate at the moment.

We are only four lines into the play when the Quarto text begins to show an aspect of Iago that is lost to the Folio reader. Roderigo's opening 'Tush' had been cut in an overzealous moment; he is obviously exclaiming about something Iago has been telling him as they walk onstage. Iago counters with a far stronger phrase, also eliminated by the Folio: "Sblood, but you'll not hear me!' At this moment we know nothing about the man and perceive only that there seems to be a different level of feeling or at least a different way of expressing it. Iago's style will remain exclamatory throughout the scene, with 'by the faith of man', a scornful 'forsooth', and other affirmative phrases thrown into his long speech in a successful effort to excite people.[17] Later we may begin to suspect that he affirms to assure belief, much as Falstaff did, although he skirts the truth with more consciously evil intent.

By line 34, Roderigo has caught some of Iago's fervour against Othello, and announces, 'By heaven, I rather would have been his hangman.' It is the first example of Iago's ability to turn things to his own use. Roderigo's earlier anger has shifted from Iago, where it presumably was when the play opened, and Iago now has money and a willing tool in his plan to destroy the Moor. By now we may be beginning to question Iago's style of speech as well as his actions. Is he more profane than the civilian Roderigo merely because he is a soldier, or does he have an innate impatience independent of his military profession? At one extreme, is he righteously angry at missing promotion and properly jealous not only of his general but also of the less soldierly, more courtly Cassio? At the other extreme, is he a very good actor, aware of when an oath will impress, just as he knows when to remain suggestively silent?

One is tempted to suspect a mixture of vulgarity and calculation as the scene progresses. Within moments he is awakening Brabantio by shouting 'Zounds' and a most unsavoury description of Desdemona's elopement with Othello. Emilia will later comment on the seaminess of her husband's mind. Here, what we see is a sense of the language that will most quickly arouse a father's anger and perhaps undermine the marriage. Brabantio ignores Roderigo's comparatively mild occasional comments, paying more attention to the 'profane wretch' who seems so direct and excited. Unconsciously apposite when he calls Iago a 'villain', he too will quickly transfer his anger to another. One notices that even in his great distress, however, Brabantio uses no oaths; by comparison, the arousal of Cassio and Othello will seem even stronger.

Having stirred the establishment as effectively as radicals today often do with obscenities, Iago returns to Othello and encourages the Moor not to confront the 'raisèd father and his friends' (I, ii, 29), here trying unsuccessfully to create and play on a furtiveness that will later serve him so well with the shamed Cassio.[18] Shakespeare seems almost to be having a bit of fun when he has Iago swear, 'By Janus, I think no,' as Othello asks whether Brabantio's party is coming. The appropriateness of the phrase should be obvious to even the most slow-witted member of the audience after the opening scene. Warburton, in the eighteenth century, expounded on it, however, in one of the few notes one finds on the oaths: 'There is great propriety in making the double Iago swear by Janus who had two faces. The address of it is likewise remarkable, for as the people coming up appeared at different distances to have different shapes, he might swear . . . without suspicion of any other emblematic meaning.'[19] Even without this elaborate excuse of different appearances, Iago would scarcely be questioned on his ironically appropriate oath. At this moment, presumably, only Roderigo and the audience know that here is one of the men 'Who, trimmed in forms and visages of duty,/Keep yet their hearts attending on themselves./. . . throwing but shows of service on their lords' (I, i, 50–2).

A second pattern begins as Cassio enters. Iago uses the much milder 'faith', seemingly harmonising with the attitudes of the person he is addressing where this is important. Although Cassio may be courtier-like in his polite attention to Desdemona, and certainly is a member of the gentry, he is so far from fashionable swearing as to be ashamed of his later oaths. Iago presumably realises that he will respond badly to the abusive anger that worked with Roderigo or Brabantio, and although the metaphor is a bit off-colour it is mildly averred: 'Faith he to-night hath boarded a land carrack.' The explanation has a 'Marry' thrown in, almost punningly in the manner of Richard III (*Othello*, I, ii, 50, 53; *Richard III*, I, iii, 97–9).

By contrast, Othello exudes dignity and restraint, never indulging in the badinage that sometimes characterises Hamlet. It is hard to imagine him uttering the 'music vows' whose honey so satisfied Ophelia. His 'faith' has far deeper meaning than the same word from Iago; when he emits something stronger, he can only be frighteningly beside himself. In fact, any theory that the Quarto is corrupt whenever Othello says 'zounds' is missing just this point, which Shakespeare seems to be establishing very carefully. At the Senate hearing, the contrast between Othello and those around him is emphasised. A soldier since he was seven, he is calmly and poetically able to spin the events of the past into fascinating stories without depending on the 'epithets of war'. He has embraced the religion of the Venetians he serves, although later he will prove to have remembered the sibyl who wove his mother's magic handkerchief. There is a simple sincerity as he denies that he used magic to win Desdemona, and demonstrates the kind of oath that is at this moment very meaningful: his story begins, 'as truly as to heaven/I do confess the vices of my blood', and narrates her reaction, 'She swore, i'faith, 'twas strange, 'twas passing strange' (I, iii, 122–3, 160). Steevens says this shows 'what kind of swearing was done by both [Desdemona and Mary Queen of Scots]; not a bold and masculine oath put into the mouth of Desdemona, such as Elizabeth frequently used, but a more earnest affirmation upon her faith and honour, which she had considered as the same with a solemn appeal to God'.[20] Steevens implies that this sort of language was exclusively feminine, but in this play the same mildness belongs to Cassio and Othello before Iago has done his work. Othello solemnly describes the nature of his love in the same vein: 'Vouch with me, heaven, I therefore beg it not/To please the palate of my appetite . . ./But to be free and bounteous to her mind' (I, iii, 261–5). At this point, he is able to ignore Brabantio's warning with a confident 'My life upon her faith', although 'Honest Iago' has stored this seed of doubt for future nurturing. Heilman points out the irony that Desdemona will in fact remain faithful, but Othello will have to pay with his life for swerving from his earlier assurance.[21]

Events in Venice are almost over. Later, there will be a fleeting memory as ambassadors bring news of Brabantio's death and remark on the precipitous change in the general. But the play shifts to the isolation of Cyprus, where Desdemona is out of her element, and the scheming Iago can work more effectively on an Othello whose attentions must be partially on affairs of state when he would prefer to be at home with a wife he barely knows. Iago scoffingly promises the despondent Roderigo, 'If sanctimony and a frail vow betwixt an erring barbarian and a supersubtle Venetian be not too hard for my wits and all the tribe of hell, thou shalt enjoy her' (I, iii, 352–4). We hate to think Iago's hellish wit can override Othello's heaven-witnessed honour, but we watch as he unerringly makes the marriage vows consume like straw in the heat of Othello's jealousy.

In what may have been a good psychological move to keep us from thinking Othello less the hero and more the gullible stranger who is defenceless against machinations, Shakespeare shows us the manipulation of a group of Venetians who by Elizabethan standards should have been aware of all kinds of trickery. Our second glimpse of Lieutenant Cassio, the theoretician with a 'daily beauty in his life', reveals the polished gentleman, perhaps a bit overly courteous as he greets Desdemona, whom he has described as a paragon. Iago has been joking coarsely in front of Desdemona, but he has carefully kept to an innocuous 'In faith' or 'marry' as he watches Cassio kiss Emilia, and comments to Desdemona about his wife's sharpness of tongue. Cassio's attention shifts to Desdemona, however, and the simplest, most innocent gesture will be seen through a grotesque lens that magnifies and distorts it. To himself Iago rejoices: 'He takes her by the palm. Ay, well said, whisper! With as little a web as this will I ensnare as great a fly as Cassio. Ay, smile upon her, do! I will gyve thee in thine own courtship' (II, i, 166–9). Cassio would explain his kissing of his fingers to Desdemona, his smiles, his whispers, just as he had earlier excused his kissing Emilia: ''Tis my breeding/That gives me this bold show of courtesy.' Iago recognises it as fashion, yet he will not picture it that way.

In his subtlety, however, he will not approach Othello directly.

He first points out to Roderigo that Cassio is a rival for Desdemona, then in his oblique way plans to fashion a confrontation between rival suitors that will make him seem the innocent bystander. When Roderigo discounts what he has seen as 'courtesy', the 'truthful' ensign corrects him, using an oath that is not only appropriate to the soldier but also seems to grow organically out of the gestures that are being talked about. He insists it was 'Lechery, by this hand! an index and obscure prologue to the history of lust and foul thoughts'. Convinced, Roderigo agrees to provoke Cassio, aware only that he will be 'displanting' his rival, never suspecting the ultimate goal of his seemingly honest mentor, and even willing to risk a stroke or two from Cassio's truncheon (II, i, 211–78).

The logistics of the scheme are complicated, and depend on the sort of lucky timing that Iago can make best use of. As Heilman points out, Iago's helpfulness consists of stirring up noise[22] after plying Cassio with comradely drink. Cassio knows he has a poor head for wine, but yields, although trying to demur with a "Fore God' as Montano offers him liquor. Soon this supposed paragon is repetitiously averring that Iago's songs are good, "Fore God'. The phrase immediately strikes us as stronger than his wonted words, and it is clear that with his oath-tossing he has indeed become, as Iago has coarsely prophesied, 'as full of quarrel and offence/As my young mistress' dog'.

After some class-conscious maundering about souls to be saved, and an attempt to distinguish right from left, Cassio goes off, vaguely puritanical, to attend to affairs. Iago slanders him to Montano as a habitual drunkard, and the false impression seems confirmed when, two dozen lines later, Cassio returns pursuing Roderigo and shouting, 'Zounds, you rogue! you rascal!' (II, iii, 139). It is the only time he uses the word in the play, and Iago will soon make much of it as he describes the events in apparent detail, including his notation of 'Cassio high in oath; which till to-night/I ne'er might say before' (II, iii, 225–6).

With the alarum bell ringing and cries of mutiny, Othello comes in from another interrupted night with his bride and finds the excitement at its height. Montano, who had earlier used a comradely 'as I am a soldier', now shouts, 'Zounds, I bleed still. I am hurt to th' death./He dies!' (II, iii, 153–4). It is no surprise that Othello is angered to find his commands 'Not to outsport discretion' so flagrantly ignored, the still nervous island aroused in the middle of the night, and the Governor of Cyprus wounded by the lieutenant sent to protect him. At a glance he sees that Iago is the only one to remember 'place and duty', and with the irony so evident in the play Othello charges him 'on thy love' to explain what has happened. In *Romeo and Juliet* the truthful Benvolio was doubted when he was called upon in similar circumstances to relate the sequence of events to the newly arrived Prince. Here, Iago's slanted retelling, bound only by his self-love, is believed implicitly.

Othello's attitude changes, and he recognises that 'Now, by heaven,/My blood begins my safer guides to rule'. Ironically, although he knows the danger when 'passion, having my best judgment collied,/Assays to lead the way', he will soon be powerless to avoid its pull (II, iii, 194–7). In the middle of line 197, the Quarto inserts a 'Zouns' that emphasises the extent of his agitation. At this point, however, 'By heaven' is stronger than anything we have heard him utter before and, although the minced expletive does indicate his great anger more precisely, it breaks up the rhythm. It fits with his precipitous dismissal of his lieutenant, but it also seems to put this emotion on a par with his fury with Desdemona. At this juncture, Iago has arranged events so that Montano and Cassio are moved to the strongest of oaths. He has not yet gained so much control over Othello. It is not, as Alice Walker suggests, that Othello could not use such a word. He is a soldier. He has heard it. And the later example has an artistic function. But this one seems out of place and suspect.

Iago's schemes are beginning to bring to the surface various characteristics that people have not previously seen in Othello, but the Moor still is able to shift back to the milder vein. Desdemona is his 'sweeting' and he looks forward to a resumption of 'balmy slumbers'. Iago, the consummate actor, also shifts again to 'Marry' and 'I protest' as he returns to his role of sympathetic advice-giver. The sorrowing Cassio turns to him and dismally recalls his behaviour: 'Drunk! . . . squabble! swagger! swear! and discourse fustian with one's own shadow!' (II, iii, 268–70).

With the bruised Roderigo, Iago again speaks more firmly and, after adding up their gains, reminds us of the passage of time with his 'By the mass,'tis morning!', a phrase which the Folio scrupulously changes to 'In troth', although Iago seems to reserve this kind of language for Cassio.[23] By its care, in fact, the Folio has levelled out some distinctions that may in themselves seem minor, but show Iago's adeptness at doing what will impress people most. As he says, 'we work by wit, and not by witchcraft,' and his twisted wit makes him enjoy words as well as the turmoil that he has just created.

Shakespeare has a technique of introducing a very different voice after particularly tense scenes, and the Clown and Musician provide a minimal contrast with their puns and 'marry's. The average person who easily recalls *Macbeth*'s Porter or *Hamlet*'s gravediggers would probably be hard-pressed to remember just where the Clown and Musician appear, for only a few lines later Iago has returned to create more confusion. Now he is ready to work directly on Othello, with Desdemona as the innocent tool in the destruction of her marriage. In her elopement and insistence that she accompany Othello to Cyprus, she has already demonstrated a firmness of spirit. Now she shows a well-meaning persistence, gently urging that 'I' faith' Cassio is humbled and penitent, and that Othello must see him. She has sworn little in the first three acts, and never by more than her faith. Here, however, as she presses, she adds, 'By'r Lady, I could do much.' As if to prove this, she refuses to be cut off by Othello's 'I will deny thee nothing' and continues her suit, ignoring a hint of impatience in his answers (III, iii).

I have spoken of the chameleon quality of Iago's choice of words, and pointed ahead to the way Othello is raised to stronger and stronger language. In this scene, one also notes the beginning of a pattern in Desdemona's use of oaths. Although the Folio took pains to excise this reference to the Virgin, it is very much in keeping with a train of thought that runs through the play. Iago comments that Desdemona could even make Othello renounce his baptism, were she so inclined (II, iii, 326–31), and Othello himself chides the brawlers 'for Christian shame' that they have seemingly turned Turks. Desdemona is decidedly Christian in her outlook and later, in moments of stress, she will call on heaven, on her Christianity and on her hopes of salvation as, during the horror that is Act IV, she denies accusation after accusation that she cannot understand. The only break from this religious pattern, in fact, comes when she is still looking upward for something to swear by and ironically echoes Iago's choice in III, iii, as she finally declares in helpless dismay, 'What shall I do to win my lord again?/... for, by this light of heaven,/I know not how I lost him' (IV, ii, 149–51). As she faces the final threats and accusations, she denies any sin and begs heaven for mercy, insisting 'by my life and soul' that she never gave the handkerchief to Cassio (V, ii, 49). Time and again, Shakespeare's characters have sworn by their lives alone. Here, however, as at moments in *Hamlet*, the thought of the afterlife is very much in people's minds.[24] In fact, we are reminded of Hamlet in reverse when Othello declares that he would not kill her 'unpreparèd spirit'. But he has a horror of perjury and, unable to accept the truth as he conducts his private trial, he accuses her still further.

> By heaven, I saw my handkerchief in's hand!
> O perjured woman! thou dost stone my heart,
> And mak'st me call what I intend to do
> A murder, which I thought a sacrifice.
>
> (V, ii, 62–5)

Iago has led Othello this far, convincing him that his honour has been insulted by the physically foul actions of the woman he had thought a paragon. One wonders if Othello would have been able to complete the killing, however, had he not taken a vow. Although it comes relatively late in the play, his oath is like those of many revengers who dedicate themselves to righting a wrong. Like Hamlet, those revengers often have their tasks set much earlier in a play. Here, we have watched the Moor moving gradually to a point where he believes his wife must die. After stronger and stronger exclamations, he makes his final vow, which Iago carefully seconds.

The difference between Folio and Quarto texts becomes most telling as we follow this progress. Othello's exclamatory 'By heaven, he echoes me' (III, iii, 106) is censored to a more sorrowful and less internalised 'Alas, thou echoest me'. Sorrow will indeed come later. But here something new is being opened to him, and he is startled and determined to know the worst. Soon, in a speech trimmed by the Folio, he thinks he is pressing Iago with his 'By heaven, I'll know thy thoughts' (III, iii, 162). This is precisely the illusion of control Iago wants, for he can now dole out insinuations with a seeming unwillingness and mysteriousness that increase Othello's unease. To a man of the Moor's honour and horror of perjury, Iago's very truthful 'I dare be sworn I think that he is honest' is meaningful and, were the process to stop here, there would be no poison working. But, with a cleverness related to Antony's technique in undermining the honourableness of Brutus' conspiracy, Iago makes 'honest' seem a very doubtful term when applied to any but himself. 'Jealousy', apparently started by an innocent warning against it, becomes a leitmotif, and Othello is driven to exclaim, 'O misery!' (III, iii, 171).

In fewer than a hundred lines, Othello's mind has been turned a new way, and despite his attempt to seem unruffled when Iago comments, 'I see this hath a little dashed your spirits. . . . I' faith, I fear it has,' we know that he is disquieted (III, iii, 214–15). His 'By heaven' contrasts with the milder 'I' faith' that is one of Iago's hallmarks as, supposedly driven by love for his leader, he voices 'doubts' he would rather keep quiet. The Moor recognises the war that has started in his mind, and knows he is bidding farewell to content as he sadly admits, 'Thou hast set me on the rack./I swear 'tis better to be much abused/Than but to know't a little' (III, iii, 335–7). He is over-reacting, saying goodbye to his life's occupation as a soldier, and for a moment he recovers, giving us one of those tantalising moments of hope that characterise some of Shakespeare's tragedies. He wavers, as if two halves of his mind were at war: 'By the world/I think my wife be honest, and think she is not;/I think that thou art just, and think thou art not' (III, iii, 383–5).[25]

He had already called Iago a 'villain' and demanded 'ocular proof' that his wife is a 'whore'. Otherwise, he had vowed, 'by the worth of mine eternal soul,/Thou hadst been better have been born a dog/ Than answer my waked wrath!' (III, iii, 359–63). If Iago fails, there is a vow backing the promise of vengeance. Recovering quickly, Iago explains that there have to be some qualifications to that 'ocular proof', and when Othello accepts these seemingly reasonable limits he also makes his more formal vow of revenge on Desdemona. It is a terrible control that succeeds his violent threat to 'tear her all to pieces!' (III, iii, 431).

Shakespeare had already experimented with the sweeping words he felt characterised a noble Moor when he created Portia's suitor with his oath in *The Merchant of Venice*. He takes Othello farther, and in a more sustained way, with ranging imagery and hyperbole.

> O, that the slave had forty thousand lives!
> One is too poor, too weak for my revenge. . . .
> Arise, black vengeance, from the hollow hell! . . .
>   my bloody thoughts, with violent pace,
> Shall ne'er look back, ne'er ebb to humble love,
> Till that a capable and wide revenge
> Swallow them up.
>   *He kneels.* Now, by yond marble heaven,
> In the due reverence of a sacred vow
> I here engage my words.
>   (III, iii, 442–62)

The wild speeches, broken by Iago's counsel of 'Patience', have led to a climax with a physical pose that makes his threat to Desdemona even more serious than his warning to Iago. And again Iago seemingly matches his master's mood, though his love of darkness makes his echoing oath particularly unpleasant:

>   Do not rise yet.
>   *Iago kneels.*
> Witness, you ever-burning lights above,
> You elements that clip us round about,
> Witness that here Iago doth give up
> The execution of his wit, hands, heart
> To wronged Othello's service!
>   (III, iii, 462–7)

Within ten more lines, Cassio and Desdemona's deaths have been decreed, and Iago is made lieutenant. His wit has apparently succeeded! Echoing the person he wishes to impress, although omitting the elements of sacredness and reverence from his vow, he has now isolated Othello farther from those who might somehow stop the course of events.

Were it possible for Othello's suspicions to be allayed at this point, Desdemona innocently makes sure that they are not. Iago has used the handkerchief in his conversation with Othello. She, rather than saying she has dropped it, pretends she refuses to get it. Fear and wonder mix when Othello tells the import of the embroidered piece of silk, and we have a hint of the way she must have reacted to his strange tales when he first visited her father's house. Now, however, there is an urgency in his behaviour that is new to her, and though we yearn for her to tell the truth we realise that it would probably do little good. Instead, she takes an even more fatal tack by defensively changing the subject to Cassio. The two who have been in harmony so recently now play their different tunes:

Othello:	The handkerchief!
Desdemona:	I pray talk me of Cassio
Othello:	The handkerchief!
Desdemona:	A man that all his time
	Hath founded his good fortunes on your love,
	Shared dangers with you –
Othello:	The handkerchief!
Desdemona:	I' faith, you are to blame.
Othello:	Zounds!

                                       (III, iv, 92–8)

The 'Away' substituted by the Folio scarcely fits with Othello's own precipitous exit. In the Quarto, this strongest of oaths exhibits in one explosion the peak of pressure to which his anger and exasperation have risen. Like Hamlet, Othello has demonstrated tension as surely by the progression of his swearing as by the general tone of his conversation. Without this progression, we could understand perfectly well what is happening. But 'Zounds', uttered here in response to pleas from a woman to whom he would have denied nothing only a few hours before, shows that indeed 'Chaos is come again'.

In lines surrounding these exclamations, Shakespeare exercises his technique of relief. Cassio, despite his unrest, is again mild, averring twice to Bianca by his faith (III, iv), and again using that and the innocuous 'marry' as he talks of his courtesan to Iago (IV, i). Now that the precipitous decline has been started, Iago can again seem the mild and calm man to all these advice-seekers. He echoes the weak asseverations used by others, never approaching the 'Zounds' that came so easily to him at the beginning of the play when he was showing apparent outrage. In conversation he reminds Othello of the handkerchief, and is answered with 'By heaven, I would most gladly have forgot it!' The insinuations continue, and soon Othello is uttering a jumble of thoughts, explosively punctuated, just before he falls into his trance:

> Lie with her! Zounds, that's fulsome. – Handkerchief – confessions – handkerchief! . . . I tremble at it. . . . It is not words that shakes me thus. – Pish! Noses, ears, and lips? Is't possible? – Confess? – Handkerchief? – O devil!
>
> (IV, i, 36–43)

As he comes to, afraid he is being mocked, he hears the slightly echoing 'No, by heaven', as Iago bends over him in pretended concern.

Iago truthfully confirms the identity of the handkerchief – 'Yours, by this hand!' – when the carefully staged conversation with Cassio has ended. The trick has worked as well as Don John's charade to convince Claudio in *Much Ado about Nothing*. It is Desdemona, not Iago, who will be chopped 'into messes'! Surely those who would be offended by finding 'Zounds' on Othello's lips and insist that there is inappropriateness and textual corruption would have to admit some problems with these images of Senecan bloodiness that are also coursing through his mind.

Othello previews his attitude toward his wife's deathbed oaths in the next scene as he sends Emilia to guard the door, then questions the kneeling Desdemona, 'Why, what art thou?' Her response, 'Your wife, my lord; your true/And loyal wife,' produces an angry and to her totally puzzling command that she ritualise her answer in a rite of perjury:

> Come, swear it, damn thyself;
> Lest, being like one of heaven, the devils themselves
> Should fear to seize thee. Therefore be double-damned –
> Swear thou art honest.
>
> (IV, ii, 35–8)

The continuing interchange, with other references to heaven, produces the series of avowed denials of wrong-doing noted earlier. Desdemona is finally left dazed and able to turn only to Iago and Emilia for help. Lodovico has already remarked that, even though he should swear it, a report of Othello's behaviour 'would not be believed in Venice' (IV, i, 235–6). Iago now pretends equal puzzlement, while Emilia unwittingly suggests the villainous knavery that must be the cause. The audience, knowing how right she is, senses a new note in Iago's impatience, a genuine uneasiness, although he is able to continue his act of concern, just as Othello, after his first outburst, was able to turn calmly back to Desdemona.

Emilia's suggestion is not the only speech in the play when someone on stage says what we in the audience long to hear. Othello came close when he called Iago a villain. Roderigo will carry matters even farther by confronting Iago and declaring angrily that he is being 'fopped', and that Iago's 'words and performances are no kin together'. There is real danger in his threat to go directly to Desdemona because of course Iago has forwarded none of the gifts supposed to win Desdemona's favour. But Iago is again able to redirect the young man's anger, silencing his protestations and creating the fiction that he has merely been testing his mettle. We can almost predict the tone of this speech – mild, conciliatory, and even echoing Roderigo's word-choice with 'I protest I have dealt most directly in thy affair'. Again Roderigo expresses a willingness to set upon Cassio at night. This time, Iago plans to be a silent bystander and assure the necessary deaths. Roderigo knows too much, and the scheme seems certain to gain for Iago the security he needs. Here, he is still enough in control to plan carefully. Later, when his wife suspects, he will have to use his sword speedily and openly on her. This is indeed the night that will make or fordo him quite.

The play lacks the falling-off and building-up in the fourth and fifth acts that so often characterises Elizabethan dramatic construction, but there needs to be a slight lessening of tension. It comes in IV, iii, with the frank realism of Emilia. Desdemona has just finished her prophetic talk of shrouds and sung the doleful Willow Song. She asks her more experienced attendant if there are indeed women who 'do abuse their husbands/In such gross kind?' Horrified by Emilia's 'Why, would not you?' she declares, 'No, by this heavenly light!' She means it as a straightforward oath, but Emilia immediately puns a bit and, as Heilman notes, boldly claims the night: 'Nor I neither by this heavenly light./I might do't as well i' th' dark' (IV, iii, 64–5).[26] In a scene reminiscent of some of the exchanges between Juliet and her nurse, Emilia continues, revealing more of her attitude toward marriage:

In troth, I think I should; and undo't when I had done it. Marry, I would not do such a thing for a joint-ring, nor for measures of lawn, nor for gowns, petticoats, nor caps, nor any petty exhibition; but, for all the whole world – 'Ud's pity! who would not make her husband a cuckold to make him a monarch? I should venture purgatory for't.

(IV, iii, 70–6)

Ironically, this woman who has herself been (presumably wrongly) suspected of infidelity will soon begin to assemble the facts that will cause her husband's fall rather than his rise. Here, her eminently practical standards contrast to Desdemona's shocked 'Beshrew me if I would do such a wrong/For the whole world'. We are forcibly struck by this declaration when we know that she is the target of a revenge plan that no proofs of goodness could reverse.

The final scene of the play divides into two parts – the murder of Desdemona and the discovery of Iago's villainy with Othello's resultant suicide. The oaths also divide into two groups. First there are those sincere avowals and countering accusations of perjury from Desdemona and Othello. Then there are the more exclamatory expressions. Iago admits he said Desdemona was false, and Emilia blasts back, 'Upon my soul, a lie! a wicked lie!' (V, ii, 182). When things have gone wrong before, Iago has managed to maintain a façade of control, even helping the wounded Cassio while trying to shift blame on to Bianca. This time, however, he fails. Emilia continues to talk, and when Othello mentions the handkerchief her 'O God! O heavenly God!' signals the impending revelation. Iago's 'Zounds, hold your peace!' marks the first time that Iago feels as desperate as Othello had earlier. Emilia, who had punned on Desdemona's oath, is now in earnest, and avouches 'By heaven' she is not lying as she ignores her husband's shouts and threats. There is no time now to arrange a midnight silencing, and Iago only compounds the charges against himself when he stabs her in his rage.

In this respect, at least, the play ends justly. The man who has for so long roused others to peaks of emotion displayed in acts of violence and strong oaths is by circumstances forced into the same pattern. He had tried to make others a bit like himself. Many of his soliloquies hinge on jealousy and sex, and he has aroused jealousy not only in Othello, but also to a lesser degree in Roderigo. There is in him a latent violence that he is able to bring out in others. Only at the end does it show in him for the rest of the people to see. Emilia has experienced the 'seamy side' of his mind at some earlier time. We have known it all along as we have seen the pieces of his plot work together for his self-aggrandisement and even enjoyment in destroying others. Finally, all he can do is kill an innocent woman, and then fall silent, while near the bodies of his victims many of the people he has so long separated and manipulated come together against him.

Obviously there are some people in the play who swear on their own, but many of the patterns of oaths are linked to patterns of action that Iago has created. On a garrisoned island, there are no blaspheming soldiers. Clowns, musicians and servants are kept muted. For the most part, the oaths, along with other aspects of speech, reveal growing tension in much the same way that they signalled the increasing stresses in Hamlet as he tried to manipulate events and carry out his assigned revenge.

Chapter 6

In Response to Censorship

When it became apparent that the Lord Chamberlain would not permit the Rock musical *Hair* to open uncut in London, the première was delayed until the end of censorship. Two years later, in 1970, the producers argued successfully against any enforced cuts when the show was briefly banned in Boston, Massachusetts. They insisted, as have many twentieth-century authors, that deleting certain words or scenes can destroy a carefully created effect. With the exception of Davenant's appeal to Charles I, mentioned in Chapter 1, we lack reports of similar authorial triumphs in the Stuart era. Extant records point, rather, to acceptance of the censor's dicta. Jonson may have muttered caustically, but he did answer charges about *The Magnetic Lady*. There seems to be no question that the spiciness added by the actors would be cut; as we saw in the opening chapter, the determination was not one of removing offending words, but of levying fines and fixing blame. We have also previously noted the revisions made by Johnson and the cuts made by the publishers of Shakespeare's First Folio.

Theatre people had already learned to live with other controls, avoiding the imprisonment and fines that could be levied for 'unchaste, seditious, or otherwise improper plays' under the Act of Common Council of 1574.[1] When they sold plays to printers, theatre companies or playwrights were cognisant of a warning to the wardens of the Stationers' Company, in 1599, that 'noe playes be printed except they be allowed by such as have authority'.[2] It was not an age to protest at one man's power as arbiter of the blasphemous. After all, Jonson and others had seen the inside of the Marshalsea because of *The Isle of Dogs*.

Nowhere does Shakespeare make so direct a comment on the hypersensitivity of the more puritanical mind as Jonson does in *Bartholomew Fair*,[3] and he is always more prone to make fun of the lover who swears meaninglessly than to laugh at the 'yea and nay' sayers. If one reads the post-1606 plays with an eye especially alert for oaths, one is impressed by Shakespeare's singularly effective adjustment to the new law in many instances. With the earlier plays, it is another matter. Although a remarkable amount slips through in some that were first printed after 1606 – one thinks of the 1622 Quarto of *Othello* – plays extant both in early Quartos and the Folio suggest that Jonson's technique of revising was never followed. *Hamlet*, for example, is much purified in the Folio, as compared with the 1604 Quarto. Here and elsewhere, when we have evidence of changes, they are pedestrian and generally weaken the play. Shakespeare seems to have let the earlier works take their chance, and had we only a Folio version of *Othello* or *Hamlet* we would often have no indication that Shakespeare ever intended stronger words to be uttered.

On the other hand, plays written after 1606 do exhibit certain tendencies that seem to show Shakespeare, aware of the way oaths could enrich the texture of a play, carefully fitting his writing to the letter of the law. He was at an advantage over Jonson and some others in that he chose to write tragedies and romances, plays removed from the everyday London life that others often purported to show. Shakespeare was to work on only one more play set in vaguely contemporary England – *Henry VIII*. The *Merry Wives of Windsor* and the chronicle histories set in the relatively recent past were products of the 1590s. *Cymbeline*, *King Lear*, and even *Macbeth*, although British, give Shakespeare an opportunity to let religious influences other than Christian suffuse a good part of the action. In these, and in plays set in the classical world, even a bawd or scurrilous tavern-haunter could swear quite naturally by a pagan deity, and not exhibit the extravagances of some of Jonson's Londoners, who must pride themselves on being able to swear 'by Pharoah'. There may be inconsistencies, particularly in the romances, but the possibility of remaining non-Christian is there.

Actually there is not a sharp temporal dividing-line. Shakespeare set some earlier action, ranging from the Senecan bloodbath of *Titus Andronicus* to the fairy-world confusions of *A Midsummer Night's Dream*, in a non-Christian world. Little in the early Quartos of these two would have offended Buck. One cannot say that Shakespeare set more of his later plays in pagan lands or times merely to avoid the law. But it is certainly fortuitous that the post-1606 plays, with the possible exception of *The Tempest*, occur either in a pre-Christian world or in one where the religious picture seems confused. Obviously the Italy of *Cymbeline* is Renaissance, and England with Edward the Confessor establishes part of the cosmology of *Macbeth*. But Roman legions battling the Britons, and the Weird Sisters who haunt the Scottish heath lend both a pagan air. The law ignored pagan gods, and a soldier could appropriately utter 'By Hercules' with impunity. Shakespeare has given himself the freedom to go beyond mere comments that people are swearing, or the mild 'faith' when stress, native profaneness, or formal avowals require examples appropriate to the characters.

Perhaps the audience would less readily grasp the relative strength of oaths by pagan gods, for their familiarity was with the Christian references. But we may recall that Nowell argued against swearing by other gods,[4] even though the law considered these oaths less weighty. Presumably within the scope of a play the audience, or at least part of it, would be acute enough to realise that Jupiter was very important to a Roman. Many, in fact, would have known a great amount of classical mythology, and brought this knowledge to the play. And Shakespeare often mentioned the pagan gods in other ways, too, to create a sense of their importance to the characters.

King Lear probably had its inception in the autumn of 1605, but records of a command performance and later entry with the Stationers suggest that it was a reasonably new play when performed at court on 26 December 1606. Certainly its treatment of oaths differs from that in *Othello* and *Hamlet*, the preceding tragedies. The Quarto, printed in 1608, and the Folio are virtually identical, so far as oaths are concerned, and there is variety that is lacking in the Folio *Hamlet* or *Othello*, where we can see changes made for a censor. It seems to me that Shakespeare either foresaw the impending legislation or finished the play after it was in effect.

In *King Lear*, the sense of of higher powers is most ambivalent. Modern criticism has frequently emphasised the detachment of the gods and the despair of the blind Gloucester, staggering toward suicide in a play where efforts at kindness lead to one's mutilation. Yet all the good characters think of deities, while the evil ones are more prone to think of themselves and even to swear, on infrequent occasions, by their own attributes. Goneril or Regan may say 'faith', but Cornwall ironically emphasises his 'life and honour' and Edmund replies 'by my honour'. With no pattern of divine mercy, one irony is avoided by the absence of references to Christ, whose name suggests grace. In his feigned madness, Edgar speaks of the Foul Fiend, but otherwise has a sense of powerful but unidentified rulers. Albany takes the action of the sword-wielding servant as evidence of vengeance from above. Lear has a momentary belief that the gods throw incense on sacrifices such as himself and Cordelia, but soon reverts to questioning. These instances seem scarcely to balance the bad, although the villains, with their mundane concerns, are ultimately defeated.

The oaths of Lear demonstrate the inconsistencies about divinity. He calls in turn upon classical deities, some vague and unnamed 'gods', and Nature herself, giving us a sense of an uncertain

cosmology that functions unpredictably. The terrible oath against
Cordelia helps underline this breadth of reference:

> by the sacred radiance of the sun,
> The mysteries of Hecate and the night,
> By all the operation of the orbs
> From whom we do exist and cease to be,
> Here I disclaim all my paternal care.
>
> (I, i, 109–13)

The obvious and the mysterious alike are included in an oath that
becomes more important to him than human relationships or good
sense. The reference to the power of heavenly bodies over human
existence accords well with Gloucester's alertness to the eclipses. Kent
attempts to reason with the old man, but Lear, whose oaths are the
most numerous in the play, shifts again to the classic with 'Now
by Apollo'.

It becomes apparent that Kent's life is completely bound up with
that of his king, and his echoing 'Now by Apollo, King,/Thou
swear'st thy gods in vain' mixes a harmony with his ruler and an
attempt to affirm by the current deity that Lear is in error (I, i, 160–1).
His echoing seems in no way to make fun of Lear's choice of words.
Kent is in turn reminded of his allegiance (presumably once sworn)
by a king whose attention is on vocal affirmations of affection.
He must play his role in the scenario Lear has constructed or be
banished, and of course Kent, like Cordelia, cannot make empty
declarations.

Lear will retain 'The name, and all th' addition to a king', and we
note that his vision of himself in the part includes a steadfastness to
vows. Ironically, this oath is as much of a superfluity as the retinue;
more store is placed on intransigence than on any possibility that he
may have been mistaken. He singlemindedly justifies the banishment
decree because 'thou hast sought to make us break our vows,/
Which we durst never yet, and . . ./To come betwixt our sentence
and our power' (I, i, 168–70). With a simple 'By Jupiter,/This shall
not be revoked', he formalises and reiterates the banishment. The
absoluteness is re-emphasised in his description to Burgundy of a
Cordelia 'Dow'red with our curse, and strangered with our oath'.
At the suggestion that he reconsider the dowry, he declares, 'Nothing.
I have sworn. I am firm.' This scene has the heaviest concentration
of oaths in the play, with only Edgar's accusations at the tournament
in V, iii, rivalling it. This suggests that Shakespeare is making
artistic use of the formality of swearing, as well as achieving much
more with oaths in this play.

There is an echo of this formality, and the need to affirm and remain
true, in the harrowing mock-trial scene. Lear had included the

perjured among the enemies of the great gods as he faced the storm (III, ii, 54), and lashed out at those who simulated virtue. Now, in the hovel, he mixes fantasy and reality, setting up his panel of 'justices' and accusing a joint-stool Goneril. Although there is a vestige of his earlier swearing, in his distraction he is now ironically closer to the truth as he affirms, 'I here take my oath before this honourable assembly, [she] kicked the poor king her father' (III, vi, 46–8).

In an earlier scene, Lear had invoked the King of Gods to deny Kent's report of Cornwall and Regan's cruelty. It is as if 'By Jupiter, I swear no!' is strong enough to make Kent bate his accusation (II, iv, 20). But Kent counters with what might in other circumstances be comic, and here has a certain absurdity: 'By Juno, I swear ay.' One has a vision of the goddess confronting her husband! The phrase, which first appears in the Folio, may have been an actor's clever addition, but it is akin to the first act exchange and seems a natural outgrowth of the verbal cleverness Kent exhibited with Cornwall earlier. Here, he is willing to risk more of Lear's anger by echoing him to try to make him realise the truth. It is a measure of the change that he undergoes that Lear, who is so positive here, will later not be willing to 'swear these are my hands' (IV, vii, 55).

One tends to overlook Kent's ability to parody, thinking of him merely as blunt and steadfast. But, after tripping Oswald, he angrily points out the discrepancy between appearance and reality when such slaves wear swords, then replies to the chiding Cornwall, ''tis my occupation to be plain'. Cornwall's disdainful 'This is some fellow/Who, having been praised for bluntness, doth affect/A saucy roughness' (II, ii, 90–2) produces a sardonic response:

> Sir, in good faith, in sincere verity,
> Under th'allowance of your great aspect,
> Whose influence, like the wreath of radiant fire
> On flick'ring Phoebus' front . . ..
>
> (II, ii, 100–3)

The asseverations in the lines are meaningless, part of his attack on emptiness covered by fair-sounding phrases. His references in the whole speech range from Camelot and Sarum to the classical Phoebus and Ajax, and, if we recall that only a twenty-line glimpse of Edgar separates this scene from its continuation, Kent's echoing of Lear fits in perfectly. It is classical but sardonic, and part of the effort to point out the truth.

This may be labouring a simple exchange, but it does show how the mature Shakespeare used oaths in close conjunction with other details to build character, all the while fitting the words into a non-Christian frame of reference that would escape the censor. Lear has noted Nature as a goddess; he has referred to the classical deities. Gloucester addresses a vague collection of 'kind gods' shortly before his blinding. An occasional 'faith' or 'marry' or reference to one's own attributes completes the catalogue of actual examples. But, when a person recalls an oath, we tend to remember the original act, and in this play a simple 'I have sworn' often carries weighty memories.

By contrast, Edmund lightly calls his honour to witness his faith-fulness to Regan, and quite unperturbedly admits, 'To both these sisters have I sworn my love' (V, i, 14 and 55). It is an airiness that Edgar would not share even as Poor Tom, where he gives a garbled version of the Ten Commandments, including: 'swear not; commit not with man's sworn spouse'. He includes a fictive description of himself as the fashionable serving man who 'swore as many oaths as I spake words, and broke them in the sweet face of heaven' (III, iv, 77–8 and 84–5).

Later, when a semblance of social order has been restored and a formal challenge and tournament supplant the swirling of storms, madmen, and battles of good French against bad English, Edgar will again emphasise an oath. The opening scene, with its flourishes, maps and attendants, is balanced by the appearance of heralds and men in armour. We seem to have stepped from ancient Britain into the medieval world of *Richard II*, and Edgar's challenge to his brother stresses honour as he speaks of 'The privilege of mine honours,/My oath and my profession'. 'I protest', he adds, 'thou art a traitor,/False to thy gods' (V, iii, 130–5). No matter who the gods are, the point of perjury is easily understood, and something that Edmund has already admitted to us. This may seem less serious than some of the other accusations, but it is basic, for a non-perjuring Edmund would never have been able to commit the other crimes which were based on lies and a lack of faith. We think of Lady MacDuff's definition of a traitor as 'one that swears and lies' (*Macbeth*, IV, ii, 47), and in a play where many people adhere to their oaths, even wrongheadedly, the faithless opportunism of Edmund and his counterparts is made obvious.

If one charts the occurrence of oaths or mention of them in the Shakespeare canon, one is struck by the richness of the history plays. This could be attributed in part to the inclusion of much about honour and allegiance, although that emphasis also comes to the fore in the Roman plays. But one cannot discount the fact that the earlier non-Roman tragedies – *Romeo and Juliet*, *Othello* and *Hamlet* – almost match the histories, and have anywhere from seventy-five to a hundred examples or references. With *King Lear*, however, the number drops into the thirties, and plummets to about a dozen in

Macbeth, a play written and first acted when the statute was new. There is a slow climb through *Antony and Cleopatra* and *Timon of Athens*, and the number is up to about forty for *Coriolanus*. Of the romances, *The Tempest*, which is the most patently Christian, is on a par with *Macbeth*, while *The Winter's Tale* and *Cymbeline* match *King Lear* and *Coriolanus* in numbers.

Remarkably, the two earlier Roman tragedies, *Julius Caesar* and *Titus Andronicus*, also had comparatively few oaths, with talk of honour or revenge providing the occasion for most of them. It was in *Romeo and Juliet* that Shakespeare began to use swearing effectively in a wider range of ways, to help suggest coarseness or impetuosity as well as faith and tension. He reached a peak of freedom and artistic achievement in *Hamlet* and *Othello*, just before the new law forced an adjustment. By 1606, however, Shakespeare not only had had practice in working with a few pagan oaths, but also possessed the skill to employ the mildest oaths effectively by limiting their numbers so that they, too, could stand out at important moments rather than being submerged in a mass of casual swearing.

There is danger in postulating the way Shakespeare faced his censorship problem. But the result, we see, can be effective, and far closer to the earlier tragedies in terms of seriousness than the topical swearing Jonson introduced in his satires. Probably one should not compare those plays with Shakespeare's tragedies. But in *Sejanus* Jonson presumably felt unable to use his witty inventiveness and instead almost eliminated oaths where he might well have emphasised Roman honour by employing the same techniques of limit and focus found in *Coriolanus* and to some extent in *Antony and Cleopatra*. In the former, the plebeians do not swear, despite their excitement, and in both the upper classes have a few mild casual utterances, but concentrate predominantly on matters of honour. Oaths, when they come, underline the non-Christian cosmology. Shakespeare might have been careless with such anachronisms as a striking clock, but he generally avoids the anachronistic swearing that characterised the mystery plays, where Old Testament characters habitually called the rood or the Trinity to witness. He had been careful in *Titus Andronicus* and *Julius Caesar*, and we expect equal attention to detail in the later plays.

Antony and Cleopatra comes closest to the non-classical, pre-1606 tragedies in its variety of phrases and treatment of oaths. The reason lies partially in Cleopatra's 'infinite variety'. Her own infrequent oaths are used carefully, and always effectively. The play has barely opened when she underlines an observation with what one might call a stock phrase: 'As I am Egypt's Queen,/ Thou blushest, Antony'. We have heard her referred to as a 'gypsy', 'a tawny front' and a 'strumpet' in a mere thirteen lines. She has just taunted Antony, and in one additional line now tells the un-initiated that she is a queen and lets us know that her sarcastic remarks have produced a reaction in an Antony sensitive about his part in the Roman government. We will later realise that she sometimes lacks dignity, but is always aware of her position as queen, an awareness that will suffuse the last scene of the play when our final sight is of her crowned and stately as Octavius comments on her royalty.

Later in the first act, when she is testy in Antony's absence, Charmian banters about Julius Caesar. The strength of Cleopatra's outburst proves that she cannot be teased, and that an underling must be sensitive to her moods. The interchange about her love for Antony culminates in a threat: 'By Isis, I will give thee bloody teeth/If thou with Caesar paragon again/My man of men!' (I, v, 70–2). Her flash of temper and undignified vow point ahead to her treatment of the messenger who brings news of Antony's marriage to Octavia.

Isis is mentioned at other times in the play, too, often in supplica-tion, and helps to differentiate Egypt from the Rome of Hercules and Jupiter. (Differentiation is more important here than it was between the Greeks and Trojans of *Troilus and Cressida*!) Enobarbus and the soldiers will call upon the masculine gods who connote power and strength, while Cleopatra turns to an enchantress goddess who sug-gests many things, including fertility. It is some measure of Antony's absorption into this world that he, whose god is Hercules, should make a parting vow to Cleopatra, 'By the fire/That quickens Nilus' slime, I go from hence/Thy soldier' (I, iii, 68–70). The phrase is neither attractive nor characteristic of the great Roman and military man, but it seems more appropriate to the kind of lusty life that characterises their unconventional relationship than the 'By Pharoah' Jonson relied upon. Not only does it imply fecundity from a source other than Isis, but it also carries an idea of Egyptian heat and fits with Antony's later talk of Nile floods, the sowing of grain, and even the crocodiles, at the feast on Pompey's galley.[5]

The mixture of hurt and anger that Cleopatra exhibited has its counterpart in the last oath Antony utters in her presence. She has received Thidias, Caesar's representative, and Antony, fresh from challenging Octavius to combat, is led back by Enobarbus. When he hears Cleopatra's fulsome talk of kisses, he blasts out, 'Favours? by Jove that thunders!' With only slightly more control than she had shown toward the messenger, he decrees a beating for the emissary. The oath here underlines explosive anger.

Maynard Mack makes the curious observation, 'When Antony will swear an oath, he cries, "Let Rome in Tiber melt and the wide arch Of the ranged empire fall!" When Cleopatra will swear, she cries, "Melt Egypt into Nile! and kindly creatures Turn all to serpents!" [6] These great phrases, full of the imagery of size and scope that characterises the language of both the lovers, are not oaths in any proper sense. They do not even work as a sort of curse – 'Let Rome melt if I prove false.' There are, however, other instances when oaths are used or past vows become important. They are stock situations, such as Octavius' accusation that Antony has denied promised arms, and the Roman concern with honour as he refutes the charge. At the end of his life, Antony reminds Eros, 'Thou art sworn' to 'kill me/. . . when I bade thee' (IV, xiv, 62, 67, 82). Others, too, think of faith and loyalty as they near death. Enobarbus calls upon the night and 'thou blessèd moon' to witness his repentance for changing sides (IV, ix, 5, 7–10). Earlier, in Rome, he had appropriately sworn 'By Jupiter' as he argued with Lepidus (II, ii, 6), but here, in the dark, with Enobarbus no longer the steadfast Roman, the moon, noted for changeability, seems absolutely suitable.

Conversely, the soldier who urges a fight by land thinks of himself as a Roman, and quite fittingly declares, 'By Hercules, I think I am i' th' right' (III, vii, 67). His exasperated outburst, ironically by the patron god who will soon leave Antony, differs from the polished phrases of Dolabella, who advises Cleopatra honestly of Caesar's plans for her and the schedule for the return to Rome. Cleopatra had asked about the plans, and in the last real oath of the play he shows the compulsion he is under: 'Madam, as thereto sworn, by your command/(Which my love makes religion to obey)/I tell you this . . .' (V, ii, 198–200). Dolabella's love of her has transformed her request and his promise into a religious act, and he almost raises her to a deity. It is the last demonstration of her power, of the way men elevate this woman who had once dressed as Isis, before the serio-comic scene with the country fellow prepares the way for her suicide.

In *Antony and Cleopatra* the oaths range from the satiric to the angry, a variety not found in the other Roman plays. It is Cleopatra herself who is able to have the momentary satiric detachment, while the men concentrate on the honour so important to soldiers and occasionally burst out under tension – aspects also found in the Queen. One feels that here Shakespeare was again using oaths confidently, if not so effectively as he had in *Hamlet* or *Othello*.

Macbeth, probably written a year or two earlier, is almost barren of oaths despite the sincerity of the Scots. (Of course, we have only the Folio text, and if *Macbeth* was written before 1606 there might have been cutting with no attempt at authorial revision.) We cannot compare it with *King Lear*, despite proximity of date and ancient

British setting, for the cosmology of Macbeth is more patently
Christian, and appropriate oaths would have been more exceptionable than those in *King Lear*. The Weird Sisters, reminiscent of the
ancient Scottish Norns, may give a pagan overtone, and Lady
Macbeth may call upon some vague spirits, but the people in England
refer to Christendom and heaven, and most of those in Scotland are
aware of angels and God. Even Macbeth worries that he cannot echo
the grooms' 'amen', while Banquo believes he stands 'In the great
hand of God', and young Siward is called 'God's soldier'.

The poetic density of *Macbeth* makes us wish that we could see
more oaths, for they would probably function at least as organically
as many of those in *Hamlet*. We do find Lady Macbeth reminding
her husband of an oath of regicide we have not heard him take.
As has been frequently pointed out, she understands him. Her
references are to his manhood as she creates the horrible image of
dashing out a baby's brains 'had I so sworn as you/Have done
to this' (I, vii, 58–9). Macbeth has thought fleetingly of his
prior allegiance to Duncan as his king, but the suggestion of
cowardice and of violating a recent oath is far more meaningful
to this man who prides himself on his manhood and bravery. He
lacks a Cassandra to point out the unworthiness of his pledge, and
Lady Macbeth, who had averred that he was greater than either
Glamis or Cawdor, 'by the all-hail hereafter', now leads him farther
along the path to a meaningless life.

Beyond these two early examples, we have very little, although
each instance is telling. Malcolm points out, as part of a speech
putting himself firmly on God's side, that he has never forsworn.
Lady Macduff and her son talk of swearing in a poignant scene
where one of Shakespeare's wise-innocent children tries to understand events.

Son: What is a traitor?
Wife: Why, one that swears and lies.
Son: And be all traitors that do so?
Wife: Every one that does so is a traitor and must be hanged.
Son: And must they all be hanged that swear and lie?
Wife: Every one.
Son: Who must hang them?
Wife: Why, the honest men.
Son: Then the liars and swearers are fools, for there are liars and
          swearers enow to beat the honest men and hang up them.
                                                    (IV, ii, 46–57)

Of course, he is eventually proven wrong. But in the Scotland he
knows under Macbeth this seems an honest appraisal, and we know

he will not live to see his father and the others bring in an order where the liars and swearers will not outnumber the honest men.

The view we are left with in the remaining post-1606 tragedies is less hopeful. Apemantus' grace seems to fit his society: 'Grant I may never prove so fond/To trust man on his oath or bond' (*Timon of Athens*, I, ii, 62–3). Coriolanus will learn about friends who will break their vows, and conversely Aufidius will accuse him of forswearing because he has spared Rome.

Timon of Athens may be the slightly earlier play. Some of the ideas and speeches seem to place it close to *King Lear*. On the other hand, the lives of Alcibiades and Coriolanus are parallels in Plutarch, and the styles of the two plays suggest that they were written within a year or two of each other, perhaps about 1608. For oaths, they are good examples of the post-1606 tragedies set in pagan Rome and Athens, providing Shakespeare with further opportunities for phrases that can be appropriately strong for the characters involved, rather than mere classical substitutions in an otherwise Christian milieu.

Shakespeare seems more at pains to establish a sense of the classical gods in *Coriolanus*. He never lets a 'marry' slip in, even though that had virtually no meaning for his audience. (It does occur in *Timon of Athens*, *Julius Caesar* and *Titus Andronicus*.) Actually, his notion of ancient Athens seems far less whole and consistent than his vision of Rome. He had had a curious *mélange* in *A Midsummer Night's Dream*; his share of *The Two Noble Kinsmen* was to be medieval in feeling; and his sources for the Timon and Alcibiades story were far less complete than the Roman material he was gleaning from North for the other plays. If any of *Timon of Athens* was completed before May 1606, and subsequently cut for the censor, this would imply an additional weakness in the conception of the play, where only classical deities should have been mentioned.

As he frequently does, Shakespeare here uses identical phrases for people of varying honesty and social class. We are expected to realise that faithful Flavius is sincerely calling the gods to witness that his grief is true, while the opportunistic Lucius, declaring 'before the gods' that he cannot furnish money, is only speaking words and deserves our antipathy for his perjury. Despite a few instances of good faith, Apemantus' scepticism seems warranted. The play has hardly opened when the 'thrifty' old Athenian calls 'the gods to witness' his intention of dispossessing his daughter for loving Timon's servant. The old man's anger evaporates with amazing speed when Timon in turn pledges on his honour that he will give Lucilius enough money to make him a worthy son-in-law.

There is a series of oaths, some, like Timon's vow to ignore

Apemantus' railing or Servilius' attestation of his master's need, sincerely meant (I, ii; III, ii). Others, like Lucius' response to Servilius, are patently false. In between fall some that may be sincere, but are on questionable points. The old Athenian's avowal is one. Another is the First Stranger's protestation that he would help Timon if asked, where policy triumphs over conscience and he does not volunteer aid. The servants seem most sincere in their swearing, while the upper classes with their greed and hollow protestations are cold and despicable by comparison.

The selection just noted seems rather unfocused, and this is a fault with the swearing throughout the play. Seldom is there the sense of the importance of an oath that we found in *King Lear*. In part, this is because the swearer often appears for only an instant, or is a servant commenting on an action he is merely witnessing. There is one pivotal accusation, when the Second Senator classifies Alcibiades' friend as 'a sworn rioter', but this is merely descriptive, and we do not see Alcibiades swear vengeance on the city that puts his friend to death and decrees his own banishment. When he meets the embittered Timon, however, he is ready to turn against the city and ripe to listen to the urging of a vow that will steel him in his vengeful purpose. At the end of a catalogue of the sins of the Athenians, Timon exhorts him to 'Swear against objects', so that neither the cries of mothers and babes nor the sight of priests bleeding can pierce his ears and eyes (IV, iii, 123–7).

In front of them are two examples of the corruption: Alcibiades' mistresses, Phrynia and Timandra, anxious to share in Timon's new-found gold. Timon aims the final discussion of vows in the play at these women and others of their type, urging them to keep at their trade and bring destruction of another sort to the greedy. Physical corruption will match, on the one hand, the chaos of conquest threatened by Alcibiades and, on the other, the internal rot and lack of honour that he has already seen repay his own generosity. Typically, they ask whether Timon has more gold, and he snarls back:

> Enough to make a whore forswear her trade,
> And, to make whores, a bawd. Hold up, you sluts,
> Your aprons mountant. You are not oathable,
> Although I know you'll swear, terribly swear,
> Into strong shudders and to heavenly agues,
> Th' immortal gods that hear you. Spare your oaths;
> I'll trust to your conditions. Be whores still. . . .
>
> (IV, iii, 134–40)

Whores were proverbially forswearers. Here, however, Timon is not interested in the stock judgment. He has learned about the faith of men and now will use the worst of them in a fitting revenge.

His last misanthropic view of life includes a curse upon men and an injunction against any hollow oaths that these women will give up their trade. Although his misanthropy includes far more than his refusal to believe oaths, this speech shows very well the distrust that has replaced the faith and trust he exhibited in the opening acts. He accepts the attitude Derek Traversi saw in Apemantus' grace – a kind of rejection of humanity in himself and others.[7]

Lest the play end on a totally pessimistic note, Shakespeare does allow Alcibiades to relent toward Athens, although not toward his personal enemies. We never see him take the oath Timon urged, and there is in his final compromise a promise of the restoration of some honour to the city. He gives his glove, rather than an oath, as a token of his pledge that he will not plunder if the Senators open the gates to him. In the play so far, vows have often emphasised a lack of honour, coming from liars or servants. Something different is needed here, and to an object-oriented city, where the quality of the spirit was a small consideration, a glove seems more appropriate than words of honour.

By contrast, in *Coriolanus* oaths again became more personal and run the gamut from the exclamations of Coriolanus in his anger to the increasingly frequent comments about the oaths of others. Although 'faith' is occasionally used by a person as carefully delineated as Valeria or by one as quickly drawn as the Second Officer in II, ii, it could apply to pagans. There is an anachronistic "Sdeath' to greet the news that the people have tribunes. But the frame of reference is almost exclusively to Roman gods or, in Aufidius' case, to the elements. Again, the oaths are skilfully used to show tension, to support other elements of characterisation, and to aid in establishing a cosmological background for the action.

Coriolanus, as we might expect, is the most frequent user – a sort of Hotspur among the Romans, bursting out in anger or standing upon his honour. Of the roughly forty examples of or references to swearing, well over half concern him. There is almost a tenderness in his oaths as he talks to the women, fierceness as he follows his political or military course, and even sarcasm in his comment on 'my sworn brother, the people' (II, iii, 92). His range of oaths is far broader than one might expect from an essentially single-minded man, but at the same time completely in accord with his personality. There are no flowing phrases, but instead a reliance on either the visible, the actions important to him, or the gods one would expect to find in a Roman's frame of reference.

Aufidius points out that, if they chance to meet, he and Marcius are 'sworn between us we shall ever strike/Till one can do no more' (I, ii, 35–6). With this determination, it is not surprising that

Marcius is angry at the populace and their lack of prowess, or infuriated at their receiving power. That is a spineless action that 'By Jove himself,/. . . makes the consuls base!' (III, i, 107–8). He crowns a sweeping indictment of the system with the equally sweeping 'What may be sworn by, both divine and human,/Seal what I end withal!' (III, i, 141–2). His ensuing comments on 'double worship', with references to wisdom and ignorance, fit organically, though seemingly unconsciously, with the phrasing of the oath.

Earlier, the same ranging from divine to human comes in a series of outbursts. He curses the retreating Romans and exclaims, 'Pluto and hell!' in much the same way Hotspur would use 'Zounds!' Unlike Shakespeare's less powerful swearers, he can add a threat to the shrinking soldiers: 'by the fires of heaven, I'll leave the foe/And make my wars on you!' (I, iv, passim). Two scenes later, exhausted and bloody, he pleads for a fresh attack on Aufidius, although Cominius cannot share his determination to fight so recklessly. In an attempt to move the general, Marcius mentions their shared experiences and 'th' vows/We have made to endure friends' (I, vi, 57–8). When Corioles has been captured, there is a return to the exclamatory with his 'By Jupiter, forgot!' as he tries to recall the name of the captured citizen who had earlier offered him succour (I, ix, 89).

We notice the same variety in the third act, where he runs the gamut of simple oaths in another verbal attack on the people. He snarls at the tribunes, 'Why then should I be consul? By yond clouds,/Let me deserve so ill as you, and make me/Your fellow tribune' (III, i, 50–2). The sarcasm is not lost on Brutus and Sicinius, who have heard the same tone of voice before. Menenius, more politically accomplished, urges restraint, and a Senator ineffectually echoes the advice when Coriolanus counsels yielding nothing to the plebeians. He rejects the suggestion that he has spoken in choler and would change his opinion in a milder moment: 'Were I as patient as the midnight sleep,/By Jove, 'twould be my mind!' (III, i, 85–6). Coriolanus is positive enough in his speech patterns, but the oaths lend even more emphasis to his combination of rigidity and irascibility in this politically disastrous confrontation. One feels that he can even be impatient with his own oaths, finding Jupiter, fires of heaven, or clouds inadequate to match his exasperation, and turning to the more sweeping 'divine and human' witnesses.

Coriolanus, the oaken man who will be shattered rather than bend, is very much the child of Volumnia, who glories in his exploits, although she would be cleverer at dissembling until she had political power. One might expect her to set a pattern for her son's oaths, but Shakespeare allows her only a dismayed 'forsooth' (III, ii, 85). The result is that, although she is proud and strong-willed, she lacks some of the ultimate fierceness and stiffness that oaths help make apparent in Coriolanus. If she influenced his choice of words at all, it may have been by her reference to the mysteries of the gods and the heavens, and by a propensity to think of herself as Juno-like in her anger. In moments of stress, her son will think, too, of the gods and heavens as witnesses to his declarations. Valeria, attuned to Volumnia's way of thinking, is also limited to the mildest asseverations, with the exception of an 'on mine honour' as she registers her delight at heroic exploits. She is one of the few women who will think of this as an oath, and it is in keeping with her Roman values. By contrast, Virgilia's abstinence from even the mildest 'faith' helps emphasise the gentleness that differentiates her from the other women.

When we finally see them all together in the pleading scene, the tenderness of love, the pathos of the kneeling women, and the remembrance of family ties all seem to combine to produce a different selection of oaths from Coriolanus. Although aware of his vow to defeat Rome, he speaks softly to them and excuses breaking his vow. 'Those doves' eyes', he observes with misgivings, could 'make gods forsworn'. He is, after all, only human, despite the exaggerated nature of his feats. Virgilia's kiss draws another oath of his faith to her: 'Now, by the jealous queen of heaven, that kiss/I carried from thee dear; and my true lip/Hath virgined it e'er since' (V, iii, 46–8).

Again, his choice of words is appropriate to the situation – not Jove here, but Juno. Coriolanus is struggling not to be forsworn, but his mother's long speech turns him. Even Aufidius admits he was moved, and Coriolanus responds simply, but with characteristic positiveness, 'I dare be sworn you were' (V, iii, 194).

If we recall the vow Aufidius mentioned in the first act, we are not surprised to find that he is still sworn to destroy his enemy. The plebeians had hooted Coriolanus out of the city, calling him a traitor and implying that he had broken vows of allegiance to Rome. Now Aufidius will make the accusation that he breaks 'his oath and resolution like/A twist of rotten silk' (V, vi, 94–5). Aufidius' 'wrath or craft' will eventually overcome a man incapable of guile. The Volscian had once declared, 'By th' elements,/If e'er again I meet him beard to beard,/He's mine or I am his' (I, x, 10–12). In the last act he is conscious that his actions may be dishonourable, but uses his long-sworn enmity to justify his plotting.

Having taken pains with the oaths of his major characters, Shakespeare does not blur the focus by giving the Roman or Volscian populace any but the most mild and pedestrian phrases. Only Aufidius' servant is allowed a bit more bluster, including a *post facto* 'By my hand, I had thought to have strucken him with a cudgel' (IV, v, 150–1), a phrase that in an instant characterises the braggart who is faster with words than with actions. Others, from the Tribune Brutus to the Volscian watchman, speak of Coriolanus' oaths, either not to appear in the market-place, or not to relent and pardon the Romans, both of which are broken (II, i, 220–3; V, ii, 47–8). Coriolanus dominates the thoughts of the audience partly because he dominates the thoughts of so many other characters. The old friend, Menenius, who incidentally runs second in the number of oaths, demonstrates this focus. He will be sworn there is great news of Coriolanus' exploits, yet when he greets the victor he delares perceptively, 'by the faith of men,/We have some old crab-trees here at home that will not/Be grafted to your relish' (II, i, 177–9). When Coriolanus is banished, Menenius parts with a handclasp and a seemingly sincere regret that he is too old or, 'by the good gods, I'd with thee' (IV, i, 56–7). He never calls on specific gods, as Coriolanus does, and seems to prefer the more earthy human faith, which is completely in keeping with the rest of his speech. The result is that in oaths, as in other matters, Coriolanus stands out, and his vows are an appropriate part of his intransigence, explosiveness and sense of his own greatness. Were Shakespeare to give Menenius or Aufidius even half the number, he would in a small way undercut the dominance of his hero.

The romances continue to enjoy the advantages of the non-Christian setting, with *The Winter's Tale* depending on a Delphic oracle, *Cymbeline* in pre-Christian Rome and Britain despite the Renaissance Italy of the Iachimo scenes, and the collaborative *Pericles* storm-tossed around a pagan eastern Mediterranean. Even *The Tempest,* with most of the characters blown from Renaissance Italy, is isolated on an island where spirits in the guise of a harpy, Ceres and Juno make us forget momentarily the Christian cosmology that probably should be noted. In *The Two Noble Kinsmen,* Fletcher and Shakespeare have returned via Chaucer to ancient Greece. Obviously the collaborative works will show us less of Shakespeare's abilities to use oaths throughout a whole play, although they do demonstrate further how he could wield them in limited situations to help draw a character. We will focus on the works wholly by him, however, the better to understand this special aspect of his technique in the last years of his career.

In the romances, the tensions characters feel are presumably just as severe as those in the tragedies – the jealousy of Leontes, the anguish of Posthumus, the anger of Polixenes as his son elopes. But the demand for a happy ending seems to lead Shakespeare to present the emotions in a more quickly developed form, so that the sense of an irreversible downhill momentum is not so great. In addition, there seems to be such a multitude of characters and separate

incidents (*The Tempest* excepted structurally) that we are not allowed
to concentrate on one person as long as we would be in a tragedy.
When people die, we are not allowed to concentrate on reactions –
Antigonus' grisly end mingles with the discovery of Perdita. Finally,
there is often some reassuring early action or manifestation of
good, such as Prospero's assurance that the storm has harmed
no one, or the Doctor's care to give Cymbeline's queen a substitute
for the poison.

Under these circumstances, what use did Shakespeare make of
oaths? Again, as in the comedies, there might be a bit of satire of
fashionable pretension. There is occasional emphasis of a strong
feeling. In *The Winter's Tale* and *Cymbeline* there is more talk
about swearing, with oaths affirming one's steadfastness or truthful-
ness. Again, there is the detachment of having the lesser characters
talk about what the major figures have sworn. *The Tempest* is
relatively barren ground, for Prospero does not trust an oath when
it must compete with desire, and the others are mild, with only
Stephano giving an indication of profane potential. At times, what
we might expect is not there. Autolycus, who could well be the
casually swearing rogue criticised in pamphlets, does not swear to
the quality of his shoddy wares, and has only a scoffing line
about Trust as 'sworn brother' to Honesty (*The Winter's Tale*, IV,
iv, 589). Boult and Bawd in *Pericles*, despite their exasperation,
remain mild of oath. Cloten comes closer to the expected, as we
noted in the third chapter, and the Clown in *The Winter's Tale*
will provide some amusement as he learns to swear.

Cymbeline exemplifies the restraint that we find in the romances,
however, where Iachimo demonstrates the villain's ability to calculate
the effect of swearing, and Imogen underlines her distress in a mild
way. At the end of the play, King Cymbeline orders Iachimo
to give testimony about his treachery freely 'Or, by our greatness
and the grace of it,/Which is our honour, bitter torture shall/Winnow
the truth from falsehood' (V, v, 132–4). The testimony before the
King is the culmination of a series of oaths and perjuries that have
almost brought disaster to Imogen by destroying Posthumus' trust
in her. Iachimo had agreed 'By the gods' to play his part in the wager
(I, iv, 139). On his return to Rome with a 'token' of Imogen's
'faithlessness', he announces that he will 'confirm with oath' the
details of his visit. His 'By Jupiter', 'By my life' and 'I'll be
sworn' are used with calculation to convince Posthumus, whose
momentary doubts are allayed by the fact that Iachimo has sworn
by the king of the gods (II, iv, 64, 121, 136, 143). Remembering
that Imogen's attendants are 'sworn and honourable' and would not
steal her ring to do a stranger's bidding, Posthumus angrily dis-
parages 'the vows of women'. When Iachimo cleverly begins to

suggest doubts, he is adamant: 'No swearing./If you will swear you have not done't, you lie' (II, iv, 143–4). Posthumus himself does not swear in the play, but he is a man of such honour that a liar can count on his taking the vows of others very seriously. A cluster of oaths and references to them has worked to win the wager for Iachimo.

In the last act, Iachimo does tell the truth, and reforms so that he can appreciate Imogen as the truest princess 'That ever swore her faith' (V, v, 417). Although she occasionally swears, Imogen makes a good match for Posthumus, for she lacks the ability of comedy heroines to comment jokingly and satirically about the oaths of others. Disguised, she carries farther the serious note of Viola rather than the swashing pose of Rosalind. Shakespeare does not make her even a slightly fashionable swearer in her doublet and hose, nor a satiriser of lovers' vows.

Like Posthumus, she is not unaware of oaths. She tells Pisanio how her father had separated her from Posthumus ere 'I could make him swear/The shes of Italy should not betray/Mine interest and his honour' (I, iii, 28–30). Cloten, like Proteus, is spurned despite his serenading musicians and his avowals of continued devotion. 'Faith' and 'By th' very truth of it, I care not for you', almost her strongest expressions, underline her declaration of displeasure. This delicacy of oath is apparent even in her dismay at losing the bracelet, when she laments 'Shrew me/If I would lose it for a revenue/Of any king's in Europe,' a phrase Heilman glosses as a 'mild, polite oath' used merely for emphasis (II, iii, 142–4).[8]

Later, when accused of falsehood, she will join the number of women who charge men with perjury by bitterly exclaiming, 'Men's vows are women's traitors!', although she does not understand the truly traitorous reason behind his action (III, iv, 54). We see more of the mildness of her language when we compare her words in disguise with those of Belarius, whose contextually much stronger 'By Jupiter' merely emphasises his pronouncement that she is 'an angel'. Under the greater stress of awaking beside the headless body that she mistakes for Posthumus, she will only say 'Good faith'. Earlier, half-dazed, she had dreamily asked the distance and exclaimed, ''Od's pittikins, can it be six mile yet?' For accuracy's sake, Shakespeare should have invented some classical-sounding phrase or at least one taken from nature, and not resorted to this minced diminutive. But the form is unusual in his works, and comes almost always from a relatively gentle or helpless person. Old Gonzalo, in *The Tempest*, utters a similarly minced 'By'r Lakin' instead of 'By our Lady'. As pressures for court regulation grew stronger, more and more people in the streets may have been using the same phrases, just as Snout and Silence used them in

A Midsummer Night's Dream and *The Merry Wives of Windsor*. Both Gonzalo and Imogen are admirable figures, both at the moment distressed and exhausted by events. Imogen's utterance fits well with her speech, too, for a few lines later she will be asking for a bit of what little pity may be left in heaven.

As we scan the romances, we find other women swearing even less than Imogen. Cymbeline's queen, in all her evil, at least never additionally jeopardises her soul by uttering any oaths. It is only in *The Winter's Tale* that there is any comparison. As we saw earlier, women in the plays generally swear less, and seldom come up to Hotspur's standards. This is more than Shakespeare's own sense of appropriateness. Even in Plato's time there was a tradition of dsitinctive oaths for the different sexes, and it is said that 'These two great men [Demosthenes and Socrates] swore so freely that they exhausted the supply of oaths commonly used and had to borrow from the women. So "by Athena" was a favourite oath of Demosthenes, and "by Hera" of Socrates'.[9] Hazelwood assigned a milder, minced oath to his wife,[10] and Queen Elizabeth shocked many by not speaking in a 'ladylike' fashion. In the romances, 'faith' and 'I'll be sworn' seem generally to have been sufficient, even if the men were calling on pagan gods, their own lives, or heaven.

Only once does Shakespeare deceive the audience about a matter of death, and that is in *The Winter's Tale*, where we believe Paulina's report to Leontes. When this serious woman, who has already dared 'be sworn' about Hermione's innocence, later says she will swear to the death and challenges Leontes, 'If word nor oath/Prevail not, go and see,' we are convinced in the same way that other false swearers have convinced many characters (III, ii, 201–2).

The pattern of oaths in this play begins almost playfully as Hermione persuades Polixenes. 'I had thought, sir, to have held my peace until/You had drawn oaths from him not to stay,' she responds to Leontes, and challenges the visitor to swear he will leave (I, ii, 28–9). Her ensuing banter points out once again the shifting ground we are on in trying to determine just what was an oath at this time. A simple 'verily', probably on a par with 'forsooth', can be added to our list and recognised again in Anne Bullen's 'Verily/I swear' (*Henry VIII*, II, iii, 18–19).

Hermione: You'll stay? . . .
Polixenes: I may not, verily.
Hermione: Verily?
        You put me off with limber vows, but I,
        Though you would seek t'unsphere the stars with oaths,
        Should yet say, 'Sir, no going.' Verily. . . .

How say you?
My prisoner or my guest? By your dread 'Verily,'
One of them you shall be.

(I, ii, 44–56)

Despite her comment, Polixenes, whose strongest expression is 'By my white beard' when he learns of Florizel's wedding plans, here never swears, but merely accedes with great courtesy. Leontes' suspicions shatter her innocent delight, and Hermione is suddenly using an oath very seriously as with dignity she denies the accusation: 'No, by my life,/Privy to none of this.' Shakespeare has followed this pattern before with a shift from the bantering to a very serious regard for oaths, and we think of Hotspur's great emphasis on an oath of honour. Here, of course, the change is more precipitous. Camillo has reported that the self-infected Leontes, 'with all confidence . . . swears,/. . . that you have touched his queen/ Forbiddenly (I, ii, 412–15). In a play where the moon and planets are mentioned in other ways, Camillo, too, turns to the heavens as he tells of Leontes' intransigence.

> Swear his thought over
> By each particular star in heaven and
> By all their influences, you may as well
> Forbid the sea for to obey the moon
> As or by oath remove or counsel shake
> The fabric of his folly, whose foundation
> Is piled upon his faith.

(I, ii, 422–8)

Fewer than four hundred lines have passed since Hermione was persuading Polixenes, and for the moment nothing can convince Leontes of her innocence. With typical dignity, she will not resort to frantic oaths to try to defend herself, and her single 'by my life' later is appropriate when her life will soon apparently be sacrificed.

We are reminded fleetingly of *King Lear* as the court tries to persuade Leontes he is in error, but oaths he has sworn are only spoken of. The formal swearing in this play comes later, forming the third part of a pattern in the first three acts. Meanwhile, there are other pledges in support of Hermione, including Antigonus' on his honour to geld his innocent daughters if the charges prove true (II, i, 143–8). Two scenes later he must defend his own reputation, denying 'by this good light' that he is part of a nest of 'traitors'. His allegiance will soon be tested in a formal situation where he is commissioned to take Hermione's child to some 'desert place'. With the precipitous speed that has marked so much in the play, Leontes asks what he will venture 'To save this brat's life', and swears him on a sword to carry the child off. Despairingly, Antigonus responds, 'I swear to do this, though a present death/Had been more merciful' (II, iii, 183–4). Ironically, he is the one who will perish in the jaws of savage nature, and just before his death he recalls this scene, mentioned also by the Hermione of his vision, for he feels 'most accursed . . ./To be by oath enjoined to this' (III, iii, 29, 51–2).

Leontes ritualises his insistence on his correctness by staging the trial, with the Delphic Oracle's message to be delivered as the culmination of his condemnation. Preparation for the reading is formalised with another of the ritual vows common in Shakespeare, as the officer instructs Cleomenes and Dion to 'swear upon this sword of justice' that they have indeed been to Delphos, received the oracle from the priest, and brought it unopened to the court (III, ii, 123–9). They immediately swear and the seal is broken. The irony of having a 'sword of justice' at a patently unjust trial is followed by the irony that this carefully-prepared-for oracle will be declared 'mere falsehood' when, like Cordelia's response, it does not fit the ruler's plan.

The Winter's Tale has presented a pattern of oaths starting with the somewhat humorous, going to the serious, and ending in formalised ritual. The pattern will now be reversed as more serious oaths follow at the palace or in pastoral Bohemia, and then give way to some comic examples with the Clown-turned-gentleman. Earlier, a single 'marry' had sufficed for the young shepherd. But association with Perdita changes his status once her identity is revealed, and he is swept along to Sicily and given the surface appearance of rank. With costume comes changed behaviour. He announces he is now worthy to fight Autolycus, who had 'denied to fight . . . this other day' because he was 'no gentleman born', and suggest that Autolycus mend his life. When the rogue accedes, the Clown magnanimously declares: 'I will swear to the prince thou art as honest a true fellow as any is in Bohemia.' The old shepherd, less impressed with frivolities, advises, 'You may say it, but not swear it.' With this touch, Shakespeare has strengthened his portrayal of the conservative older man in contrast to his son, who argues:

Clown: Not swear it, now I am a gentleman? Let boors and franklins say it, I'll swear it.
Shepherd: How if it be false, son?
Clown: If it be ne'er so false, a true gentleman may swear it in the behalf of his friend. And I'll swear to the prince thou art a tall fellow of thy hands and that thou wilt not be drunk; but I know thou art no tall fellow of thy hands and that thou wilt be drunk. But I'll swear it.

                                                  (V, ii, 151–8)

Like the young gentlemen we spoke of in the third chapter, he hopes swearing will seem to make a truth. Shakespeare stops short of the welter of 'appropriate oaths' the Clown might have used, merely suggesting what this minor character has become. Had Jonson written the play, Autolycus would probably have taken the fool into training in a more fully developed satire. Totally missing from the Clown are the more threatening aspects that Cloten somewhat grotesquely assumes when he swears in turn to kill Pisanio, violate Imogen and kill Guiderius, vows that we hear about in detail only after his death. Cloten, although a more complicated figure, was too inept, too clownish to succeed as a villain, despite his genuine anger. With the young shepherd, however, Shakespeare has returned to the less complicated figure who merely apes fashion.

Just as Posthumus is a contrast to Cloten, so Florizel is the opposite of the Clown. He is not interested in surfaces, and would never, like the Clown or old shepherd, forswear himself out of fear (V, i, 199). His mild oaths and references to those he has sworn, both of faith to Perdita and of firm purpose to escape rather than break that faith, are concentrated in IV, iv, and elicit a response from homesick Camillo, on his honour, to send the young couple where they will be helped (IV, iv, 518).

Cymbeline and *The Winter's Tale* have virtually the same incidence of oaths or references to swearing, but the former shifts more randomly from the casual to the serious swearing, without the peak of formality that marks the latter. In neither does Shakespeare make full use of the pagan setting in choosing oaths, although in both, with the exception of "Od's pittikins' and an occasional 'marry', he avoids the anachronism of Emilia's 'God's Lid' in his part of *The Two Noble Kinsmen*, a phrase stronger than anything appearing in the other romances.[11]

There are a few phrases that should be noted, however, not because they are particularly important in these plays, but because Shakespeare employed them more frequently in the later plays while avoiding references to God or Christ. He had had some practice with them in earlier works, and one has only to recall Titus Andronicus' vow 'by my father's reverent tomb' (II, iii, 296), or the reference to maidenheads by Juliet's nurse. Often the oaths, although not so ingenious as Jonson's, fit more subtly into the text. The Jailer, sincerely puzzled by Posthumus' attitude toward death, will call his conscience to witness (*Cymbeline*, V, iv, 198-9). Earlier, Guiderius and Arviragus try to decide on a plan of action. Raised simply in the country, Arviragus declares 'By this sun that shines' that he will fight the Romans. Guiderius agrees to defy Belarius: 'By heavens, I'll go' (IV, iv, 34, 43). With a natural sense of honour and dignity impelling the boys, the sun and heavens are far more appropriate to them than the classically oriented 'By Jupiter' that came casually from Belarius, the former courtier. Furthermore, from what we have seen of Cloten and Iachimo, and what we hear from Belarius of the 'two villains, whose false oaths prevailed/ Before my perfect honour', we find little to recommend the faith of the court. By turning to nature, Shakespeare has found another subtle way of contrasting these upright boys who have respected and protected Imogen to those who lack true honour. One could continue the list with references to the honour of one's parents, one's own life or spirit, and other things in nature, but it would become a tedious catalogue. The important thing is that Shakespeare is using this linguistic resource effectively and more frequently now that there is a need to be religiously inoffensive.

Pericles, despite its authorial problems, follows the same principles as the other romances. Pander, Boult and Bawd, Marina and Lysimachus all use the 'marry' and 'faith' that were part of the average Jacobean's vocabulary. Pander and his friends seem most 'English' – figures who could easily swarm on to the scene of *Bartholomew Fair* or many other plays, though not so witty as Armin, for example, would have made them.[12] Although they, like Pompey in *Measure for Measure*, do little swearing, they comment not only on the sexual reform that Marina is working, but also on the astonishing fact that her goodness would turn swearers into priests (IV, vi, 11).

More in keeping with the distant setting, Gower, despite his medieval connotations, introduces an awareness of Diana, other gods and fortune, and with it a frame of reference for upper-class swearers. Thaisa becomes Diana's votaress and the goddess, in a vision, underlines her words with the singularly appropriate 'by my silver bow' (V, i, 249). After Cleon has vowed, with a self-curse, to take care of Marina, or 'The gods revenge it', Pericles responds 'By bright Diana' that he will not cut his hair until his daughter is married (III, iii, 24, 28). Earlier, in a part of the play perhaps not Shakespeare's, Simonides reported to the assembled knights that they might have no access to his daughter, for she had shut herself up for twelve months more in 'Diana's livery', adding, 'This by the eye of Cynthia hath she vowed,/And on her virgin honour will not break it' (II, v, 11–12). Simonides is putting words into his daughter's mouth, but they are appropriate to this woman, prized by knights, who will bear a daughter that is the epitome of maidenly modesty and take refuge in Diana's temple.

The restraint of those who use their oaths with care and devoutness contrasts to the overdone protestations of a weaker person, such as Cleon, whose wife points out the absurd lengths he will go to, as one 'that superstitiously/Doth swear to th' gods that winter kills the flies'

(IV, iii, 49–50). She knows he will yield to her murderous suggestions, despite his claims of innocence. Midway between the two is Leonine, repeatedly mindful of his pledge to kill Marina, but unhappy in the task and willing to perjure himself by reporting her death after the pirate raid (IV, i).

If we consider only\ the last three acts of the play, where credit is given unanimously to Shakespeare, we find little change in the incidence of oaths. 'Jove' and 'Juno', mentioned with mechanical appropriateness by Simonides in II, iii, have, however, given way to the more fitting Cynthia or Diana, who controls the last part of the play. Pericles indulges in some symbolic vows and becomes increasingly unkempt in keeping them. But there is not the focus Shakespeare often achieved with oaths concentrated in the mouths of major characters. The only pattern, in fact, is the tendency of the more noble people to speak of the pagan gods, while the lower class uses phrases common to Shakespeare's audience.

One yearns to find in *The Tempest* some culminating subtlety of pattern and use of oaths, but were this the only post-1606 play we might be tempted to assume that Shakespeare almost ceased to use oaths, or that he did not adapt to the law and his work was censored. There is another way of explaining part of the thinness, however, and it lies in the result of Prospero's control. The drunken Stephano, in no way attuned to Prospero's values, will threaten to punish Trinculo, will brag of his prowess in swimming, and will finally threaten to destroy Prospero. He uses trite, occasionally appropriate, occasionally ironic phrases: 'by this hand', 'by this light', 'on my honour'. Gonzalo, the man most admired by Prospero, seems opposed to oaths. He reminds us of the recovering Lear, for he will not swear as he wonders about the reality of Prospero's revelation. He even makes fun of the equally nonplussed Boatswain, who had evidently incurred his enmity with shipboard invective: 'Now, blasphemy,/That swear'st grace o'erboard, not an oath on shore?' (V, i, 218–19). Yet amazingly Gonzalo alone rivals Stephano in the number of oaths uttered, with a scattering of mild phrases to underline despair and uncertainty. It would be going too far to suggest that because Prospero, who does not trust oaths, so completely controls the play there is little swearing. Despite the fact that this control removes much of the dramatic tension, characters themselves are under great stress. But our attention focuses on Prospero, not on any developed anguish of Ferdinand or Alonso. As a result of his magic, the only thing that many of the people can swear to is their puzzlement. Ferdinand does aver 'as I am a man' that he is no usurper, and he will later declare sincerely 'As I hope/For quiet days, fair issue, and long life' that his love for Miranda will not become lust (I, ii; IV, i, 23–4). But Prospero affects to believe neither statement, warning the young man that 'the strongest oaths are straw/To th' fire i' th' blood. Bc more abstemious,/Or else good night your vow!' (IV, i, 52–4). In the formality of the masque, Iris echoes Prospero's thoughts by emphasising that this man and maid have vowed 'that no bed-right shall be paid/Till Hymen's torch be lighted' (IV, i, 96–7).

Control is the key in the play, and casual swearing does not fit with it. Even Caliban, in his frustration and anger, does not dilute his curses with oaths, in the same way that Margaret's curses in *Richard III* were allowed to stand out. Prospero, narrating his past history, might have sworn a bit to underline his anger, but he uses only direct statements. In many of the scenes of the play, in fact, emotion is shown briefly, and our attention is on some aspect of magic, rather than on the character reacting to it. Emotions tend to become formalised and distanced.

The Tempest most probably dates from 1611; *Henry VIII* seems to be the product of 1613; *The Two Noble Kinsmen*, so authorially problematical that it is omitted from most modern editions, apparently falls close to *Henry VIII*. In *The Two Noble Kinsmen*, we are back in pagan Greece, and with a plot that centres on the emotions of two young men. Theseus, in a passage probably by Fletcher, can exclaim approvingly and appropriately of Palamon and Arcite, 'By th' helm of Mars, I saw them in the war' (I, iv, 17). Later, when both men are desperately in love with a woman seen from afar, the shackled Palamon angrily declares, 'By all oaths in one/I, and the justice of my love, would make thee/A confess'd traitor!' (III, i, 33–5). As he continues to listen to Arcite's flowing words, Palamon becomes more exasperated, wishing he were free so that 'By this air,/I could for each word give a cuff' (III, i, 103–4). Theseus later calls upon Castor as witness (III, vi, 136).

But neither Shakespeare not Fletcher makes full use of the possibilities to swear by the old gods, or to derive oaths from the particular surroundings. Although Mars and Venus preside over the final combat, the feeling of the play, with its tourney and knightly courtesy, is medieval. One unimportant oath, Cicely's 'by wine and bread', is remarkable in showing a blend by having the elements that suggest the mass but make no specific religious reference (III, v, 47). As in many of the late plays, the most interesting oaths are unimportant, and the sense of increasing tension, reinforced by sworn declarations, is missing except for that third-act outburst by Palamon, and the continuation of the conflict into the fourth scene. Even there, the phrases are trite and seem less forceful than they did in III, i. Formality suffuses the end of the play, and promises are made with elaborate courtesy. There are no casual or fashionable swearers and, except for the frenzy of the Jailer's Daughter, all those emotions that might have continued to be sponstaneously expressed are quickly pushed by Theseus into the mould of formal combat.

It is with some delight that we turn finally to *Henry VIII*, despite its problem of attribution. It may have presented a challenge to its authors, for it is set in almost contemporary England, yet embraces themes of honour and allegiance, with people under pressure, that would require the sort of oaths used in the pre-1606 chronicle histories. Like *Richard II*, *Henry VIII* lacks the glimpses of lower life that provided a contrast in the *Henry IV* plays. Jonson, showing that stratum of English society, was at liberty to create a 'by St George, the foot of Pharoah', or mincing phrases such as 'S' deynes' or 'slud',[13] which Falstaff and his cronies never needed to explore. But most of these phrases will hardly do for the nobility who are swearing seriously, rather than fashionably individualising their oaths. Nor, evidently, did Shakespeare feel it was appropriate for King Henry to use the 'Jupiter' suitable in the religiously hazy world of *King Lear*. (Classical gods are not part of the history-play vocabularies.) Indeed, Richard III's references to St Paul are almost the only oaths on a proper name not God's or Christ's in this group of plays. The English nobles will turn to God, or to those lesser phrases about faith, the mass, or the Virgin that refer to their Christian religion.

In *Henry VIII* the pattern is not changed significantly, despite legal pressures, as characters react to arrests, trials and other political manoeuvrings with suitable outbursts. The play, in fact, has more oaths or references to swearing than any of the other later works, and almost half of them occur in the six scenes definitely attributable to Shakespeare.[14] 'Zounds' and ''Sblood' do not appear, of course, but Shakespeare succeeds in creating a sense of King Henry's explosiveness without them. In fact, despite the authorial uncertainties of the play, we get a good final sense of the way Shakespeare concentrated a series of oaths to help give one person a dominance and a positiveness that are lacking in others. Of course, Henry is king, his word is law, and he can be mercurial in his commands and attitudes. Even without the oaths, this would be apparent. But expletives give him an increased decisiveness, helping to draw his character a bit more memorably.

Before the pattern is established, Shakespeare emphasises the honour of others. The Duke of Buckingham's surveyor pawns his soul to affirm, with questionable honesty, that he has heard his master utter oaths to the detriment of Cardinal Wolsey. The Duke, in turn, had accused Wolsey of buying and selling his honour (I, ii, and I, i). Political factions begin to become obvious.

While the men strive for power, Anne Bullen and an Old Lady reminiscent of the Nurse in *Romeo and Juliet* have a rather comic exchange as the Old Lady doubts Anne's declaration that 'Verily' it is 'better to be lowly born' than to have to suffer as Queen Katherine has.

Ann: By my troth and maidenhead,
                I would not be a queen.
Old Lady: Beshrew me, I would,
                And venture maidenhead for't; and so would you. ....

The argument continues as Anne shrugs off an accusation of hypocrisy:

Anne: I swear again, I would not be a queen
                For all the world.
Old Lady: In faith, for little England
                You'ld venture an emballing.
                                                    (II, iii, 23–47)

We, like the first audience, know how quickly Anne will yield to Henry's dominant personality, and see the irony of her protestation combined with the *double-entendre* sexual allusions of the Old Lady who quite frankly sees the temptations that will arise. With this introduction, incidentally, we are not surprised that the Old Lady insists 'By this light, I'll ha' more!' as her tidings of Elizabeth's birth produce a reward she considers too small (V, i, 171). The exchange is a typically Shakespearian concentration on oaths that stands out above the occasional 'faith' or 'On my conscience' that anonymous men use to react to events in a series of non-Shakespearian passages. But even it pales by comparison with the use of oaths to reinforce the portrait of a domineering and self-centred king whose attitudes and declarations provide turning-points for the plot.

What chance has Buckingham, no matter how false the evidence, when his sovereign has ended the scene with the emphatic tag-lines, 'By day and night,/He's traitor to th' height!' (I, ii, 213–14)? Later, defending Cranmer, he will note how easy it is to procure perjuries, but here the thought seems not to have crossed his mind. Earlier, he had cut Katherine off with 'By my life,/This is against our pleasure' (I, ii, 67–8). He will frequently call upon his honour or his position as he underlines his declarations or heightens his exclamations of impatience. Like Leontes, Henry is so firmly set upon his course that nothing will deter him, although he insists that if the marriage is proven lawful, 'by my life/And kingly dignity, we are contented' (II, iv, 224–5). With a characteristic reference to himself, he declares that the tearfully grateful Cranmer is 'honest on mine honour! God's blest mother, I swear he is true-hearted' (V, i, 153–4).

These are exempla of a whole series of oaths that usually stop just short of the legal boundaries. Changes in his position will be accompanied by the same sense of declaration, and many simple statements will gain a degree of asperity because they are embellished with an oath.

The mercurial actions of one character again beget responses of like strength. Henry's decisions lead others to swear that Anne's disclaimer of ambition was innocence or meaningless determination. Katherine, being cast aside, calls upon heaven and her conscience to witness her faithfulness. In a scene not attributed to Shakespeare, she emphasises the seriousness of perjury, especially in one so near death, as she vows the virtue of her waiting women (IV, ii).

Despite problems of authorship, *Henry VIII* is, for our purposes, more satisfactory than many of the last plays which are wholly Shakespeare's, and especially *The Tempest*, where there is no authorial problem. There is obviously a planned use of oaths in the scenes that fit the metrical tests of Shakespeare's later style, and far less pattern in the scenes attributable to the collaborating hand. It is the technique that we first glimpsed in *The Taming of the Shrew* and *Richard III*, with a focus on one person to emphasise his character and the result of his actions.

In these last eleven plays we have seen not the simple 'toning down' of oaths that Hazelton Spencer noted when he wrote of the *Richard III* texts,[15] but a full-blown compliance with the regulations.[16] Occasionally there is a phrase that does not show the 'fear and reverence' required when one is mentioning 'the holy name of God or of Christ Jesus', and there may have been a few cuts. But so much slips through into the Folio texts of the earlier plays that it seems unlikely that these later works would be as consistently in keeping with the law had not Shakespeare himself adapted his writing. Occasionally he will let the audience supply their own examples, as Jolenta does in *The Devil's Law-Case*: 'I do call any thing to witness/That the divine law prescribed . . ./To strengthen an oath.'[17] But he did this also in *As You Like It*. More often, he has the advantage of being explicit in a non-Christian world. The shock value might not have been so great as for ''Sblood' or 'Zounds', but to an audience attuned to the subtleties of imagery, and as practised in listening as many Jacobeans were, the seriousness of the phrases would soon have been apparent. After all, it is not the oath by itself, but swearing in context with the many other facets of the plays that creates the effectiveness.

Notes

INTRODUCTION

1 E. R. C. Brinkworth, *Shakespeare and the Bawdy Court of Stratford* (London: Phillimore, 1972).

2 Keith Thomas has an excellent section on cursing in *Religion and the Decline of Magic* (London: Weidenfeld & Nicolson, 1971).

3 Renatus Hartogs and Hans Fantel, *Four-Letter Word Games: The Psychology of Obscenity* (New York: Dell, 1968), p. 12.

4 Samuel Johnson, 'Preface' to *The Plays of William Shakespeare* (1765), in *Samuel Johnson on Shakespeare*, ed. W. K. Wimsatt, Jnr (New York: Hill & Wang, 1960), p. 34.

5 Marvin Spevack, *A Complete and Systematic Concordance to the Works of Shakespeare*, 8 vols (Hildesheim: Georg Olms Verlagsbuchhandlung, 1968–75).

6 *The Comedy of Errors, The Two Gentlemen of Verona, As You Like It* and *Twelfth Night* were first printed in the Folio, as were the later *All's Well that Ends Well* and *Measure for Measure. The Taming of the Shrew* and *The Merry Wives of Windsor* can also be added to the list if one discounts the 'Bad' Quartos.

7 John S. Farmer, notes to *Six Anonymous Plays*, Second Series (London: Early English Drama Society, 1906), p. 426. Although a random opening is usually rewarding, pp. 145–56 are especially valuable.

CHAPTER 1. THE MOUTH-FILLING OATH

1 *Henry IV, Part One*, in William Shakespeare, *The Complete Works*, general editor Alfred Harbage (Baltimore: Penguin Books, 1969), III, i, 245–54. All quotations and line references, unless otherwise noted, are from this edition. The spelling has been anglicised.

2 R. C. Gent, *The Times' Whistle or A Newe Daunce of Seven Satires*, ed. J. M. Cowper (London: Early English Text Society, 1871), satire 2, 11. 733–5.

3 Randle Cotgrave, *A Dictionarie of the French and English Tongues* (London, 1611), n.p.

4 Martin Mar-Prelate (John Penry?), 'An Epistle to the Terrible Priests of the Convocation House', in *Puritan Discipline Tracts*, ed. John Petheram (London, 1842), pp. 6, 4.

5 Julian Sharman, *A Cursory History of Swearing* (London: Nimmo & Bain, 1884), p. 105.

6 Jonson, *Every Man In His Humour* (1601), I, iii, 55–77, shows Cob most aware of what Bobadilla has taught him. The speech is in I, iv, in the 1616 Folio.

7 Roger Ascham, *The Scholemaster*, ed. Edward Arber (Boston: D. C. Heath, 1910), p. 114.

8 Samuel Rid, *Martin Mark-All, Beadle of Bridewell, His Defence and Answere to the Belman of London* (London, 1610), sig. D1.

9 Ibid., sig. C4.

10 *As You Like It*, II, vii, 150; *Henry IV, Part Two*, IV, v, 124.

11 G. L. Hosking, *The Life and Times of Edward Alleyn* (London: Cape, 1952), p. 80.
12 Richard Bernard, *The Isle of Man; or The Legall Proceeding of Man-Shire Against Sinne* (London, 1627), p. 27.
13 Hesiod, *Works and Days*, trans. Dorothea Wender (Baltimore: Penguin Books, 1973), p. 67, 11. 280–4.
14 Alexander Nowell, *A Sword Against Swearers and Blasphemers* (London, 1611), sig. A1v.
15 Ibid., sig. A4v.
16 Ibid., sig. C8v.
17 Ibid., sig. E2v. Sig. E is completely devoted to such examples.
18 Thomas Adams, *The Gallants Burden, A sermon Preached at Paules Crosse* (London, 1612), p. 16.
19 Babington on the Ten Commandments, quoted in the appendix to the forewords of Phillip Stubbes, *Anatomy of the Abuses in England in Shakespeare's Youth*, ed. F. J. Furnivall (London: N. Trübner for the New Shakespeare Society, 1877–82), pt 1, p. 82*.
20 *Al-Man-Sir or, Rhodomontados of the Most Horrible Terrible and Invincible Captain Sr Fredrick Fight-all* (London, 1672), p. 36. The French translation dates from 1607 and the English from 1630.
21 James P. Malcolm, *Anecdotes of the Manners and Customs of London from the Roman Invasion to the year 1700* (London, 1811), p. 75.
22 Thomas Adams, 'The Sinners Passing-bell' and 'Englands Sicknesse', in *Works* (London, 1630), pp. 261–2, 320.
23 Robert Boyle, *A Free Discourse Against Customary Swearing and A Dissuasive from Cursing* (London, 1695), p. 48.
24 Babington on the Ten Commandments, p. 116.
25 Boyle, *Discourse*, p. 93.
26 Andrew Boorde, *A Dyetary of Helth*, ed. F. J. Furnivall (London: N. Trübner for the Early English Text Society, 1870), p. 243.
27 *Hay any-worke for Cooper, being a reply to the Admonition to the People of England* (London, 1845; reprint of a fragment of *c.* 1589), p. 8. The press seems to have been seized before the work was completed, and few of the fragmentary tracts circulated.
28 Andrew Gurr, *The Shakespearean Stage, 1574–1642* (Cambridge: Cambridge University Press, 1970), p. 141.
29 G. B. Harrison, *A Second Jacobean Journal* (Ann Arbor: University of Michigan Press, 1958), p. 126.
30 'Damning Blasphemy', *Time Magazine*, 16 May 1969, p. 72. The statute specified a fine of twenty-five cents for the first word and fifty cents for each additional one.
31 Boyle, *Discourse*, pp. 99–113 passim.
32 Gerald D. Nokes, *A History of the Crime of Blasphemy* (London: Sweet & Maxwell, 1928), pp. iv, 14.
33 Sharman, *Cursory History*, p. 31.
34 Sharman notes that a Quartermaster Bowtholmey had his tongue bored with a hot iron, and was then discharged, in 1649 (p. 129).
35 Nowell, *Sword Against Swearers*, sig. D4v. The Scottish Parliament under Mary, in 1551, fixed penalties, and William Dunbar, in 'The Sweirers and the Devill', writes 'A prelate of Kirk, earl, or Lord' would be fined twelve pence for the first offence, and banished or imprisoned for a year at the fourth occurrence. (See Sharman, *Cursory History*, p. 120.)
36 Nokes, *History of the Crime*, p. 20, citing R. V. Bysett.
37 E. R. C. Brinkworth, *Shakespeare and the Bawdy Court of Stratford* (London: Phillimore, 1972), pp. 122, 128.

38 *Quarter Sessions Records for the County of Somerset*, vol. I (James I – 1607–25), ed. E. H. Bates, Somerset Record Society Publications no. 23 (n.p., 1907), pp. 3, 96.
39 *North Riding Record Society, Quarter Session Records*, ed. J. C. Atkinson (London, 1884), vol. I, p. 65.
40 A. H. A. Hamilton, *Quarter Sessions from Queen Elizabeth to Queen Anne* (London: Sampson, Low, 1878), p. 154.
41 Sharman, *Cursory History*, p. 130.
42 Brinkworth, *Bawdy Court*, p. 149.
43 Sharman, *Cursory History*, p. 130.
44 *State Papers Domestic* for 1595, p. 12, cited in Sharman, *Cursory History*, pp. 118–19. It is an interesting coincidence that *A Midsummer Night's Dream*, remarkably free from oaths except for the satiric fun made of fashionable swearing, may have been performed in this same year for the wedding of Burghley's granddaughter, Lady Elizabeth Vere.
45 Sharman, *Cursory History*, p. 124.
46 Frederick Chamberlin, *The Sayings of Queen Elizabeth* (London: John Lane, 1923), p. 121.
47 Ben Jonson, *Every Man In His Humour* (London, 1601), I, i, 156, 170, in *Ben Jonson*, ed. C. H. Herford and Percy Simpson (Oxford: Clarendon Press, 1927), vol. 3.
48 Chamberlin, *Sayings of Queen Elizabeth*, p. 292. Chamberlin adds more instances in *The Private Character of Queen Elizabeth* (London: John Lane, 1921).
49 Nathan Drake, *Shakespeare and His Time*, vol. 2, p. 160, quoted in Sharman, *Cursory History,* p. 97 n.
50 George Peele, *The Old Wives Tale*, ed. Frank S. Hook, in *Life and Works*, 3 vols. (New Haven, Conn: Yale University Press, 1970), vol. 3, 1. 76.
51 E. K. Chambers suggests that 'it is conceivable that the personal taste of James may have required a similar revision of plays selected for Court performances at an earlier date' (*The Elizabethan Stage* (Oxford: The Clarendon Press, 1923), vol. 3, p. 360).
52 Nokes, *History of the Crime*, p. 19.
53 21. Jac. 1. c. 20. (1623).
54 Joannes Ferrarius, *A Woorke of Joannes Ferrarius Montanus Touchynge The Good Orderynge of a Common Weal*, Englished by William Bavande (London, 1559), ff. 52, 53.
55 Boyle, *Discourse*, pp. 4–9.
56 Christopher Hill, *Society and Puritanism in Pre-Revolutionary England* (London: Secker & Warburg, 1964). Chapter 11 is devoted to oaths as rites.
57 Nowell, *Sword Against Swearers*, sig. C5v.
58 Boyle, *Discourse*, pp. 27–8.
59 Ibid., pp. 122–3.
60 Gervaise Babington, *A Verie fruitfull Exposition of the Commandements by way of Questions and Answers* (London, 1590), pp. 118, 113–14.
61 Thomas Elyot, *The boke named the Governour* (London, 1531); John Earle, *Micro-Cosmographie* (London, 1628); Thomas Lupton, *All for Money* (London, 1578): all cited by A. R. Humphreys in Shakespeare, *Henry IV, Part One*, New Arden Edition (London: Methuen, 1966), note on II, i.
62 Sharman, *Cursory History*, p. 93. It is retained in the Folio *Romeo and Juliet* when Capulet utters it in III, 5, 177.
63 Noel Perrin, *Dr Bowdler's Legacy* (New York: Atheneum, 1969), ch. 4.
64 Quoted in Virginia Gildersleeve, *Government Regulation of the Elizabethan Drama* (New York: Columbia University Press, 1908), p. 128.
65 Chambers, *Elizabethan Stage*, vol. 1, p. 303.
66 Gildersleeve, *Government Regulation*, p. 112.

67 Chambers, *Elizabethan Stage*, vol. 1, p. 322.
68 British Museum Lansdowne MS. 807. Folios 34, 37 and 37*v* (which has marks on two-thirds of its length) are most heavily censored.
69 3. Jac. 1. c. 21., cited in Nokes, *History of the Crime*, p. 125.
70 Sharman, *Cursory History*, pp. 125–6.
71 Boyle, *Discourse*, pp. 31–2. It is a practice still noted by Arthur Bedford a century after Shakespeare: 'They change the Letter, and keep to the Meaning . . . and therefore are in this respect as guilty of the Sin as such who never mince the matter.' Arthur Bedford, *Serious Reflections On the Scandalous Abuse and Effects of the Stage* (Bristol, 1705), p. 25.
72 *Hamlet*, IV, v, 61. Nicholas Breton, 'The Toyes of an Idle Head' (1577–82), in *Works in Verse and Prose*, ed. Rev. Alexander B. Grosart (Edinburgh: Chertsey Worthies Library, 1879), vol. 1, p. 30. John S. Farmer and W. E. Henley, *Slang and Its Analogues* (London, 1890), p. 370. The phrase may have come from J. H. S., although Ritson suggests a reference to St Gisela. *Hamlet: A New Variorum Edition*, ed. H. H. Furness (Philadelphia: J. B. Lippincott, 1877), vol. 1, p. 334. In both *Misogonus* and *Godly Queen Hester* it is used by a man.
73 Eric Partridge does note a use with sexual overtones from the time, but says such use is more common in the eighteenth century (*A Dictionary of Slang and Unconventional English* (New York: Macmillan, 1961)).
74 Farmer, *Slang*, p. 347; *A merry and pleasant Comedie called Misogonus*, ed. John S. Farmer, in *Six Anonymous Plays*, Second Series (London: Early English Drama Society, 1906), IV, i, p. 227.
75 Farmer, *Slang*, p. 335. Nicholas Breton, *A Mad World My Masters and Other Prose Works*, ed. Ursula Kentish-Wright (London: Cresset Press, 1929), vol. II, 14 n.
76 Babington, *Exposition of the Commandements*, pp. 117, 112.
77 Ibid., p. 112.
78 Boyle, *Discourse*, pp. 28–9.
79 Ibid., pp. 29–32.
80 Stubbes, *Anatomy*, pp. 131–3.
81 Ibid., pp. 133–4.
82 Robert Crowley, *Of Blasphemous Swerers*, in *Select Works*, ed. J. M. Cooper (London: Early English Text Society, 1872), pp. 18–19.
83 Stubbes, *Anatomy*, p. 131.
84 Babington, *Exposition of the Commandements*, pp. 113–15.
85 Nicholas Breton, *The Good and the Badde, or Descriptions of the Worthies, and Unworthies of this Age* (London, 1616), p. 18, character 25.
86 Ben Jonson, *The Alchemist* (London, 1612).
87 Breton, *The Good and the Badde*, pp. 20–4, characters 27, 31.
88 R. C., *The Times' Whistle*, ll. 1946–7, 2054–5.
89 Hill, *Society and Puritanism*, p. 399, quoting Overbury, *Crumms fal'n from King James Table*, in *Miscellaneous Works*, p. 257.
90 Boyle, *Discourse*, pp. 23–6.
91 Nowell, *Sword Against Swearers*, sig. C1.
92 Ferrarius, *Good Orderynge of a Common Weal*, ff. 134, 136.
93 R. C. *The Times' Whistle*, ll. 669–80.
94 Thomas Dekker, *The Seven Deadly Sinnes of London*, quoted in William P. Holden, *Anti-Puritan Satire, 1572–1642* (New Haven, Conn: Yale University Press, 1954), p. 56.
95 *How a Man may Choose a Good Wife from a Bad*, in Robert Dodsley's *A Select Collection of Old English Plays*, ed. W. C. Hazlitt (London, 1874; reprinted New York: Benjamin Blom, 1964), vol. 4, p. 62 (III, iii).
96 Ben Jonson, *Bartholomew Fair*, ed. C. H. Herford, Percy Simpson, and Evelyn

Simpson (Oxford: The Clarendon Press, 1938), vol. 6, p. 17 (Induction, 11. 149–52).

97 Stubbes, *Anatomy*, p. 145. Similar arguments are advanced in Gosson's *School of Abuse* and Babington's *Exposition of the Commandements*.

98 *Romeo and Juliet*, I, iii, 2.

99 William Averell, *A mervailous combat of contrarieties* (London, 1588), sig. A1v. There is a similarity between this dialogue, with its parable-like plea for order in the realm, and Menenius' fable in *Coriolanus*, although here the problem is not dissident workers but Papists.

100 Robert Armin, *Fools and Jesters: with a reprint of R. Armin's Nest of Ninnies*, introduction and notes by J. Payne Collier (London: Shakespeare Society, 1913), p. 40.

101 *Wily Beguiled*, in Hazlitt's Dodsley, Blom reprint, vol. 4, pp. 369, 304.

CHAPTER 2. OATHS AS STRUCTURE

1 Charles Cowden Clarke commented on the number of repetitions of similar words used by Constance in the first sixty-two lines of the scene (*The Shakespeare Key* (London, 1879), p. 629).

2 Frederick Chamberlin, *The Sayings of Queen Elizabeth* (London: John Lane, 1923), p. 5.

3 Arnold Oskar Meyer, *England and the Catholic Church* (London: Kegan Paul, Trench, Trübner, 1916), pp. 79, 285, 358–70.

4 *Part 1*, 11. 1007–9 (scene v), *Narrative and Dramatic Sources of Shakespeare*, ed. Geoffrey Bullough (New York: Columbia University Press, 1962), vol. 4, p. 99.

5 Toby Lelyveld, *Shylock on the Stage* (Cleveland: Western Reserve University, 1960); and Marlowe, *The Jew of Malta*, ed. Richard Van Fossen (Lincoln: University of Nebraska, 1964), p. xvii.

6 Harley Granville-Barker, *Prefaces to Shakespeare, Second Series* (London: Sidgwick & Jackson, 1930), pp. 93, 97.

7 Ibid., pp. 102–4.

8 George Santayana, *Interpretations of Poetry and Religion* (New York: Charles Scribner's Sons, 1924), p. 148. Santayana goes on to liken them to 'pebbles tossed about in the unconscious play of expression. The lighter and more constant their use, the less their meaning.'

CHAPTER 3. FASHIONABLE SWEARING

1 Congreve later pointedly stated that laughter is properly directed at those exaggerated qualities over which a person has some control. Although insanity could be an object of amusement, Jonson and others speak of their plays as criticisms of the foibles of society. William Congreve, 'Concerning Humour in Comedy', in *Comedies*, ed. Bonamy Dobrée (Oxford: University Press, 1925). Jonson, prologues to *The Alchemist* and *Volpone*, ed. C. H. Herford and Percy Simpson, vol. 5 (Oxford: The Clarendon Press, 1937).

2 *Hyck Scorner*, in *Specimens of Pre-Shakespearean Drama*, ed. J. M. Manly (Boston: Ginn, 1897).

3 *Youth*, in *Six Anonymous Plays*, Second Series, ed. John S. Farmer (London: Early English Drama Society, 1906).

4 Nicholas Udall, *Ralph Royster Doyster*, in *Tudor Plays*, ed. Edmund Creeth (New York: W. W. Norton, 1966), I, i, 36.

5 Plautus, *Miles Gloriosus, The Braggart Warrior*, trans. Paul Nixon (Loeb Classical Library, Cambridge, Mass.: Harvard University Press, 1950), vol. 3. The oaths tend to be mainly by Heracles.

6 Ben Jonson, *Every Man In His Humour*, Quarto (London, 1598), E4.

7 Ben Jonson, *Every Man Out of His Humour*, Quarto (London, 1604), 12*v*.

8 Barnaby Rich, *The Honestie of This Age* (London, 1614).

9 Philip Stubbes, 'Supplication to Henry VIII', in *Four Supplications, 1554* (London: Early English Text Society, 1871), p. 53.

10 Roger Ascham, *The Scholemaster*, ed. Edward Arber (London, 1897), p. 54.

11 Robert Boyle, *A Free Discourse Against Customary Swearing and A Dissuasive from Cursing* (London, 1695), p. 37.

12 Philip Stubbes, *Anatomy of the Abuses in England in Shakespeare's Youth*, ed. F. J. Furnivall (London: N. Trübner for the New Shakespeare Society, 1877–82), pp. 132–3.

13 Richard Brathwayte (Brathwaite), *Loves Labyrinth or The True-Lover's Knot* (London, 1615), E2.

14 Joannes Ferrarius, *A Woorke of Joannes Ferrarius Montanus, Touchynge The Good Orderynge of a Common Weale*, Englished by William Bavande (London, 1559), f. 136*v*.

15 Barnaby Rich, *The Fruites of Long Experience* (1604), pp. 32–3, quoted in Gert Geoffrey Langsam, *Martial Books and Tudor Verse* (New York: King's Crown Press, 1951), p. 109.

16 Hazelton Spencer, introductory note to *Every Man In His Humour*, in *Elizabethan Plays* (New York: D. C. Heath, 1936), p. 254.

17 To avoid confusion, I shall generally use the better-known character-names from the Folio.

18 Jonson, *Every Man In His Humour* (Folio), in Spencer, II, v, 17–23.

19 Jonson, *Every Man In His Humour*, Quarto, C2*v*.

20 Quoted in Julian Sharman, *A Cursory History of Swearing* (London: Nimmo & Bain, 1884), p. 38.

21 John Russell Brown, *Shakespeare and His Comedies*, 2nd ed. (London: Methuen, 1964); H. B. Charlton, *Shakespearian Comedy* (London: Methuen, 1961).

22 H. H. Furness, *Twelfth Night: A New Variorum Edition* (Philadelphia: J. B. Lippincott, 1901), p. 80 n. Furness points out that in *Othello*, II, i, there is also a reference to 'the vouch of very malice it self'.

23 Robert Heilman, introduction to *Cymbeline*, in Shakespeare, *The Complete Works* (Baltimore: Penguin Books, 1970), p. 1292.

24 Nathaniel Field, *Amends for Ladies* (1618), quoted in Sharman, *Cursory History*, p. 56.

25 The same sort of interchange was taking place much later, in Thomas Jordan's *Wealth out-witted*, where Featherbrain, a prodigal, has sworn his love for Felicina, and she rejects his oath, going a bit farther in her accusation: 'Think you after your fluent prodigality . . . to undo some weak ey'd Virgin, by your vows and Oaths. . . . Indeed, I will not take your oath' (*Wealth out-witted* (London, n.d.), pp. 20–1).

26 Shakespeare, *The First Sketch of Shakespeare's Merry Wives of Windsor*, ed. James Orchard Halliwell (London: New Shakespeare Society, 1842), p. 48.

27 *Jack Drum's Entertainment*, ed. John S. Farmer, Tudor Facsimile Texts (London: 1912), D1–D1*v*.

28 Ben Jonson, *The Case Is Altered* (London, 1609), G4*v*.

29 *The first part of the True and honorable history of the Life of Sir John Old-Castle, the good Lord Cobham* (London, 1600), p. B1*v*. (Priests and curates in general are called 'Sir', so with Hugh Evans or Sir John there is no question of knighthood.)

30 *The Taming of A Shrew*, ed. F. S. Boas (New York: Duffield, 1908), induction, ii, and I, i, 326.

31 Richard Hosley, introduction to *The Taming of the Shrew*, in Shakespeare, *The Complete Works* (Baltimore: Penguin Books, 1969), p. 80.

32 Jonson, *Every Man In His Humour*, Quarto, D2, G1*v*, E2*v*, E3, G2.
33 Ibid., C3*v*, G2.
34 Ibid., E1*v*–E2.
35 *How a Man may Choose a Good Wife from a Bad*, in Robert Dodsley's *A Select Collection of Old English Plays*, ed. W. C. Hazlitt (London, 1874; reprinted New York: Benjamin Blom, 1964), vol. 4, p. 35 (II, iii).
36 David, Lord Barry (Lording Barry), *Ram Alley*, ed. John S. Farmer, Tudor Facsimile Texts (London: 1913), G–G2. The piece was acted by children.
37 Daniel C. Boughner, *The Braggart in Renaissance Comedy* (Minneapolis: University of Minnesota Press, 1954).
38 Sharman, *Cursory History*, p. 106.
39 Boughner, *The Braggart*, p. 168.
40 Gospel According to St Matthew, 5: 37.
41 Shakespeare, *Henry IV, Part Two*, ed. R. P. Cowl, Arden Shakespeare (London: Methuen, 1923).
42 Sir Thomas Elyot, *The Governour*, quoted in E. K. Chambers, *The Elizabethan Stage* (Oxford: The Clarendon Press, 1923), vol. 1, p. 239.
43 Whether Shakespeare was responsible for the additions, we will probably never know; the Quarto is, after all, a corrupt text. They do demonstrate the fact that oaths were considered an integral part of dialectal speech, as Shakespeare also showed with Dr Caius' French accent.
44 *Literary Remains of Edward VI*, ed. J. G. Nichols (London, 1857), quoted in Sharman, *Cursory History*, p. 97.
45 Richard Brathwaite, *A Strappado for the Divell:* Epigrams and Satyrs alluding to the time, with divers measures of no lesse Delight (London, 1615), pp. 64, 53.
46 George Chapman, *May-Day* (London, 1611).
47 *The Swearing-Master, or, A conference between Two Country-Fellows Concerning The Times* (London, 1681).

CHAPTER 4. OATHS OF AIR AND OF HONOUR

1 Joannes Ferrarius, *A Woorke of Joannes Ferrarius Montanus, Touchynge The Good Orderynge of a Common Weale*, Englished by William Bavande (London, 1559), ff. 136–136*v*. Perkins spoke similarly: 'For when all other humane proofes doe faile, then it is lawfull, to fetch testimonie from heaven. . . . In this case alone, and never else, it is lawfull to use an Oath.' William Perkins, *The Whole Treatise of the Cases of Conscience* (Cambridge, 1608), p. 179.
2 'The distressed Virgin', no. 1 in a collection of thirty-three seventeenth-century *Ballads* in the British Museum.
3 *A New English Dictionary*, ed. James A. H. Murray (Oxford: The Clarendon Press, 1905). West, listing offences, calls perjury a 'Slaunder against God', and defines it as any 'lie affirmed by oathe'. William West, *The Second Part of Symboleography* (London, 1611), pp. 87–8.
4 Thomas Adams, 'Plaine Dealing', *The Sacrifice of Thankefulnesse* (London, 1616), p. 22.
5 Richard Bernard, *The Isle of Man; or The Legall Proceeding of Man-Shire Against Sinne* (London, 1627), pp. F2–F2*v*.
6 David, Lord Barry (Lording Barry), *Ram Alley*, ed. John S. Farmer Tudor Facsimile Texts (London: 1913), p. B4. *The Swearing-Master: or, A conference between Two Country-Fellows Concerning The Times* (London, 1681), p. 3.
7 Richard Brathwaite, *A Strappado for the Divell: Epigrams and Satyrs alluding to the time, with divers measures of no lesse Delight* (London, 1615), pp. 41–3. Nicholas Breton expressed similar distrust in 'Wit and Private Wealth' when he noted that swearing and lying had become common and therefore 'so little believed I wonder they do not leave it' *(Works in Verse and Prose*, ed. Rev.

Alexander B. Grosart (Edinburgh: Chertsey Worthies Library, 1879), vol. 2, p. 6).

8 Gervaise Babington, *A Verie fruitfull Exposition of the Commandements by Way of Questions and Answers* (London, 1590), pp. 112, 135. Henry Parrott, *Laquei ridiculosi: or Springes for Woodcocks* (London, 1613), no. 143.

9 See Chapter 1. Alexander Nowell, *A Sword Against Swearers and Blasphemers* (London, 1611), p. C5v.

10 Babington, in his *Exposition of the Commandements*, pointed out that under civil law an infidel might swear by his own gods. The emphasis is on finding an object the swearer respects (p. 118).

11 Jonson, *The Poetaster* (London, 1602), p. L4. In *Every Man In His Humour*, Thorello has doubts about Piso's reluctance to swear, and finally about 'whether his oath be lawfull', deciding to 'ask counsel ere I do proceed' (*Every Man In His Humour* (London, 1598), pp. F2v–F3).

12 Joseph Hall, *Characters of Vertues and Vices* (London, 1608), p. 75.

13 Julian Sharman noted that Quakers and Puritans often opposed oaths of piety and statecraft because they were so closely allied with those of malice (*A Cursory History of Swearing* (London: Nimmo & Bain, 1884), p. 34).

14 Although not dealing with these oaths to any extent, Fredson Bowers gives much background on the sense of honourable obligation that revengers feel in a wide range of plays (*Elizabethan Revenge Tragedy, 1587–1642* (Princeton: Princeton University Press, 1940)).

15 *The Two Gentlemen of Verona, A Midsummer Night's Dream, As You Like It*.

16 Sharman, *Cursory History*, p. 96.

17 We must remember that, like the majority of the comedies, *The Two Gentlemen of Verona*, *As You Like It* and *Twelfth Night* are only in the Folio, while *Cymbeline* is post-1606. *The Merchant of Venice*, whose Quarto would have escaped the censor, shows the disguised Portia in a court scene, where any casual swearing would be out of keeping with her role as the young and serious lawyer, and the attention must be focused on Shylock's vows.

18 William W. Lawrence, *Shakespeare's Problem Comedies* (New York: Macmillan, 1931), examines this test in the context of wider literary convention.

19 Nicholas Breton, 'The Court and the Country', in *A Mad World My Masters and Other Prose Works*, ed. Ursula Kentish-Wright (London: Cresset Press, 1929), vol. 1, p. 189.

20 Oscar James Campbell, *Shakespeare's Satire* (London: Oxford University Press, 1943), and *Troilus and Cressida: A New Variorum Edition*, ed. Harold N. Hillebrand (Philadelphia: J. B. Lippincott, 1953), point out the irony of Cressida's vows.

21 Richard Whitford, *A Werke for householders, or for them that have the guyding or gouvernaunce of any company* (London, 1537), p. Ciiv, regards this sort of oath to a person in power as particularly binding.

22 Henry Hitch Adams, *English Domestic or Homiletic Tragedy, 1375–1642* (New York: Benjamin Blom, 1971), p. 24.

23 Francis Beaumont, *The Knight of the Burning Pestle*, in *Elizabethan Plays*, ed. Hazelton Spencer (New York: D. C. Heath, 1936), II, i, 58–9.

24 Geoffrey Chaucer, *Troilus and Criseyde*, in *The Poetical Works of Chaucer*, ed. F. N. Robinson (Boston: Houghton Mifflin, 1933), bk 4, ll. 1541–7.

25 Ibid. Jove, Venus, and Cupid are named in bk 3, ll. 150, 186–7.

26 *Richard II*, III, iii, 105–20. The tomb over Edward III's bones, the mutual royalties of their bones, 'the buried hand of warlike Gaunt', and his 'worth and honour' are all cited as part of Bolingbroke's pledge.

27 Joseph Hall, *The Lawfulness and Unlawfulness of an Oath or Covenant* (Oxford, 1643), p. 94.

CHAPTER 5. OATHS AND TRAGIC TENSION

1 This line appears only in the First Quarto (III, vii, 220).
2 Although it was a tradition that Richard used it, G. Wilson Knight points to the paradox of the un-Christian Richard swearing by Paul (*The Sovereign Flower* (London: Methuen, 1966), p. 26).
3 Quotations are from *Hamlet*, ed. Willard Farnham, in Shakespeare, *The Complete Works* (Baltimore: Penguin Books, 1969), unless otherwise noted.
4 *Hamlet: A New Variorum Edition*, ed. H. H. Furness (Philadelphia: J. B. Lippincott, 1877), vol. 1, pp. 112–13. Julian Sharman in his *A Cursory History of Swearing* (London: Nimmo & Bain, 1884), pp. 26–7, notes the military origin of oaths, saying that the sword was eventually consecrated. *The Winter's Tale: A New Variorum Edition* also has a note on the oath taken on the sword by a Master of Defence when his degree was conferred (p. 111, quoting Halliwell). In *The Spanish Tragedy* Lorenzo makes Pedringano swear on a sword, and threatens to use it on him if he has told an untruth (Thomas Kyd, *The Spanish Tragedy*, ed. Charles T. Prouty (New York: Appleton-Century-Crofts, 1951), II, i, 87–93). There is a perversion of this sort of oath when Falstaff says Glendower 'swore the devil his true liegeman upon the cross of a Welsh hook' (*Henry IV, Part One*, II, iv, 321–2).
5 Benno Tschischwitz, quoted in *Hamlet: A New Variorum Edition*, vol. 1, p. 111.
6 Loc. cit.
7 Marvin Spevack, *A Complete and Systematic Concordance to the Works of Shakespeare*, vol. 5 (Hildesheim: Georg Olms Verlagsbuchhandlung, 1970), p. 2599.
8 *Hamlet: A New Variorum Edition*, vol. 1, p. 111.
9 Renatus Hartogs and Hans Fantel, *Four-Letter Word Games: The Psychology of Obscenity* (New York: Dell, 1968).
10 Edward Strachey, *Shakespeare's Hamlet: An Attempt to find the Key to a Great Moral Problem* (London: J. W. Parker, 1848), quoted in *Hamlet: A New Variorum Edition*, vol. 1, pp. 266–7.
11 *The First and Second Prayer Books of King Edward the Sixth* (London: J. M. Dent, 1920), p. 407. *Mucedorus* also has references to picking and stealing with the same assumption of audience recognition (I, iv, 128; IV, ii, 56).
12 John Marston, *The Scourge of Villanie* (1599), ed. G. B. Harrison, Elizabethan and Jacobean Quartos (New York: Barnes & Noble, 1966 [reprint of 1925 ed.]), satire VII.
13 Marvin Rosenberg, *The Masks of Othello* (Berkeley: University of California Press, 1961), p. 47.
14 Robert B. Heilman, *Magic in the Web* (Lexington: University of Kentucky Press, 1956), p. 20, citing George Rylands, *Words and Poetry* (New York: Payson & Clarke, 1928), p. 163; Heilman, pp. 116–17, 106 and 39.
15 Alice Walker, *Textual Problems of the First Folio* (Cambridge: The University Press, 1953), p. 31.
16 Ibid., p. 142.
17 Heilman points out that even here there is an organic quality. 'His oath, "by the faith of man,/I know my price" (1, 1, 10–11) might seem a random one but for the fact that it occurs in a context in which he compares Cassio to a "spinster" (24), sneers at "Many a duteous and knee-crooking knave" (45), and decrees a treatment for the type, "whip me such knaves!" (49)' (*Magic in the Web*, p. 108).
18 E. E. Stoll pointed to this as he noted various ways Iago worked on Othello's imagination, in *Othello: An Historical and Comparative Study* (New York: Haskell House, 1964 [reprint of 1915 ed.]), p. 21.
19 William Warburton, quoted in *Othello: A New Variorum Edition*, ed. H. H. Furness (Philadelphia: J. B. Lippincott, 1886), p. 35.

20 George Steevens, quoted in *Othello: A New Variorum Edition*, p. 60.
21 Heilman, *Magic in the Web*, pp. 18, 192.
22 Ibid., p. 142.
23 R. Grant White, in 1861, said that this was a playhouse emendation, made for the sake of rhythm, not from scruples, although Malone and others attribute it to the censor (*Othello: A New Variorum Edition*, p. 153).
24 Oaths and other statements included, *Othello* and *Hamlet* have more references to heaven than any of the other tragedies, with *Romeo and Juliet* a distant third.
25 William Empson comments on this word-choice: 'Othello swears *by the world* because what Iago has said about being honest in the world, suggesting what worldly people think, is what has made him doubtful' ('Honest in Othello', in *The Structure of Complex Words* (Norfolk, Conn.: New Directions, n.d.), p. 225).
26 Heilman, *Magic in the Web*, p. 68.

CHAPTER 6. IN RESPONSE TO CENSORSHIP

1 E. K. Chambers, *The Elizabethan Stage* (Oxford: The Clarendon Press, 1923), vol. 1, pp. 275, 283.
2 Ibid., vol. 3, p. 169.
3 Jonson, *Bartholomew Fair*, 'Induction', *Works*, ed. William Gifford (London: Routledge, Warne & Routledge, 1860), pp. 306–7.
4 Alexander Nowell, *A Sword Against Swearers and Blasphemers* (London, 1611), pp. B6, C1.
5 Despite Sir Thomas Browne's doubts, the theory of spontaneous generation was held well into the seventeenth century.
6 *Antony and Cleopatra*, ed. Maynard Mack, in Shakespeare, *The Complete Works* (Baltimore: Penguin Books, 1969), p. 1169.
7 Derek Traversi, *An Approach to Shakespeare* (New York: Doubleday, 1969), vol. 2, p. 173.
8 *Cymbeline*, ed. Robert B. Heilman, in Shakespeare, *The Complete Works* (Baltimore: Penguin Books, 1969), p. 1306.
9 Plato, *Gorgias*, ed. E. R. Dodds (Oxford: Clarendon Press, 1959), p. 195.
10 cf. 'Fashionable Swearing', note 20.
11 Shakespeare and Fletcher, *The Two Noble Kinsmen*, ed. George Lyman Kittredge, in *Complete Works of Shakespeare* (Boston: Ginn, 1938), V, iii, 97.
12 Robert Armin, *The History of the two Maids of More-clacke*, in *Works*, ed. Rev. Alexander B. Grosart, in Occasional Issues of Unique or Very Rare Books, Vol. 14 (Manchester, 1880).
13 Jonson, *Every Man in His Humour*, in *The Workes of Beniamin Jonson* (London, 1616), p. 15.
14 The scenes generally accepted without question as Shakespeare's are I, i and ii; II, iii and iv; III, ii, 1–203; and V, i.
15 Hazelton Spencer, *The Art and Life of William Shakespeare* (New York: Harcourt, Brace, 1940), p. 165.
16 See E. K. Chambers, *Elizabethan Stage*, vol. 1, p. 277, for additional comments on this aspect of Puritan opposition to the theatres.
17 John Webster, *The Devil's Law-Case* (London, 1623), pp. F3v–F4.

Bibliography

The Bibliography has been divided into primary and secondary sources. Dates for the primary works are given in square brackets if they are appreciably earlier than those of the editions used. Brief comments indicate either the focus or the applicability of the secondary material.

PRIMARY SOURCES

Adams, Thomas:
   The Gallants Burden, A sermon Preached at Paules Crosse. London, 1612.
   The Sacrifice of Thankefulnesse, Sermon of December 3, 1615. London, 1616.
   Works. London, 1630.
Al-Man-Sir or, Rhodomontados of the Most Horrible Terrible and Invincible Captain Sr Fredrick Fight-all. London, 1672.
Armin, Robert:
   Fools and Jesters: with a reprint of R. Armin's Nest of Ninnies. Edited by J. Payne Collier. London: Shakespeare Society, 1913 [1608].
   The History of the two Maids of More-clacke, With the life and simple maner of John in the Hospitall. London, 1609.
   The Works of Robert Armin, actor. Edited by the Rev. Alexander B. Grosart. Occasional Issues of Unique or Very Rare Books, vol. 14. Manchester: C. E. Simms, 1880 [*c*. 1600].
Ascham, Roger. *The Scholemaster*. Edited by Edward Arber. London, 1897, and Boston: D. C. Heath, 1910 [1570].
Averell, William:
   A Dyall for dainty Darlings; A Glasse for all disobedient Sonnes; A Myrrour for vertuous Maydes. London, 1584.
   A mervailous combat of contrarieties. London, 1588.
Babington, Gervaise:
   A Verie fruitful Exposition of the Commandements by way of Questions and Answers. London, 1590.
   The Ten Commandments, 1588. New Shakespeare Society Transactions, 1877–9, Part 1. London, 1879.
Ballads. London, British Museum collection of thirty-three seventeenth-century ballads, black-letter, with woodcuts.
Barry, David, Lord [Lording Barry]. *Ram Alley*. Edited by John S. Farmer. Tudor Facsimile Texts. London, 1913 [1611].
Bates, The Rev. E. H. (ed.). *Quarter Sessions Records for the County of Somerset*. Vol. 1, 1607–25. N.p., 1907.
Bedford, Arthur. *Serious Reflections On the Scandalous Abuses And Effects of the Stage*. Bristol, 1705.

Bernard, Richard. *The Isle of Man; or The Legall Proceeding of Man-Shire Against Sinne.* London, 1627.

The Bible. Edited by the Rev. C. I. Scofield. New York: Oxford University Press, 1917.

Bicknoll, Edmond. *A Swoord agaynst swearyng.* London, 1579.

Boorde, Andrew. *A Dyetary of Helth.* Edited by F. J. Furnivall. London: N. Trübner for the Early English Text Society, 1870 [1547].

Boyle, Robert. *A Free Discourse Against Customary Swearing and A Dissuasive from Cursing.* London, 1695.

Brathwayte (Brathwaite), Richard:
Barnabae itinerarium: Barnabees journall. London: Penguin Press, 1933 [1638].
Loves Labyrinth or The True-Lovers Knot. London, 1615.
A Strappado for the Divell: Epigrams and Satyrs alluding to the time, with divers measures of no lesse Delight. London, 1615.

Breton, Nicholas:
The Good and the Badde, or Descriptions of the Worthies, and Unworthies of this Age. London, 1616.
A Mad World My Masters and Other Prose Works. 2 vols. Edited by Ursula Kentish-Wright. London: The Cresset Press, 1929 [1635].
Works in Verse and Prose. Edited by the Rev. Alexander B. Grosart. 2 vols. Edinburgh: Chertsey Worthies Library, 1879.

Bullough, Geoffrey (ed.). *Narrative and Dramatic Sources of Shakespeare.* 8 vols. New York: Columbia University Press, 1957–75.

C., R., Gent. *The Times' Whistle or A Newe Daunce of Seven Satires.* Edited by J. M. Cowper. London: Early English Text Society, 1871.

Chapman, George. *May-Day.* London, 1611.

Chaucer, Geoffrey, *Troilus and Criseyde,* in *The Poetical Works of Chaucer.* Edited by F. N. Robinson. Cambridge, Mass.: Houghton Mifflin, 1933 [1482].

Congreve, William. *Comedies.* Edited by Bonamy Dobrée. Oxford: Oxford University Press, 1925.

Cotgrave, Randle. *A Dictionarie of the French and English Tongues.* London, 1611.

Crowley, Robert. *Select Works: Epigrams, etc.* Edited by J. M. Cowper. Early English Text Society Extra Series, no. 15. London, 1872 [c. 1550].

Dekker, Thomas. *The Seven Deadly Sinnes of London.* London, 1606.

Earle, John. *Micro-Cosmographie.* London, 1628.

Elyot, Thomas. *The boke named the Governour.* London 1531.

The Famous Victories of Henry the fifth. London, 1617 [1598].

Farmer, John S. (ed.). *Six Anonymous Plays.* Second Series. London: Early English Drama Society, 1906.

Ferrarius, Joannes. *A Woorke of Joannes Ferrarius Montanus, Touchynge The Good Orderynge of a Common Weale.* Englished by William Bavande. London, 1559.

Field, Nathaniel. *Amends for Ladies, With the merry prankes of Moll Cut-Purse.* London, 1639.

The First and Second Prayer Books of King Edward the Sixth. London: J. M. Dent, 1920.

The first part of the True and honorable history of the Life of Sir John Old-Castle, the good Lord Cobham. London, 1600.

Gosson, Stephen. *The School of Abuse.* Edited by J. Payne Collier. Shakespeare Society Publications, no. 2. London, 1841 [1579].

Hall, Joseph:
Characters of Vertues and Vices, in *Works.* Edited by J. Pratt. Vol. 6. London, 1808 [1608].
The Lawfulness and Unlawfulness of an Oath or Covenant. Oxford, 1643.
The Remedy of Prophanenesse. London, 1637.

Hamilton, A. H. A. *Quarter Sessions from Queen Elizabeth to Queen Anne.* London: Sampson, Low, 1878.

Harington, John. *Epigrams Both Pleasant and Serious.* London, 1615.

Hawes, Stephen. *The Conversyon of Swerers.* Edinburgh: The Abbotsford Club, 1865 [1509].

Hay any-worke for Cooper, being a reply to the Admonition to the People of England. London, 1845.

Hesiod. *Works and Days.* Translated by Dorothea Wender. Baltimore: Penguin, 1973 [*c.* 700 B.C.].

How a Man may Choose a Good Wife from a Bad, in Robert Dodsley's *A Select Collection of Old English Plays.* Edited by W. Carew Hazlitt. London, 1874. Reprint New York: Benjamin Blom, 1964. Vol. 4 [1602?].

Howgil, Francis. *Oaths no gospel ordinance but prohibited by Christ.* London, 1666.

Hyck Scorner, in *Specimens of Pre-Shakespearean Drama.* Edited by J. M. Manly. Boston: Ginn, 1897 [1510?].

Jack Drum's Entertainment. Edited by John S. Farmer. Tudor Facsimile Texts. London, 1912.

Johnson, Samuel. *Samuel Johnson on Shakespeare.* Edited by W. K. Wimsatt, Jnr. New York: Hill & Wang, 1960.

Jonson, Ben:
The Alchemist. London, 1612.
Bartholomew Fair, in *Works.* Edited by William Gifford. London: Routledge, Warne & Routledge, 1860 [1614].
Ben Jonson. Edited by C. H. Herford, Percy Simpson and Evelyn Simpson. 11 vols. Oxford: Clarendon Press, 1925–52.
The Case is Altered. London, 1609.
Every Man in his Humour. London, 1598, 1601.
Every Man out of His Humour. London, 1604.
The Poetaster. London, 1602.
The Workes of Beniamin Jonson. London, 1616.

Jordan, Thomas:
A Cure for the Tongue-Evill Or, a Receipt against Vain oaths. London, 1662.
Wealth out-witted or, Money's an Ass. London, n.d. [1668?].

Kyd, Thomas. *The Spanish Tragedy.* Edited by Charles T. Prouty. New York: Appleton-Century-Crofts, 1951 [1592].

Lupton, Thomas. *All for Money.* London, 1578.

Marlowe, Christopher. *The Jew of Malta.* Edited by Richard Van Fossen. Lincoln: University of Nebraska Press, 1964 [1594].

Marston, John. *The Scourge of Villanie*. London, 1598.

Martin Mar-Prelate [John Penry?]. 'An Epistle to the Terrible Priests of the Convocation House', in *Puritan Discipline Tracts*. Edited by John Petheram. London, 1842 [1589?].

Mucedorus, in *The Shakespeare Apocrypha*. Edited by C. F. Tucker Brooke. Oxford: The Clarendon Press, 1971 [1598].

A New English Dictionary. Edited by James A. H. Murray. 20 vols. Oxford: The Clarendon Press, 1888–1928.

Nichols, J. G. (ed.). *Literary Remains of Edward VI*. London, 1857.

North Riding Record Society: Quarter Session Records. Edited by J. C. Atkinson. Vols. 1 and 2. London, 1884.

Northbrooke, John. *A treatise against Dicing, Dancing, Plays and Interludes*. Edited by J. P. Collier. Shakespeare Society Publications vol. 14. London, 1843 [1577?].

Nowell, Alexander. *A Sword Against Swearers and Blasphemers*. London, 1611.

Parrott, Henry. *Laquei ridiculosi: or Springes for Woodcocks*. London, 1613.

Partridge, Eric. *A Dictionary of Slang and Unconventional English*. New York: Macmillan, 1961.

Peele, George. *Life and Works*. Edited by Frank S. Hook. 3 vols. New Haven: Yale University Press, 1970.

Perkins, William. *The Whole Treatise of the Cases of Conscience*. Cambridge, 1608.

Plato. *Gorgias*. Edited by E. R. Dodds. Oxford: Clarendon Press, 1959 [c. 375 B.C.].

Plautus. *Miles Gloriosus, The Braggart Warrior*. Translated by Paul Nixon. Loeb Classical Library. Cambridge, Mass.: Harvard University Press, 1950 [c. 200 B.C.].

Porter, Henry. *The Pleasant Historie of the two angrie women of Abington*. London, 1599.

Powell, Walter. *A Summons for Swearers, and a law for the lips in reproving them*. London, 1645.

Prynne, William. *Histrio-Mastix: The Players Scourge*. London, 1633.

The Puritaine Or the Widdow of Watling-street. London, 1607.

Rich, Barnaby. *The Honestie of This Age*. London, 1614.

Rid, Samuel. *Martin Mark-All, Beadle of Bridewell, His Defence and Answere to the Belman of London*. London, 1610.

S., Mr, Master of Art. *Gammer Gurton's Needle*, in *Medieval and Tudor Drama*. Edited by John Gassner. New York: Bantam, 1971 [1560?].

The Second Maiden's Tragedy. British Museum Lansdowne MS. 807 [1611].

Shakespeare, William:

   The Complete Works. General editor Alfred Harbage. Baltimore: Penguin, 1969.

   A New Variorum Edition of Shakespeare. Edited by Horace Howard Furness, *et al*. 26 vols. Philadelphia: J. B. Lippincott 1871–1953.

   The First Sketch of Shakespeare's Merry Wives of Windsor. Edited by James Orchard Halliwell. London: The New Shakespeare Society, 1842 [1602].

   Henry the Fourth, Part One. Edited by A. R. Humphreys. New Arden Edition. London: Methuen, 1966 [1597].

Henry the Fourth, Part Two. Edited by R. P. Cowl. The Arden Shakespeare. London: Methuen, 1923 [1598].

and Fletcher, John. *The Two Noble Kinsmen,* in *The Complete Works of Shakespare.* Edited by George Lyman Kittredge. Boston: Ginn, 1938 [1613].

Sherman, John. *A True Relation of the Lewd Life and Repentant Death of one John Sherman.* London, 1641.

Spencer, Hazelton, (ed.). *Elizabethan Plays.* New York: D. C. Heath, 1936.

Statutes: An Acte to Restraine Abuses of Players. 3. Jac. I c. 21 (27 May 1606).

Stubbes, Phillip:
Anatomy of the Abuses in England in Shakespeare's Youth. Edited by F. J. Furnivall. Parts 1 and 2. The New Shakespeare Society, Series 6. London: N. Trübner, 1877–82 [1583].

'Supplication to Henry VIII'. *Four Supplications, 1554.* London: Early English Text Society, 1871.

The Swearing-Master, or, A conference between Two Country-Fellows Concerning The Times. London, 1681.

The Taming of A Shrew. Edited by F. S. Boas. New York: Duffield, 1908 [1594].

Taylor, John. *The Nipping or Snipping of Abuses.* London, 1614.

The Troublesome Raigne of John, King of England. London, 1591.

The True Tragedy of Richard Duke of Yorke. London, 1594.

Udall, Nicholas. *Ralph Royster Doyster,* in *Tudor Plays.* Edited by Edmund Creeth. New York: W. W. Norton, 1966 [1550?].

Webster, John. *The Devil's Law-Case.* London, 1623.

Whitford, Richard. *A Werke for householders, or for them that have the guyding or gouvernaunce of any company.* London, 1537.

Wily Beguiled. London, 1635 [1606].

Wither, G. *Abuses Stript and Whipt; or, Satirical Essayes, etc.* London, 1613.

SECONDARY SOURCES

Adams, Henry Hitch. *English Domestic or Homiletic Tragedy, 1575–1642.* New York: Benjamin Blom, 1971. Of minimal use for the specific study of oaths, it is thorough on the whole spectrum of drama that tried to teach moral lessons.

Aydelotte, Frank. *Elizabethan Rogues and Vagabonds.* Oxford Historical and Literary Studies, vol. 1. Oxford: The Clarendon Press, 1913. Although not helpful on language-use, it gives a broad view of those whom others show swearing.

Boland, Daniel and Sawyer, Bernard Henry. *Oaths and Affirmations.* London: Stevens, 1953. With its focus on the use of oaths in the British courts over the years, it provides some helpful legal background.

Boughner, Daniel C. *The Braggart in Renaissance Comedy.* Minneapolis: University of Minnesota Press, 1954. A thorough treatment of braggarts and their antecedents, it pays more attention to other aspects of language than to swearing.

Bowers, Fredson. *Elizabethan Revenge Tragedy, 1587–1642.* Princeton:

Princeton University Press, 1940. The standard study of such plays, it ranges widely but pays virtually no attention to oaths of revenge.

Brinkworth, E. R. C. *Shakespeare and the Bawdy Court of Stratford*. London: Phillimore, 1972. A gleaning from court records, it gives a broad perspective on what was punished, including examples of swearing.

Brown, John Russell. *Shakespeare and His Comedies*. 2nd ed. London: Methuen, 1964. A broad study with no specific treatment of swearing, it provides interesting insights against which to examine a particular element of the comedies.

Campbell, Oscar James. *Shakespeare's Satire*. New York: Oxford University Press, 1943. Although with little about oaths, it provides background on verbal satire.

Chamberlin, Frederick:
The Private Character of Queen Elizabeth. London: John Lane, 1921.
The Sayings of Queen Elizabeth. London: John Lane, 1923.
Both books give detailed reports, from contemporary records of all sorts, of the Queen's utterances, and include many oaths.

Chambers, E. K. *The Elizabethan Stage*. 4 vols. Oxford: The Clarendon Press, 1923. A basic study, it includes an excellent section on censorship.

Charlton, H. B. *Shakespearian Comedy*. London: Methuen, 1961. Like Brown's book, it ranges widely, although there is some attention to language and an occasional reference to an oath.

Clark, Eleanor Grace. *Elizabethan Fustian*. Vol. 1. New York: Oxford University Press, 1937. There is less than one might expect on oaths, with the focus on ranting.

Clarke, Charles Cowden and Clarke, Mary Cowden. *The Shakespeare Key*. London: S. Low, Marston, Searle & Rivington, 1879. A series of comments of varying worth on separate passages, it has a few relevant remarks on oaths.

'Damning Blasphemy'. *Time Magazine*, 16 May 1969, p. 72. A brief segment on what is considered blasphemous is combined with a summary of some attempts to control profanity.

Empson, William. 'Honest in Othello', in *The Structure of Complex Words*. Norfolk, Conn.: New Directions, n.d. The concentration on one word sheds light on the way Iago manipulates Othello and others.

Farmer, John S. and Henley, W. E. *Slang and Its Analogues*. London: privately printed, 1890. A useful and specific treatment, it is rich in examples as well as commentary.

Gildersleeve, Virginia C. *Government Regulation of the Elizabethan Drama*. New York: Columbia University Press, 1908. A seminal book, it has excellent broad coverage and specific examples.

Granville-Barker, Harley. *Prefaces to Shakespeare. Second Series*. London: Sidgwick & Jackson, 1930. Like all the *Prefaces*, this treats action and characters closely, with an eye to the theatre.

Gurr, Andrew. *The Shakespearean Stage, 1574–1642*. Cambridge: Cambridge University Press, 1970. A broad overview, it does touch on the theatre's reputation for disorder and encouragement of vice that the Puritans fostered.

Harrison, G. B. *A Second Jacobean Journal*. Ann Arbor: University of Michigan Press, 1958. A detailed picture of things that would have interested Jacobeans, it is created from records of the period.

Hartogs, Renatus and Fantel, Hans. *Four-Letter Word Games: The Psychology of Obscenity*. New York: Dell, 1968. The parts dealing with profanity are brief, but the psychological background is widely applicable.

Heilman, Robert B. *Magic in the Web*. Lexington: University of Kentucky Press, 1956. Although not dealing with oaths, it provides a broad and thorough study of *Othello*, with emphasis on Iago as manipulator that is good background for studying the oaths.

Hill, Christopher. *Society and Puritanism in Pre-Revolutionary England*. London: Secker & Warburg, 1964. Some specific treatment of oaths and swearing is strengthened by good background on the attitudes that led to censorship.

Holden, William P. *Anti-Puritan Satire, 1572–1642*. New Haven, Conn.: Yale University Press, 1954. Of very limited value concerning oaths, it shows how many Englishmen responded to Puritan complaints.

Hosking, G. L. *The Life and Times of Edward Alleyn*. London: Cape, 1952. Although focusing on Alleyn, it gives details about attitudes toward theatres and actors.

Johnson, Burges. *The Lost Art of Profanity*. Indianapolis: Bobbs-Merrill, 1948. Wide-ranging, it adds little to Sharman's account of the Elizabethan and Jacobean periods.

Knight, G. Wilson. *The Sovereign Flower*. London: Methuen, 1966. Although concentrating on plays of kingship, Knight includes treatment of *All's Well that Ends Well*, and works closely with word-use in ways that can be extended to swearing.

Langsam, Gert Geoffrey. *Martial Books and Tudor Verse*. New York: King's Crown Press, 1951. While saying little about profanity, it does show how soldiers and military matters were represented.

Lawrence, William W. *Shakespeare's Problem Comedies*. New York: Macmillan, 1931. Fitting *All's Well that Ends Well*, *Measure for Measure* and *Troilus and Cressida* into a wide framework of literary convention, it provides excellent background for a study of action and character.

Lelyveld, Toby. *Shylock on the Stage*. Cleveland: Western Reserve University, 1960. A broad survey, its early pages suggest Elizabethan responses to Shylock.

Malcolm, James Peller. *Anecdotes of the Manners and Customs of London from the Roman Invasion to the Year 1700*. London: Longman, Hurst, Rees, Orme & Brown, 1811. Gleanings from sources of apparently varying reliability support or expand other early seventeenth-century material about swearing.

Meyer, Arnold Oskar. *England and the Catholic Church*. London: Kegan Paul, Trench, Trübner, 1916. Not concerned with oaths, it does give some interesting parallels to *King John*'s treatment of Catholic figures.

Nokes, Gerald Dace. *A History of the Crime of Blasphemy*. London: Sweet & Maxwell, 1928. A wide-ranging survey, it contains much of interest on attitudes toward swearing and legal attempts to control it.

Partridge, Eric. *Shakespeare's Bawdy*. New York: E. P. Dutton, 1969.

Although emphasising sexual overtones, it provides useful testimony to the way meanings have been lost.

Perrin, Noel. *Dr Bowdler's Legacy*. New York: Atheneum, 1969. There is little on swearing in a book showing what offended Bowdler and his many followers.

Rosenberg, Marvin. *The Masks of Othello*. Berkeley: University of California Press, 1961. Heavily oriented toward the actor's interpretation, it also examines some critical writing and gives a broad perspective on the play.

Santayana, George. *Interpretations of Poetry and Religion*. New York: Charles Scribner's Sons, 1924. There is only a brief passage on oaths amid wide-ranging criticism of literature.

Sharman, Julian. *A Cursory History of Swearing*. London: Nimmo & Bain, 1884. Thorough, with an exceptionally rich part on the Elizabethan period, it is seldom supplanted by more recent books.

Spencer, Hazelton. *The Art and Life of William Shakespeare*. New York: Harcourt, Brace, 1940. A broad-ranging work, it provides conservative studies of the plays and much background material.

Spevak, Marvin. *A Complete and Systematic Concordance to the Works of Shakespeare*. 8 vols. Hildesheim: Georg Olms Verlagsbuchhandlung, 1968-75. Accurate and detailed, with tabulations of word-frequency, it supersedes Bartlett's concordance.

Stoll, E. E. *Othello: An Historical and Comparative Study*. 1915. Reprint New York: Haskell House, 1964. Less illuminating than other *Othello* studies noted, it does have a few useful comments on specific oaths.

Thomas, Keith. *Religion and the Decline of Magic*. London: Weidenfeld & Nicolson, 1971. One chapter emphasises cursing and, by extension, includes some attitudes toward swearing.

Traversi, Derek. *An Approach to Shakespeare*. 2 vols. New York: Doubleday, 1969. Each play is treated in turn in a conservative, reasonably thorough fashion.

Viles, Edward and Furnivall, Frederick James (eds). *The Rogues and Vagabonds of Shakespeare's Youth*. New Shakespeare Society Reprints, vol. 69. London: N. Trübner, 1880. Although with little attention to swearing, it provides background about classes that habitually swore.

Walker, Alice. *Textual Problems of the First Folio*. Cambridge: Cambridge University Press, 1953. Although not altogether accurate, it provides insights into the relation of the censor to the existence of oaths in the Folio texts of Shakespeare's plays.

Index